IMAGINED EMPIRES

Incas, Aztecs, and the New World of
American Literature, 1771–1876

Imagined Empires demonstrates that early American culture took great interest in South American civilizations, especially the Incas and Aztecs, and in so doing made a statement about the role of the United States as an empire in the emerging political order of New World colonies and states. In this examination of works by Philip Freneau, Joel Barlow, William Prescott, Herman Melville, and Walt Whitman, the long-contested concept of "indigenous origins" is given expanded meaning beyond traditional critiques of American culture. Eric Wertheimer recovers the Incas and Aztecs in Anglo-American literature, and thus sheds new light on national sovereignty, identity, and the development of an American history narrative.

Eric Wertheimer is Assistant Professor of American Studies at Arizona State University West.

Books in the series:

IMAGINED EMPIRES

INCAS, AZTECS, AND THE NEW WORLD OF AMERICAN
LITERATURE, 1771–1876

ERIC WERTHEIMER

CAMBRIDGE
UNIVERSITY PRESS

PUBLISHED BY THE PRESS SYNDICATE OF THE UNIVERSITY OF CAMBRIDGE
The Pitt Building, Trumpington Street, Cambridge CB2 1RP, United Kingdom

CAMBRIDGE UNIVERSITY PRESS
The Edinburgh Building, Cambridge CB2 2RU, UK   http://www.cup.cam.ac.uk
40 West 20th Street, New York, NY 10011-4211, USA   http://www.cup.org
10 Stamford Road, Oakleigh, Melbourne 3166, Australia

© Eric Wertheimer 1999

First published 1999

Printed in the United States of America

Typeface New Baskerville 10.5/13 pt.   *System* Penta   [RF]

A catalog record for this book is available from
the British Library

Library of Congress Cataloging-in-Publication Data
Wertheimer, Eric, 1964–
Imagined empires : Incas, Aztecs, and the New World of American
literature, 1771–1876 / Eric Wertheimer.
p.   cm. – (Cambridge studies in American literature and
culture)
Includes bibliographical references (p. 225–38)
ISBN 0-521-62229-8
1. American literature – 19th century – History and criticism.
2. Imperialism in literature.   3. American literature – Revolutionary
period, 1775–1783 – History and criticism.   4. American
literature – 1783–1850 – History and criticism.   5. Colonies in
literature.   6. Indians in literature.   7. America – In literature.
8. Aztecs in literature.   9. Incas in literature.   I. Title.
II. Series.
PS217.I47W47   1998 / 999   98-6475
810.9'358 – dc21   CIP

ISBN 0 521 62229 8   hardback

For Mili

CONTENTS

ACKNOWLEDGMENTS

Work on this project was started in 1989 at the University of Pennsylvania. From the beginning and to this day, the support and insights of Eric Cheyfitz and Betsy Erkkila have been invaluable and sustaining; they both showed me the way. The following friends, teachers, editors, and mentors from my time at Penn were also crucial to the book's development: Myra Jehlen (whom I especially thank for setting me on course), Al Filreis, John Richetti, Paul Korshin, David Shields, Cathy Davidson, Kim Benston, Amy Kaplan, Elisa New, George Justice, Elvin Padilla, John Feffer, and Jay Grossman.

More recently, I am grateful for the encouragement and input of my colleagues at ASU West, especially Emily Cutrer, Tom Cutrer, and Darryl Hattenhauer, who read and took great interest in the project through its final stages. I would also like to thank those colleagues and friends who have made work and leisure enjoyably reciprocal pursuits: Ian Moulton, David Lawrence, John Corrigan, Dottie Broaddus, Kristen Koptiuch, Gloria Cuadraz, Tressa Berman, Cat Nilan, Alberto Pulido, Arthur Sabatini, Candice Bredbenner, Dodie Peart, Dan Bivona, Scott Stevens, Mike Stancliff, and Keith Gaby. The students of ASU West have helped me to see this material through their inquisitive, skeptical eyes, and I owe them greatly.

The following foundations and institutions provided me with crucial funding: the Mellon Foundation, Haverford College, the University of Pennsylvania, and Arizona State University (Main and West campuses). I would like to thank the staffs of Penn's Van Pelt Library, the Historical Society of Pennsylvania, and the Library Company of Philadelphia (especially Jennifer Sanchez). At ASU's Fletcher Library, Dennis Isbell has been especially helpful. I am grateful as well for the responses I received in talks I gave at the following institutions: the University of California at Berkeley, George Mason University, Florida International University, and Columbia University. Sections of Chapters 1 and 3 have appeared previously as articles in *Early American Literature* and *American Literature*, respectively.

Eric Sundquist, the series editor who initially took an interest in the project and encouraged me, is a major reason why this book is seeing completion and publication. At Cambridge University Press, Anne Sanow (editor), Holly Johnson (production editor), and Walter Havighurst (copyeditor) were exceptionally constructive, thorough, and patient. I have had the excellent research assistance of Amy Davis and Beth Mooney. Any remaining errors are mine.

This book is the product of a family tradition that made thinking, reading, and principled reflection both necessary and rewarding. My parents, Stephen and Judy, as well as my grandparents, Ruth and Sylvia, have been a major source of emotional, intellectual, and practical support. Their enormous generosity is surpassed only by their humor and wisdom.

Milagros Cisneros was the inspiration for this work and these ideas. She has placed before me innumerable intellectual challenges and shown me immeasurable love; she has kept me going. I dedicate whatever is good in this book to her, with all my love. Finally, my beloved daughters Dani and Aya – I hope you read this someday: Don't tell your Mom, but this is for you too.

INTRODUCTION

ANCIENT AMERICA IN THE POST-COLONIAL
NATIONAL IMAGINARY

Writing in 1891, at the fabled dawn of the United States' imperial power in the Western Hemisphere, José Martí made a plea for new histories:

> The history of America, from the Incas to the present, must be taught in clear detail and to the letter, even if the *archons* of Greece are overlooked. Our Greece must take priority over the Greece which is not ours. We need it more.[1]

Martí's sense of the importance of teaching previously obscured history "to the letter" is surely right if we are to work toward an America that is commensurate with its utopian impulses. But just who *is* "we"?

I hope that Martí would forgive the displacement that occurs when his words are placed before a study of Anglo-American appropriations, written by an English-speaking North American, especially since this study is about the problems of creating possessive pronouns like "we" and "our" when making narratives of history and nationality. The contest and convergence of meanings pertaining to the term "America," among historical varieties of "us," is precisely the impetus behind this work. The "our" is never constant from chapter to chapter, just as the "Greece which is not ours" is always shifting; what it means to teach history "to the letter" is in constant question. Nonetheless, the terrain of study is defined throughout by a politicized sense of "our America." The effort to understand the story of "our America" – a multicultural, multinational set of relations expressing the promise of social justice – is, I believe, essential to the anti-imperialist, redemptive project Martí was engaged in. It

1

is a struggle that many of us in American cultural studies, along with those outside the academy, attempt to keep alive. The dialectical nature of the word "our" – at once signifying possession and communality, within and without academia – can serve cultural study; we need that now, more than ever.[2]

Martí's inducement leads me as well to the basic questions of my study: What did five important American writers, in the period spanning the early republic to just after the Civil War, think of as *American* history? What, for these authors, were republican America's "native" origins and where were they to be found, given the problems that cluster around both terms, "native" and "origin"? How did they imagine that history? Why *that* history?

This introduction will describe the chapter-by-chapter analyses and attempt to account theoretically for the choosing of histories and the constructing of early American identities – "what, how and why *that* history." Beginning to answer such questions requires a certain amount of cross-Atlantic interpretation, work that, perhaps surprisingly, leads to the intricate situation of "post-coloniality."[3] For such "indigenous" historicism in the newly "decolonized" republic was clearly a product of the race to construct national histories, to locate worthy antecedents for inscription into national narratives. Across the Atlantic from the western continents, Europeans were engaged in a similar project, furiously searching back, combing the annals of empire and civilization – Egyptian, Greek, Roman – trying to impart teleological, self-justifying stories of progress, renovation, and enlightenment. Eighteenth- and nineteenth-century Americans were classicists, no less than their European counterparts; but they were classicists with different geopolitical, and therefore historical, coordinates.

Of course, Europeans had started the "antiquating" of American history as early as the Renaissance, elaborating fantasies of Arcadia, Atlantis, and even Eden lying just over the geographical and temporal horizon.[4] But while Europeans of the late eighteenth century put to rest their fantasies of locating in the American hemisphere a prior utopia that would serve as a mythic engine of empire, post-colonial Anglo-Americans found the very condition of post-coloniality a spur to theorizing American classical origins. In a flourish of Columbian thinking, they "newly" contemplated the precedents and possibilities of "American civilization," pre-discovery and post-colonial. A certain form of exceptionalism believed America was a nation without precedent; but there was a vital tradition that saw exemplars in the New World. Americans of the colonies and states gazed out over a hemisphere covered with the enduring marks of Indians who, before the prospective rise of their own exceptional empire, had organized that space into empires. Thus, to call a collectivity or individual "Indian" was a more nuanced historical, political, and racial nomination than one might imagine.

Indians were not undifferentiated hunter-gatherers, this much most eighteenth-century history readers knew; after all, the New World had been the site of civilization and empire. Still, these were Indian states, which had to be fed into Enlightenment narratives of progress and decline, not to mention anticipatory narratives of national expansion across "destined" territories. These Native Americans had tampered with the "natural" teleologies of rational action and national organization.[5] How to bring them fluently under the sign "American," and even "classical republican," was the problem for the literary epic. Why they were initially so important to the literary imagination is the theoretical problem at hand for this book.

I am broadly interested in the intersection of literature and international politics, how that overlap occurs in this period of American literature and which discourses enable it to be seen and which suppress it. This is of a piece with my interest in post-coloniality; I would hope that one is not merely a gloss for the other – that American colonial culture and post-structuralist revisions of colonial ideology are not as unrelated as the dearth of such criticism might make it seem.[6] For my topic concerns the formation of an imperial self in America's literature as that self relates to other elements of American New World history – the Incas and Aztecs. At the same time, the idea of proto-republican Indian empires was cultural hybridity itself. Not surprisingly, such hybridity engendered cultural aporia and political advantage; discursive conflict bolstered the accommodations of exceptionalism, and so conditioned the imperial ambitions of the new nation. Accordingly, the authors who exemplify that "national self" both resist and exploit, both make and unmake, the empire(s) that come with thoughts of *their* New World.

The obsession with a fantastic, quasi-"primitive" origin can be seen as part of the narrative of American nationalism. Incas and

Aztecs, as historical figures of an idealized Other, were a politicized code in the early national period; one of the central inquiries of this book concerns the way this code was related to the consolidation of imperial power. By the mid-nineteenth century, pre-Columbian America, as a literary idea, had been wrung dry by a historical tradition that was serving a different order of national needs; the obsolescence of this kind of New World imagining was brought on, in part, by the emergence of the real transatlantic and North-South power of the republic. Both Melville's and Whitman's New Worlds were thus underwritten by varieties of national omission that produced both self-criticism and radical critiques of representation and imperial knowledge. Again, this book may be read as pursuing a paradigm of the literary culture of nationalism and empire, tracing a micronarrative of new epistemologies for a New World: first, the epic poems of origin, then novelistic histories of the necessary downfall of Otherness, and finally self-critical fictions of pluralism and erasure.

Beginning with a 1771 oration, my first chapter, "Commencements," examines the claims made on Philip Freneau's republican identity by the indigenous legacies of the Incas and Aztecs. In several key poems, I find Freneau struggling to articulate an epic destiny that denies its hybridity even as it utilizes a hybridized frontier logic. This chapter is critically foundational because it demonstrates just how well-versed Freneau and literary republicans like him were in the South and Central American history they claimed as native to the Anglo imagination. Chapter 2, titled "Diplomacy," focuses on Joel Barlow's quasi-epics, *The Vision of Columbus* (1787) and *The Columbiad* (1807), showing how Barlow structured America's "classical" Inca past and made it central to his exceptionalist designs, even as the Inca myth of origin vexed his concept of race. For the cosmopolitan poet abroad, New World history was a kind of symbolic museum – a place to experiment with the alluring and troubling terms of commercial self-invention. This chapter extends many of the analytical lines I begin in the chapter on Freneau, but follows them to a kind of crisis of national exceptionalism that is borne out in the formal and schematic properties of *The Columbiad.* That is, Barlow, in part because he neglects the genealogy of European exile that Freneau is careful to ascribe to Incas and Aztecs, begins to

4

foreshadow the identitarian crisis of Anglo nativism – of claiming a native proto-republican Other as the anchor of Anglo national destiny.

Chapter 3, "Noctography," bears out that crisis in its fullest dimensions. It dramatizes the issue of composition, and by implication the matter of civilization and barbarism, in William Prescott's romance histories, *The Conquest of Mexico* (1843) and *The Conquest of Peru* (1847). Prescott, who was nearly blind, wrote with the aid of a device called a noctograph, which he claimed produced hieroglyph-like writing. Pursuing the operation of the hieroglyphic style through both histories, I argue that Prescott must maintain a theory of nationalist and racist hierarchies that threaten, in the very work of his own writing, to engulf both him and an imperial America.

Chapter 4, "Mutations," reads the stories of Melville set off the coast of South America ("Benito Cereno" and "The Encantadas") in the context of emerging theories of natural history. Those theories of natural creativity, of course, were based on Charles Darwin and Charles Lyell's investigations of natural history in the same part of the world. I argue that Melville's understanding of modern history (post-Columbian, post-conquest) is bound up in similarly Darwinian questions of "creativity" and "origins," and is, in turn, articulated in the racial dimensions of both biological and national narratives. And yet Melville resists the racist implications of these early scientific epistemologies by elegizing, in ways mindful of the cultural violence of empire, the Spanish American historical and geographical setting. Here in Melville is the "time lag" or "caesura" of modernity so important to post-colonial criticism, where representation and Otherness have the space to articulate a different history, alternative to the forward "progress" of Anglo-American modernity.[7]

The concluding Chapter 5, on Whitman, called "Passage," explores the final absence of pre-Columbians from the American literary imagination. Specifically, I analyze Whitman's Columbus-inspired historical and geographical excision of non-"Manifest" America – Central and South America. Taking "Passage to India" as a crucial authorial and historicist revaluation of his life of writing, I show how Whitman's expansive vision attempts to sublimate or transcend the imperial implications of his own purification of Anglo New World pursuits. The omission of the "civilized" Indian leads me back to Whitman the nationalist author, and thus to the nexus linking the expanding nation and exportable print emblems of identity. I demonstrate how the "absence upon which we write" (to quote Whitman) is marked – how this affects his nationalist poetics, and how it alters our understanding of his relationship to the exceptional nation he attempted to delineate in print.

This book's larger narrative about nationalist thinking now can be brought into clearer focus. Freneau and Barlow begin American literary "diplomacy" by projecting a nativist national imaginary, while Prescott begins to display unresolvable symptoms of the crisis of such instrumental nativism. With Prescott the projected genealogy starts to become self-consciously introjected when the consequences of empire (among others, the Mexican-American War) begin to have ethical and formal implications for his own methods of representation; that problematic introjection of the national imaginary is continued and intensified with Whitman and Melville.

For Freneau and Barlow, New World history stretches more or less "naturally" from the discovery and conquest of "American civilizations" to national independence; the Incas and Aztecs are potent myths affirming foundational republican precepts. And yet, such historical representations bear ominous and irresolvable problems of race and empire in America. Prescott begins to show ruptures that Barlow and Freneau were able to wash in their republican optimism; he places Incas and Aztecs within a ruined past that is mysteriously, but hazardously, legible. To narrate the story of their destruction, while representing the achievements of what was destroyed, is a task that becomes treacherous for an Anglo-American and Federalist Whig in the age of the Mexican War; Prescott's skirmishes with the actors in his story become wars of representation that threaten to undermine the composition of his own national identity.

In the final chapters I press the "sign" of Columbus, and search the literary record for the pre-Columbian trace and absence. In Melville it is fading, while in Whitman the ancient American chronotope, along with the geography of all that is not North America, is erased in his post–Civil War poetry. What happened to the idea of ancient America in the mid-nineteenth century? The self-evident answer is that the United States' official history became more Anglo and monocultural even as – and perhaps because – it became more

6

multicultural in actuality; the "nativeness" of nationalism was no longer necessary. David T. Haberly, in "Form and Function in the New World Legend," elaborates on these answers by explaining why "usable pasts" were not really necessary to the nationalist project of the nineteenth century.

> During the course of the nineteenth century, the legend slowly disappeared from the literature of the United States, or changed in purpose and in form. It can be argued, in part, that the legend – which by definition looked backward rather than forward – did not have much of a chance against the forces of optimism, materialism, and progress, forces defeated only within Washington Irving's texts. Beyond this, however, the example of Nathaniel Hawthorne suggests that few American writers found it possible to discover a usable national past.[8]

Haberly's explanation is useful to a point; which is to say that the "usability" of the New World past can be read in Melville and Whitman. While some "pasts" are elevated to national prestige, others are marginalized or "fused" out of the national imaginary.[9] The past *is* "usable" insofar as it can be forgotten, denied, changed, found somewhere else.

Whitman's work presents a good example of the past's repressive use-value. Further estranging the Incas and Aztecs from an original New World history, even as he doggedly preserves the purely figural symbol of Columbus (who embodies, more than anything, the tragic ambivalence of Whitman's centrifugal globalism), Whitman participates in the literary installation of U.S. history as a process of renewal and affirmation rather than retrospection and appreciation. Myth-making of this sort tells a story about the utility of displacement in national thinking, about the necessity to forget the "origins" of New World empire in order to further empire.

One consequence of this is that the Revolutionary moment had, by the middle of the nineteenth century and its attendant crises of nationality, become the obsessive starting line for the American narrative. All other narratives of New World nationality, particularly Indian and Spanish, were obscured, fulfilling the consolidating logic of the "national forgotten"; Columbus remained as the literary and emotional "dues payer" for a still-distorted New World map. The hybridity exemplified in Freneau, Barlow, and Prescott was seen for what it was by Melville – the genealogical construction of empire. And it had become too much to bear for the self-conscious "world power" of Whitman's great hopes. In the culture at large, "Manifest Destiny" supplanted the New World imaginary; but the substitution did not nullify lingering, non-"manifest" claims.

The study of American literary nationalism's relation to hierarchies of history and Otherness is, of course, not new. Primarily, I am indebted to the work of Roy Harvey Pearce, whose enduring *Savagism and Civilization* set many of the most important terms for thinking about the place of the Indian in the Anglo-American imagination.[10] I hope to be augmenting and revising this work in important ways, adding insights enabled by more recent cultural theory and criticism.[11]

This book also has as one of its critical lineages the study of the American frontier, since the frontier concept works to constitute early American national identity at myriad levels. The traditional frontier model, beginning not just with Frederick Jackson Turner but also with Argentina's Domingo F. Sarmiento, exemplified the nostalgia and romance, not to mention racism, of nationalism; in many ways, early theorists of the frontier reproduced the worst effects of nationalism.[12] More recent theorists and historians of the frontier have shown it to be a quintessentially modern, and modernizing, formation, delineating mythic rigidities that serve capital, nation, literature, and language. Indeed, breakthroughs in thinking about the frontier are as multiple and imaginative as the site they theorize.[13] Annette Kolodny summarizes the thrust of this work in her call for a radically different frontier, urging the recovery of the interwoven structure of contact and emphasizing the falsely mythic qualities of frontier rigidities:

> We [must] let go our grand obsessions with narrowly geographic or strictly chronological frameworks and instead recognize "frontier" as a locus of first cultural contact, circumscribed by a particular physical terrain in the process of change *because of* the forms that contact takes, all of it inscribed by the collisions and interpenetrations of language. My paradigm would thus have us interrogating language – especially as hybridized style, trope, story, or structure – for the complex intersections of human encounters . . . [14]

8

Given the scope of Kolodny's injunction and the embeddedness of the frontier myth, the frontier's reassessment needs to continue. Stressing the interpenetration, intersectionality, and indeed the porousness of frontiers is a welcome revision in thinking about the hybridity of these formations. Certainly this helps us counteract the static, linear logic of borders themselves; there can be no doubt the cross-woven frontier had, as Walter Prescott Webb put it in *The Great Frontier*, "length and breadth."

But I would argue that this in some ways rather old emphasis on "zoning" the frontier underestimates one of its most retrograde purposes: it was a place for positing the edges of difference – the constructed hard lines between contiguous Others. The term "frontier," with its connotations of division and limitation, has historical and theoretical resonances that we can still learn from, since such hard significations were essential to the formation of bordered national identities. I would argue further that hybrid identities emerge under the operations of both containment *and* intersection.

That said, I would add that frontiers are not only the first stage in the sharpening of borders, they are mobile; the American frontier is not necessarily geographically specific. It is a figurative site of national origins that derives its narrative power from deciding who is "civilized" and who is "barbaric."[15] Although writers like Freneau, Barlow, Prescott, and Whitman never identify the Incas or Aztecs as products of the "frontier" as such, I treat them that way because I view their symbolic and political deployment as coextensive with an imperial imagination that was hegemonic in manifold ways; the frontier generated imperial ambition by binaristically processing each line of national, cultural, and historical difference. I am by no means the first to point out that the frontier can be geographical and psychological, and thus serve domination in its mobility – Melville was among the first to recognize this.[16]

Imperialism, as I use the word here, arises from a particular historical matrix delimited by a republican American "national imaginary" and an obsession with frontier thinking.[17] By imperialism, I mean national thinking that envisions an expansionist and portable national presence, from the beginning of America's self-recognition as being independent. I also hold that the generation of empire afforded unique symbolic maneuvers related to the condition of post-coloniality. Indeed, republican America's imperial range must

be viewed as simultaneously post-colonial and neocolonial (economic, as opposed to classic territorial, colonialism).[18] That colonial
paradox, consisting in double roles, is a feature not only of its con-
tinual identification at the frontier, but of its own exceptionalist
ideas about itself. The two national conditions, post-coloniality and
neocolonialism, are inextricable, and they may also be linked to the
orientalist discourse of ancient America – a literary-historical mode
that attempted to speak for the "mute" civilizations of the New
World.[19] This New World historicism of arrogating voices and influ-
encing territories marks the frontier, as it were, between nation and
empire, Manifest Destiny and Monroe Doctrine.

We tend to view Manifest Destiny as an aggressive form of nationalism, and the Monroe Doctrine as the diplomatic architecture
of neocolonial imperialism; I would rather view them as the twin
offspring of frontier thinking. Etienne Balibar links nationalism with
imperialism and colonialism when he writes in "The Nation Form:
History and Ideology" that modern nations are often the product
of colonization as well as the crucible of a renovated colonialism:
"In a sense, every modern nation is a product of colonization: it has
always been to some degree colonized or colonizing, *and sometimes
both at the same time*"(341, my emphasis). This is particularly true of
republican America, and as such helps to clarify the dialectical tensions of the post-colonial imaginary I am talking about.[20] Imperialism inheres in the contradictory roles nations perceive for
themselves as well as in what Balibar terms "precocious phenomena" and "articulated" wars that implicitly seem to disorient temporal continuities: "a decisive role is played by the precocious
phenomena of imperialism and the articulation of wars within colonization"(341).

America's own "precocious phenomena of imperialism" have
yielded a somewhat truncated history of imperialism, beginning for
most historians at the end of the nineteenth century.[21] I take to be
among those "precocious phenomena" the literary imaginings of
epic national glory, even before the Monroe Doctrine's neocolonial
sign was imposed on the New World map. One of my aims is to
recover, however partially, some of the origins of imperialism in
American culture by examining those epic imaginings. These origins
have seemed absent perhaps because they present to the cultural
historian a bewildering chart of impossibly coexisting locations.

They mark a gulf between the capabilities of national power and representations of national ambition, between what nations can contain and what empires can see; filling that gulf between are the identitarian problems implicit in the historical and symbolic nomination "American."

Yet if one is willing to explore the gulf between signs and power, and navigate that tide of identities (Anglo, Indian, Black, mestizo, creole, etc.), American imperialism comes into view sooner than expected. For those primordial, even precocious, thoughts of empire amidst chaos form, as I have said, an orientalism that makes Anglo-American empire seem, oddly enough, *belated*. The discourse harnessed an optimism that was innocent of imperial motive because it made claims on human progress, Columbian martyrdom, and, more problematically, the precedent of "native" empires. Incas and Aztecs, as well as the Columbus who brought about their "discovery," were deployed as a stabilizing chronotope, as both caution and incitement in the face of vast national and historical uncertainties. As the instigator of frontier thinking, the Columbian "sign" carried "precocious" symbolic power and formed a powerful relay between nationalism and neocolonialism.

In light of this discourse of American power I want to refine my theoretical framework by conjuring a panoptic conceit that offers a way into what I mean by the "national imaginary": What did these writers see when they looked outward – Miltonically, over space and time – from North America's states? How did this perspective determine identity?

The "national imaginary" works to distinguish the national from the international in the expanses that result from such epic placement of authorial perspective. It is an arrangement of global space – frontiers, borders, and histories – according to an economy of pleasure and anxiety; this mapping determines the symbolic resolution of difference and identification. Thus the writing of history, especially in the literary mode, compels the early national imaginary to account for, indeed to take pleasure in, the South American and pre-Columbian as well as the European and the "modern." At the same time, anxiety about political contingencies – requirements originating in the sphere of diplomatic dispute, the mapped shifts of sovereignty so endemic to the early American military frontier –

reinforces the subject's reworking of where the "civilized" and "barbaric" reside within the national imaginary. In short, the national imaginary functions as a scope for reading the New World's teleologies, America's imperial maps, and the literature in which, ultimately, it too is registered.

Frontiers, when viewed as a feature of the national imaginary, are then sites of origin for imperialist thinkers and, for that matter, thinkers about imperialism (I am also in a quest for sources and origins). Identity originates at the frontier because it demands definition between absolutes; one side marking the latest development in the linear spread of modernity (civilization), and the other signifying the absence, or incipient logic, of modernity – "barbarism." Organized by a kind of Derridean pressure, the frontier hones cultural difference and signifies its identifying potential; a compendium of identity-defining binaries follows. Insofar as this is true, the final two chapters may be read as deconstructions of frontier thinking and its consequences. That concluding work is necessary, in part, because of my own complicity with the critical practice of differentiating and identifying at the site of origins.

It should be clear, especially in those latter chapters, that I lean rather heavily on Lacanian conceptions of national identity while standing upon the Andersonian ground of materialist notions of print culture generating the read and imagined nation. Nationalism is related to vision as well as narrative, for they are each necessary to the process of conceiving the symbolic social fiction that is the nation – its boundaries and its cultural and historical content.[22] The fusion – Andersonian-Lacanian – is meant to account for identity in a way that complements both approaches. Moreover, both theoretical explanations bear a core that I find compellingly descriptive of the New World American: collective, and especially imperialist, thinking prompts the primary reflex of identification, rather than differentiation.

For some, "Lacan at the frontier" may have a kind of jaunty dissonance; nonetheless, his description of the self as other is suggestive for my analysis. It helps explain how a certain form of American identity, the seemingly unambiguous ego of the nation's earliest expansionist efforts, uses the frontier to formulate hybrid identities that enable the national imagination of empire. Here, in the case of the "semicivilized Indian," the frontier's line functions as a kind of semitransparent mirror.[23] It is semitransparent because the ego can see beyond the limit of its reflection to the territory beyond, the geographical space of the New World; yet the mirror returns a peculiar variant of the image of the misidentified ideal, since the site of difference becomes the occasion for a kind of nationally flattering self-recognition – Others become mirrored self-images, only at earlier stages of development.[24] I say "misidentified" not because I wish to assert essentialist historical allegiances, but because such a recognition does a faulty job, at best, of acknowledging difference in the form of culture, power, and language; indeed, "frontier thinking" is a transitional imaginary function that is not interested in the particulars of the Other beyond his identifying potential. Perhaps most importantly, in the national imaginary, while self and other are cross-referenced, self and land become metonyms. Lacanian self-mapping is thus conducive to an argument about the formation of an imperial ego that seeks (colonial and neocolonial) identification, over and against difference, with other nations, other subjects, and other territories.

The compulsion to find such identities arises from the pleasure of origins and then the symbolic satisfaction of enunciating them.[25] Autonomy, power – the features of an articulated and now aggressive identity – flow into literary discourses about the shape of the American domain. Incas and Aztecs, represented ambivalently through the Black Legend as "semicivilized," invite the Anglo epic poet to see himself in their New World experiments in civilization; in that imaginary identification, Anglo-Americans make a statement about the proximity of *all* American territory. Along that historical frontier, the "barbaric" North American Indians, who offer no useful points of imperial or political identity, are, by a contrasting logic, suitable for removal. Incas and Aztecs – the ideal Others at the site of origins – lead American writers to the sovereign claim of New World provenance *through* the historical claims of homologous, "original" identities. By imagining a community of American readers who in turn imagined earlier empires to lay claim to, early national authors and their publics imagined *their* empire.[26] Still, the logic of difference (the Lacanian other), and ultimately domination, reside within the identification. When the need for identification gave way to the realities of American power and pluralism in the nineteenth century, the possibility of neocolonial domination became more than just an imagined destiny.[27]

The Black Legend, the earliest Anglo-American history of the New World as a North-South entity, is then an origin of the American who brought the "frontier" with him – not so much as a militarized metaphor for understanding conflict, but for the aesthetic and political arrangement of national hierarchies and territories. The modality of the recently "liberated" and newly "independent" – a mobile embrace of oppressed and oppressor, at once "civilized" and "barbaric" – is what I mean when I say that American literature of empire is post-colonial. If the frontier is an internalized mark, then the counterpoint to the "civilized" resides *within* America's literature of national development as much as without. This duality fits the imperial ego for modern dominations: post-colonial American literature articulates a neocolonial sphere of relations and narratives. It is a mode that could be realized and unambiguously deployed as administrative, imperial violence with the final exit of Great Britain from the New World stage after the Civil War. The United States of America, in the second half of the nineteenth century, becomes a "world power"; and yet, in its literary maps, that had already happened.

Finally, I want to explain my use of the term "New World" at the end of this introduction because it is an apt point of departure – a means of intervening into the discourse of neocolonial American thinking and, more humbly, a method of conducting the reader into the issues raised in the first chapter.

The "New World" is yet another phrase that has functioned dramatically, yet deceptively, in a long line of literary and cultural histories of America. Too often it means simply the United States in contradistinction to the Old World of Europe (and more specifically Great Britain). But its genealogy in Renaissance thinking about politics and geography determined its meanings well into the eighteenth and nineteenth centuries. When properly historicized, the term becomes a hemispherical denotation that converts "America" into a political narrative about geographical sovereignty. For example, as used by Freneau and Barlow, "New World" is understood to mean North and South America; America is coterminous with the geography of the continents; America will assume, by Providence and by politics, the New World. My insistence on the sign "America/ South *and* North America/New World" is essential because it restores an expansive and commutative nomination whose meaning in the works of America's earliest theorists of nation and empire meant clarity of imperial purpose.

Not surprisingly, the New World sign is also conceptually pivotal in reconceiving "exceptionalism."[28] American exceptionalism is, I argue, partly a product of Anglo participation in the idealized South and Central American Others and their histories. While many critics of American exceptionalism have ascribed its power to transcend inconsistencies to religious, specifically Puritan, dynamics, I want to hold this global articulation of political power to its racialist and historicist cultural operations, to see how those produce a uniquely self-justifying nation.[29] In American cultural history, for better or worse, "frontier" and "New World" are terms whose interpretive logic lead us to "exceptionalism."

That logic loops back – providentially or imperialistically it may seem – into the term "America." I stress again the care with which I appropriate to my own purposes the post-Martían sense of the term "America." Certainly, the terms I use to differentiate U.S. America from Spanish American territories – North America, Anglo-America, and so forth – are always problematic, reflecting the cultural instabilities of both nationalist and imperialist discourses within the "American domain." The North-South, national, and linguistic distinctions between Americans are helpful, but they cannot once and for all remedy the imprecision that Americanness imparts when viewed broadly; again, the problem of "our" and the difficulty of the sign "America."

Still, this imprecision is curiously essential to my book and the revisions it undertakes. I want to suggest briefly how this might work: to begin thinking of the New World in the early moments of American history is inevitably to rethink the context of contemporary North-South issues.[30] One way to bring the United States' relationship with South and Central America into better focus is, ironically, to recall the national imaginary mapped out by the likes of Freneau and Barlow. That is, we can return to the New World, but with critical awareness of imperial modes of incorporation and fragmentation; we might start by heeding the simple advice of Martí as we reassume the frontier in order to undo it. Revising the New World of "our America" helps us learn about a hemisphere that North Americans assume responsibility for, but know little about. In the absence of such revision, North-South dynamics are silently subordinate to transatlantic relations. When America is read as having a New World history that is not always dependent on European bestowals, it is less likely that the transatlantic sphere will eclipse U.S. relations with Latin America and the Caribbean in our contemporary national imaginary. This North-South, New World, American story needs constant retelling.

The ability of the United States to advance its interests by westward expansion – through luck or well-earned "fortune" – seems to indicate for historians of American nationalism the natural limits not only of U.S. American appetites but of European power. Histories and theories of Manifest Destiny emphasize the distinctness of two *northern* worlds to the exclusion of U.S. domination of a no less "manifest" mandate to the south.[31] And yet, as I have said, the history of U.S. power is from its earliest moments – before the Monroe Doctrine – a story of imaginings and designs that understood hegemony in terms of the New World, a hemisphere. To keep that larger world in view when asking questions of literature and history is to challenge, however academically, contemporary versions of "Manifest Destiny" and Monroe Doctrine.

It is for this reason that the Black Legend's Indian empires will be treated in what follows as the historiographic and literary site of a contest over American identity – over the ongoing positioning of Anglo-Americans in the North-South New World. So Martí is a corrective still. He was, after all, invoking a polemical "our," one that demands a dignified recognition of the "America" forgotten, distorted, and scorned in struggles past – and the "America" portended and hoped for in New Worlds to come.

1

COMMENCEMENTS

PRE-COLUMBIAN WORLDS AND PHILIP FRENEAU'S
LITERATURE OF AMERICAN EMPIRE

September 25, 1771, was Commencement Day at the College of New
Jersey (later Princeton). The centerpiece of the ceremony was an
effusive poem about national potential, "The Rising Glory of America," written by two graduating seniors, Philip Freneau and Hugh
Henry Brackenridge. The word "commencement" has perhaps
never so well described a perennially inflated event, for the student
body included men who would become some of the most influential
figures in the nation's political and literary culture, among them
James Madison, Aaron Burr, Freneau, and Brackenridge.[1] As a moment for critical reflection, the ceremony has been appreciated by
many seekers of an important originary moment of early national
political and literary culture. Hans-Joachim Lang has pointed this
out, citing Kenneth Silverman, Gordon Wood, and even Evert Duy-
kinck as having employed the rhetorical excesses of that day to their
critical advantage.[2]

But even while the event has been regarded as an inauguration
of America's imperial prospects, the poem's thematic obsession with
imperial beginnings has gone largely unexamined. Delivered to an
impressive cast of young men who would commence to raise America's glory, the focus of the epic was deeply retrospective, addressing
the founding of prior British and Spanish empires in the New
World. A major problem to be dealt with in a "visionary" poem was
the conundrum of New World history, presenting to the poetic
imagination a tangled problematic of racial, cultural, and national
Otherness. What, we might ask, did the discovery of the Indian New
World by Columbus, a Genoan who sailed in the name of Spain and
Catholicism, mean to British colonials just beginning to understand

themselves as something other than British? By engaging in this retrospection, Freneau[3] rehearses stories that would be crucial to the prospective national identity of his fellow future politicians and myth-makers. Circumscribing and integrating America's origins (pre-Columbian history, discovery, and conquest) into the ceremony of nationalism, the poem makes a political asset of this secular history. Once subjected to the operations of poetry, history's problematic of Otherness could provide claims to the colonized lands of an imperial periphery as well as prospective territories within the continent and hemisphere. The New World was, after all, an entity that stood to be doubly transformed – by Columbus and soon by Princeton's best and brightest.

The poem of rising glory, for all its grandiose claims to Miltonic clarity of vision, was determinedly blind to its own hybridity, to the limits of its work as settler of colonial claims and configurer of a colonial domain within the national imaginary.[4] But those blind spots can be filled in by examining the poem's recurring obsession with the bordered, discretely national elements of New World history. In order to understand the limits of the American "visionary" poem I want to analyze two versions of "The Rising Glory of America": a 1772 reprint of the 1771 oration[5] and a substantially revised, overtly republican and national text of 1786. When examined against one another, the two versions of "The Rising Glory of America" can help us assess the emergence of a national imaginary out of, and in spite of, problematic historical legacies. In so doing, we can glimpse how poetry of this sort rhetorically processed and erased the inconsistencies and limits of American claims to imperial exceptionalism.[6]

My primary interest in this chapter is to demonstrate how the problematic of national Otherness embodied in the Black Legend can be critically resolved. Since two versions of a single, though remarkably rich, poem – "The Rising Glory of America" – do not fully account for Freneau's extensive treatment of these themes, I will then turn to other relevant work that also manifests his fascination with the pre-Columbian South American ideal. Here I want to try to undo the methodology and somewhat functionalist teleology of my earlier argument and to restore the characteristic dissonance – the clanging and harmonies of hybridity and savagist discourse – that accompanied Freneau's ambivalence. Finally, I will attempt to reinterpret the post-colonial symbology of the terms "America" and "New World," given my readings in the previous sections.

American, Old and New: Of Freneau and the Black Legend

Raised on a New Jersey farm by a father who fell victim to the post–French and Indian War depression, Freneau was consistently oppositional in his politics (first an anti-British Whig, then an anti-Federalist republican). Such politics arose from hard times that resulted in part from the economic contestations between imperial center and periphery; specifically, his father's troubles were due in large part to Britain's demonstration-of-credit of 1765. The fact that New Jersey had the largest war debt only worsened the economic and political climate for prospects of recovery. Freneau's father died not long after the Townsend Act of 1767, perhaps harassed by creditors into illness.[7]

In the wake of these personal and social misfortunes, Freneau entered Princeton in 1768. He and his fellow students were intensely political, as evidenced by the resolution of the graduating class of 1771 to wear clothes only of American manufacture. Even the notoriously contentious Whig and Cliosophe societies agreed on the emerging notion of American rights,[8] an indication that elite colonials were vigorously pursuing the discourses and philosophies that would develop a national identity.

The 1771 version of "The Rising Glory of America" passionately exalts the future of "America," that still-indistinct national concept. But it does so only after first attempting to resolve a traditionally murky relationship with a New World past that was alien to Anglo America. That alienation was resolved in the non-Spanish world by a pseudo-historical tradition known as the Black Legend. In *Oracles of Empire*, David Shields discusses the Black Legend as a grand ideological construct:

> Great Britain assured itself of the righteousness of its imperial mission by the myth of the *translatio imperii* and the humanist belief that trade engendered the "arts of peace." It also understood its righteousness in contrast to the depravity of its imperial rival, Spain. Spanish depravity, like English righteousness, formed part of a larger mythic construct. "*La leyenda negra*," the Black Legend

of Spanish imperial cruelty, proved a long-lived and potent myth. (175)

Colonials borrowed this history from the British, and such legends informed much of the founding ideology of the North American frontier, first for the British and later for the Americans. Columbus's celebrated "discovery" of the New World and the Spanish conquest of the great civilizations of America were the essential elements of this popular assertion of a British right of dominance over the New World.

In broad and incontestable terms, the legend describes the genocide that was perpetrated on the indigenous people of the American continents.[9] The stories become hyperbolic and legendary in their stereotyping of Spanish depravity. Rapacity and greed seem to arise naturally from the Spaniards' degraded social and cultural template, as the conquistadors come to symbolize all that is Spanish. The legend presents a heroic Columbus discovering a New World reminiscent of the Protestant Eden or Arcadia, a luxurious yet ordered natural domain subject to the care and wisdom of original civilizations like the Incas and Aztecs. Spaniards proceed to destroy this romantic world in the name of greed, thereby betraying the virtuous discovery – and betraying Columbus in particular, who had only meant to bring Christianity to the benighted. Hence, Columbus, the Incas, and the Aztecs all stand as New World martyrs of corrupt empire.[10]

Shields identifies three strains within the Black Legend, the most important of which originated with the Protestant imperial rivals of Spain. The power of the Black Legend was so intense among these contenders that, says Shields, the "factual, historical consideration of [Spanish colonialism] never saw print in British America or, indeed, ever enjoyed much influence subsequently" (*Oracles of Empire*, 175).[11] Shields's work on the Columbus trope and the Black Legend in prenational, British American poetry is pioneering; however, the importance of their persistence in Revolutionary American letters is still an open critical question. In the post-colonial case of Freneau, his obsession with New World history and its obsessive distribution of national and cultural difference provides the opportunity to ask important questions about the ideology of American myths and the international purposes to which they were put.

Genealogies of Exile

"The Rising Glory of America" of 1771 ("RGA" 1771) expresses inchoate, still-differentiating British, American, and New World identities. A tangle of antagonistic and complementary allegiances characterizes the poem throughout, as each identity and its corresponding history constantly suggest a reconsideration of the other. Specifically, "RGA" 1771 establishes a dialectic between the saintly tandem of Columbus and British civilization (with America an uncomfortable subset of Britain) on the one hand and the sinful conquistadors, French, and Indians on the other. In the version of 1786 ("RGA" 1786), Americans are added as a national category which both subsumes and supersedes all others. The legendary meanings of Spanish New World history are always calibrated to the moral advantage of American power on the contested frontier.[12] The elapsed years between 1771 and 1786 produce a refinement of an Anglo-American idiom of innocence with respect to those meanings. Ultimately, that innocence is made possible when the diffusion of multiple New World identities is satisfactorily rooted in a poetic genealogy of New World nations, races, and cultures.

Both "RGA" 1771 and "RGA" 1786 are lengthy blank verse colloquies spoken by three characters, each with a suggestive name: Acasto (the Aeneas-like European exile), Eugenio (the generation of a better breed), and Leander (the doomed, somewhat Columbian, lover who tragically braves the sea to reach his beloved). They exhibit in their reciprocity and contentiousness a fractured or bordered proto-national identity – the ongoing conundrum that was, to use Lois Parkinson Zamora's phrase, "the past's multilayered and unresolved presence" ("The Usable Past: The Idea of History in Modern U.S. and Latin American Fiction," in Gustavo Pérez Firmat, ed., *Do the Americas Have a Common Literature?*, 15). Against the background of a bordered inheritance, highlighted by a multivocal performance, there is a collective attempt, in both versions of the poem, to peel back the layers of New World history (viewed inevitably as a history of empires) to find the primordial template of ancient America. In so doing, the poems locate the critical differences between pre-Columbian North Americans and South Americans. The poems' concern for differentiating origins thereby sets the stage for repub-

lican articulations of imperial usurpation and the arrival of monologic American international power.

It would seem appropriate then that Leander begins "RGA" 1771
by making a respectful plea for an end to dialogue with the Old
World: "No more of Memphis and her mighty kings, / Or Alexan-
dria, where the Ptolomies / Taught golden commerce to unfurl her
sails, / And bid fair science smile . . ." ("RGA" 1771, 3; all citations
of "RGA" 1771 refer to the 1772 reprint of the 1771 oration, with
page number). Leander is calling for a momentary turning away
from British tradition so that he can define something new and live
up to the epic idea of the title. But the turn away is, as we will see,
ineffectual. Of course this is primarily due to the lack of political
independence – the birth of the nation has not yet come. But to
take the national aspirations of the poem at face value is to understand the problem of identity in the fulfillment of those aspirations.
In its attempt to voice a proto-national epic, too much of British
and European history remains entangled with that of the New
World; consequently, it is an epic in search of a hero who will ac-
tively create a distinct and independent nation. Columbus comes
closest to filling that role, but he functions better as a symbol that
allows empire to proceed and American identity to be negotiated.
And largely because of that lack of a national hero on the order of
Aeneas, what Leander is calling for in place of the old – the clear
vision of an American nation – will remain blurred throughout the
poem of 1771. "The Rising Glory of America" is thus a patriotic
epic at odds with itself, a telling embodiment of the strains within
the British-American empire itself.

Freneau politely expresses the debt owed by the acolytes of civilization to forebears whose praise should now fall silent. This litany
concludes with a familiar empire, Britain.

> No more of Britain, and her kings renown'd,
> Edward's and Henry's thunderbolts of war;
> Her chiefs victorious o'er the Gallic foe;
> Illustrious senators, immortal bards,
> And wise philosophers, of these no more.
> A theme more new, tho' not less noble, claims
> Our ev'ry thought on this auspicious day;
> The rising glory of this western world
> . . . .

Where now the dawning light of science spreads
Her orient ray, and wakes the muse's song.
                    ("RGA" 1771, 3–4)

Having cleared the historical and rhetorical ground for the new epic of a monumental, though as yet ill-defined, civilization, Acasto responds by proclaiming the need for a muse that will be adequate to such rhetorical pretensions: "And since a friendly concourse centers here / America's own sons, begin O muse!"(4). Columbus is quickly introduced as the poets attempt to sing the original moment of American history: "Now thro' the veil of ancient days review / The period fam'd when first Columbus touch'd / The shore so long unknown . . ."(4). Columbus's discovery becomes the opportunity to establish the rightness of British claims to New World sovereignty. The poets invoke the Black Legend, taking evident rhetorical delight in their rage at the Spanish, declaiming the lurid details of bloody southern conquests of Mexico and Peru.

But why, thus hap'ly found, should we resume
The tale of Cortez, furious chief, ordain'd
With Indian blood to dye the sands, and choak
Fam'd Amazonia's stream with dead! OR why,
Once more revive the story old in fame,
Of Atabilipa by thirst of gold
Depriv'd of life: which not Peru's rich ore,
Nor Mexico's vast mines cou'd then redeem.
Better these northern realms deserve our song,
Discover'd by Britannia for her sons;
Undeluged with seas of Indian blood,
Which cruel Spain on southern regions spilt;
To gain by terrors what the gen'rous breast
Wins by fair treaty, conquers without blood.
                    ("RGA" 1771, 4–5)

Eugenio follows this emphatically pro-British tirade by further buttressing the historical claims of non-Spanish Europe to New World territory. The trope of blood is the most perfect emblem of colonial righteousness. He offers a litany of explorers, beginning with John Cabot (an adopted Englishman) and ending with "illustrious Raleigh," all of whom followed a legally sanctioned, "unbloody" course of conquest.

Methods of conquest, emblematized by their relative bloodiness, are not, however, enough to differentiate the two empires, Spanish and British. A complex genealogy of difference regarding the conquered aboriginals, and by implication their conquerors, is required to explain how the Spanish conquest was an affront to reformist notions of empire. Britain's discoveries and fair conquests lead Eugenio, and then Acasto, to wonder just where North America's Indians came from. Their meditations lay the groundwork for a genealogical argument in which savagism draws on the Black Legend to sanctify the continued colonization of North America.[13]

> For in her woods America contain'd,
> From times remote, a savage race of men.
> Who shall we know their origin, how tell,
> From whence or where the Indian tribes arose?
>
> ACASTO:
> And long has this defy'd the sages skill
> To investigate. – Tradition seems to hide
> The mighty secret from each mortal eye,
> How first these various nations, South and North,
> Possest these shores, or from what countries came.
>
> ("RGA" 1771, 4–5)

Setting up "tradition" as their rhetorical straw man, Freneau and Brackenridge will attempt to surpass the limitations of traditional appeals. Though pre-Columbian New World history had been something of an enigma, we must begin to parse out just who was, and is, entitled to make sovereign claims. The poem, we are told, will clarify the mysteries of imperial retrospection by beginning an argument about those mysteries. Out of that argument will arise the criteria for theorizing pre-European Indian entitlement. The primary standards will be European racial heritage and thus modes of political economy and cultural formation.

Acasto proposes several schools of thought on Indian origins that compass geological upheaval and emigration across continents. Leander, however, finds all this to be sophistry, that Acasto is too scientific. Instead, Leander urges Acasto to "Hear what the voice of history proclaims"(7), thereby turning the scientific "prehistory" of the New World over to British imperial propaganda. His theory holds that the Carthaginians, before the Roman conquest of their empire, were driven westward across the Atlantic "by the eastern trade wind," finally landing somewhere in Brazil. These civilized if unfortunate north Africans were the ancestors of

> . . . – those whom we call
> Brazilians, Mexicans, Peruvians rich,
> The tribes of Chili, Patagon, and those
> Who till the shores of Amazonia's stream.
> ("RGA" 1771, 8)

Leander's "history" is really a prelude to yet another elaboration on the Black Legend. The glory of pre-Columbian civilizations results directly from their Mediterranean heritage (Leander identifies the Carthaginians as European) and thus their ability to "till the shores of Amazonia's stream." The destruction of such civilizations by the Spanish seems a particularly egregious betrayal of lost strains of European glory. Note in the following how Europe's agents discover "cities form'd from Europe's architecture."

> When first the powers of Europe here attain'd
> Vast empires, kingdoms, cities, palaces
> And polish'd nations stock'd the fertile land.
> Who has not heard of Cusco, Lima, and
> The town of Mexico – *huge cities form'd*
> *From Europe's architecture*; ere the arms
> Of haughty Spain disturb'd the peaceful soil.
> ("RGA" 1771, 8, my emphasis)

The idea of the city, replete with the architecture of permanence fed by fecund rural societies, has become a fetish that serves to underscore the impermanence of a totalized North American Indian culture. British colonization proceeded on the righteous claim to a civilization that would endure over time – that, like the Incas and Aztecs, would provide recognizable, and therefore solid, monuments of history.

"RGA" 1786: An Exile's Identity for the Republican

When Freneau recasts the above passage in the 1786 version, he claims something other than British imperial prerogative, something altogether strange. He seems to suggest the common roots of New

25

World civilizations, calling for a bond between civilizations that have been destroyed by Europe (Incas and Aztecs) and those threatened with imminent destruction (the United States). In so doing, Freneau's genealogy of difference, which glorifies the South American native ideal, is refined and transformed in the present to justify a variety of post-colonial prerogatives. I will return to this matter in a moment.

Another important difference between 1771 and 1786 concerns the Indians at the western frontier, who represent in the later poem a condensation of anxieties the new nation has about its own historical innocence regarding its potential to unseat the original inhabitants of the continent. In 1771, colonial American imperial guilt could be successfully palliated by anti-British rhetoric, whereas the worrisome implications of American oppression of the Indian were only aggravated by the frontier politics of 1786. While tracing the parallel origins of exiled Europeans in the New World is enough in 1771, the firmer national implications of 1786 demand more differentiation between North and South American Indians. Accordingly, Freneau plays up differences between North and South that were there in 1771, but that he did not need to dramatize. The 1786 distinction is intensified by notions of civility and savagery that derive from the Black Legend. The Legend convinces Freneau that Indians on the northern continent have no land rights.

This finds expression in "RGA" 1786, where the previous passage from 1771 is augmented by the following:

> But *here*, amid this northern dark domain
> No towns were seen to rise. – No arts were here;
> The tribes unskill'd to raise the lofty mast,
> Or force the daring prow thro' adverse waves,
> Gaz'd on the pregnant soil, and crav'd alone
> Life from the unaided genius of the ground, –
> This indicates they were a different race;
> From whom descended 'tis not ours to say –
> ("RGA" 1786, 46–7; all citations of "RGA"
> 1786 refer to *The Poems* [1786],
> with page number)

North American Indians are now represented as a truly uncivilized lot, untraceable along a characteristically eighteenth-century course

26

of ascension or decline – "a different race; / From whom descended 'tis not ours to say."[14] To have "descended" in this context is really to have been exiled from civilization, for Leander suggests that North American Indians do indeed have an origin – they are the product of a spontaneous creation, a barbaric birth from the "pregnant soil": "That power, no doubt, who furnish'd trees, and plants, / And animals, to this vast continent, / Spoke into being man among the rest" (47). The continent would seem to have been the site of its own primal creation, a place of divine nomination set apart from the unitary origin of the rest of the world. But this power of divine nomination is conferred by the epic artificer; North American Indians are akin to the continent's flora and fauna, deprived of all legitimizing agency.[15]

Yet despite what he represents as a genuinely inhibiting factor, Freneau cannot countenance that they did nothing with their share of the New World, that "no arts were here." Anglo-Americans have no such inhibitions and are justified in renaming and thereby reclaiming the continents. Godlike himself, Leander speaks into being the new reign of civilization and imperial chauvinism on the northern continent, rhetorically reestablishing a genealogy that parallels the civilized South American ideal of exile and architectural permanence. His language overflows in the present tense with the exaggerated wonder and astonishment of the explorer who has had the good fortune to rediscover the New World already civilized, retroactively made over by the industry of commercial America and the voice of the nominative artificer: "But what a change is here! – what arts arise! / What towns and capitals! how commerce waves / Her gaudy flags, where silence reign'd before!" (47).

The legal argument for North American colonization, based on distinctions between North and South American Indian land use, was well known to eighteenth-century Americans. Indeed, these justifications had served the British well, and were useful now to Americans. In 1758, the Swiss legal theorist Emmerich de Vattel reasoned from solid Black Legend premises that North American colonization was legally justified by the different economic modes employed by South American civilizations and North American tribes.

Thus, while the conquest of the civilized Empires of Peru and Mexico was a notorious usurpation, the establishment of various colonies upon the continent of North America might, if done within just limits, have been entirely lawful. The peoples of those vast tracts of land rather roamed over them than inhabited them.[16]

"RGA" 1786, in particular, distills such self-serving tonics. While the colonists' European origin and dedication to agricultural improvement are important to differentiate them from the North American Indians, the poem also begins to ally the colonists – historically, ideologically, and even racially – with the Incas and Aztecs. Following in the pre-Columbians' tradition, American colonists will create the preeminent agricultural and political culture of the New World; and, like the South American civilizations, their survival is profoundly threatened by the meddling of illegitimate European empires (i.e., those not founded by true exiles). The American poet's voice breaks the "silence" of North America by introducing a resounding historical epic that is conscious of what constitutes a "notorious usurpation," and in so doing stretches both south and east to find its exile(d) lineage and native legacy.

We can view this elevation of the South American ideal as an extrapolation of a republican view of history. Even as Freneau reaches Europe by way of South America, there is a kind of bypassing of Europe that takes part in an ahistorical discourse. Another instance of this anti-Europeanism *cum* ahistoricism is to be found in Thomas Paine's argument in the *Rights of Man*, Part II (1792), in which Paine claims that recent traditions of contract-based government are products of coercion and violence, perversions of Greco-Roman precedent as well as corruptions of new insights into natural law. Paine means to indict European (particularly British) post-Renaissance political schemes: "As time obliterated the history of their beginnings, their successors assumed new appearances but their principles and objects remained the same. What at first was plunder assumed the softer name of revenue."[17] Paul Carter discusses this ahistorical stance as a conscious break with European political traditions, an attempt to construct a new story that is in line with certain assumptions about human nature.

There was thus no point in defending modern free government by an appeal to the past; the political past, at least, did not deserve such veneration. Humanity was in a brand-new political era, Paine affirmed, and the makers of a new American government should apply the recent insights of science rather than old conjectures about government origins. Instead of drawing upon an imagined primeval condition of liberty or a real but antiquated Graeco-Roman tradition, modern revolutionaries should transfer the grand simplicities of Newtonian physics over to the craft of state-making . . . republican government . . . "is always parallel with the order and immutable laws of nature, and meets the reason of man in every part" [Paine]. (Carter, *Revolt Against Destiny*, 30)

But "ahistoricism" is not the precise term for Freneau's stance. Whether or not Paine was tired of the search for origins, others, like Freneau, were more keenly attuned to genealogies that legend had provided, and so turned their attention to "native" Americans, who, like them, and unlike loyalist exiles (whether British or Spanish), had suffered the oppressions of empire.

Indeed, Freneau was compelled to consider the past because he was committed to the fundamentally historicist standards of the epic. For Freneau and his fellow republicans, the exemplars of a world in which man and nature were governed by benign reason could be located in the Black Legend.[18] For republicans, especially agrarian anti-Federalists, that those early practitioners of Newtonian civilization were "in their own back yard" in a figurative, geohistorical domain, proved politically irresistible. The Incas and Aztecs, who by Leander's account were the forerunners of North America's exiled Europeans, had indeed established "vast empires" that subjected abundant unclaimed nature to the *orden y concierto* we find in the Black Legend; these civilizations seemed to embody, moreover, the virtues of Virgilian pastorals, but in a New World context. Paine's understanding that the American government would naturally "parallel with the order and immutable laws of nature, and meet the reason of man in every part" describes an essential virtue of all successful New World civilizations. Natural law arises axiomatically from the political perfection residing in South American history; Americans could now understand themselves as embodying and restoring that exceptional legacy.[19]

This restorationist move into the submerged history of New World governance is made from the beginning of the 1786 version of "The Rising Glory of America." Increasingly anxious to fashion a stable national identity from the heraldic gestures and ambiguity

of 1771, Freneau takes his prophecy of 1771, "I see a Homer and
a Milton rise" ("RGA" 1771, 24),[20] and fulfills it with himself in
the Miltonic role. He now relocates the Old World, British dialectic
between Jerusalem and Albion to the New World of America and
Mexico/Peru. Just as Albion was to reestablish the dominion of
God over earth in *Paradise Lost*, so America would reignite what has
been extinguished in this hemisphere. Freneau hearkens a precedent for poetic vision and national pride, distinctly Miltonic in its
quest for epic "strains" that sing Edenic moments of political paradise lost.

> Now shall the adventurous muse attempt a strain
> More new, more noble, and more flush of fame
> Than all that went before –
> Now through the veil of ancient days renew
> The period fam'd when first Columbus touch'd
> These shores so long unknown . . .
> ("RGA" 1786, 42)

In 1771, when Freneau and Brackenridge wrote "A New Jerusalem, sent down from Heaven, / Shall grace our happy earth," they
could only look forward to such Miltonic renewal. Freneau's emphasis on novelty and renovation – "new" and "renew" (in 1771
"review" was sufficient) – would seem to be a recognition of the
double transformation of two Columbian moments, the historical
and the contemporary. The contemporary transformation will be
restorative, a renewal of a paradisiacal moment in the history of
empires, when "first Columbus touch'd these shores" and imperial
Europe came upon the glorious spectacle of New World civilization.
Columbus is the historical symbol of cosmic possibility and renovation, and the contemporary symbol of an opportunity for the nation
to restore the legacy of New World civilization. The poem in 1786
thus has grander claims to nationalism in the face of northern and
southern European hegemony in North America; Columbus functions as the prophet who ordained America's counter-hegemony in
its project of premillennial restoration.

The initial moment of Columbian restoration is intensified in
"RGA" 1786 by Freneau's immediate recollection of the Black Legend, which follows in the form of a question posed somewhat rhetorically by Acasto. In this post-Revolutionary version, 1771's "But

why, thus hap'ly found" is changed to "But why to prompt your tears," as Acasto forcefully questions the rote invocation of the Black Legend. There is a sense that the repetition of the British colonial story is gratuitous – it has become sentimental, even boring: "But why, to prompt your tears, should we resume / The tale of *Cortez*..." (43). Though Freneau would now question the use of a tired British trope, he is not above retaining its most sensational aspects. His reasons for continuing the tradition are expressed in the rhetoric of yeoman ideology.

> Better these northern realms demand our song
> Design'd by nature for the rural reign,
> For agriculture's toil, – No blood we shed
> For metals buried in a rocky waste.
> Curs'd be that ore, which brutal makes mankind,
> And prompts mankind to shed a brother's blood.
> ("RGA" 1786, 43)

The corresponding 1771 passage followed with a cruder elucidation of the Black Legend; here, though, the refrain is noticeably more refined in its republican sensibilities, claiming an agrarian basis for imperial usurpations. Freneau's assertion of the superior quality of North American land – "design'd by nature for the rural reign" – serves the emerging version of republicanism that glorified such frontier virtues, as well as such frontier identifications.

In its distinction between the essential qualities of North and South America (their respective lands, dark natives, and white conquerors), the Black Legend was a way of arriving at nationalist configurations of American commerce and agriculture that would endure and clash as the republic expanded.[21] The tension between commerce and agriculture is reflected in the symbolic resonances of the Black Legend's dialectic between Columbus and the conquistadors. Columbus, for his part, is truly the commercial ideal.[22] As Freneau proclaims in 1771: " 'Tis commerce joins dissever'd worlds in one, / Confines old Ocean to more narrow bounds; / Outbraves his storms and peoples half his world" ("RGA" 1771, 17). And in 1786, a less enthusiastic yet nevertheless admiring Freneau writes of commerce in the Columbian mode, differentiating European systems of capital by figuring them into categories of civility and savagery.

Strip Commerce of her sail, and men once more
Would be converted into savages –
No nation e'er grew social and refin'd
Till Commerce first had wing'd the adventurous prow.
("RGA" 1786, 52)

The conquistadors of legend, on the other hand, serve to differentially romanticize the agricultural genius of the liquidated and enslaved South Americans, a distinction that implicitly suggests the politics of radical Jeffersonianism.

Spanish New World history, encompassing as it does two conflicting tropes of political economy, displays not only the residual dichotomy between country and court, but also emergent anti-Federalism and Federalism, a division that played itself out in debates about national expansion. Freneau is, as we've seen, subject to this ambivalence, even though the trope's deployment provides an opportunity to render a false post-Revolutionary national consensus. For him, the Black Legend's version of ancient America's discovery and conquest is more than a compendium of horrors located within history; it also exercises a crucial ideological purpose within the present. It effectively produces a justifying mode for North Americans who have been able to improve the land by removing, or exterminating, its Indians, unlike the Spanish who have reduced the Indians to slaves. The Black Legend, in Freneau's rhetorical world of peaceful imperialism, is thus a way of appropriating history in order to bolster national prospects in the present. History inhabits a quite different register for Spanish Americans; figured as a train of enslaved bodies of South American Indians, history continues to delegitimize the civilizing but warlike energies of New Spain.

The braggarts' peace in the poem, however, is blind to the nation's conflict elsewhere. A relapse into war with European rivals was anxiously being averted by Jefferson and Adams, as they tried to bring about favorable terms of trade that would antagonize neither Britain nor France, and that would place them in good position to expand into the Spanish Mississippi valley. As if to dismiss immediately any notion that "Indian hosts were slain" outside the bounds prescribed by Vattel's "just limits," Leander begins to recount the savage resistance offered by the Indians to the Anglo colonizer's improving advance.[23] We learn that the Indian is made even more savage when he is sponsored by European imperial rivals (in this case the French) who misguide the barbarous with the worst of civilizing warfare.

> . . . fierce Indian tribes
> With vengeful malice arm'd, and black design,
> Oft murder'd or dispers'd these colonies –
> Encourag'd, too, by Gallia's hostile sons,
> A warlike race, who late their arms display'd
> At Quebec, Montreal, and farthest coasts
> Of Labrador, or Cape Breton, where now
> The British standard awes the subject host.
>
> ("RGA" 1786, 48)

The Indian thus impedes the proper colonization of America by allying himself with southern European empires such as France. This would seem a curious, though not too surprising, variation on the Black Legend, where France becomes the "warlike race," and the discourse now reinforces American claims to the land based on the treachery of Catholic imperialists everywhere, who opportunistically continue to exploit savages against a still-oppressed fledgling nation.[24]

With regard to Britain, however, an obvious change has taken place since 1771. We find the same passage (with its last line, "where now / The British standard awes the subject host") in both versions of the poem; however, the politics of independence have intervened to alter its meaning. In 1771 the frontier flew British standards on the American side of the border; in 1786, by contrast, those flags fly antagonistically on the other side. Indeed, the issue of frontier forts was the major obstacle to peaceful relations in the postwar years. The quality of the word "awed" is thus transformed from a term of respectful wonder on the part of the Anglo colonial subject and the Indian in 1771 to a signal of border anxiety in 1786.

Freneau's 1786 options with the connotative possibilities of the line are emblematic of the multiple registers his orientalism had to voice. Freneau must continue to assert Anglo-American rights to the land against the Spanish, French, and Indians, and, at the same time, signal American territorial prerogatives against the British; national and cultural hegemony must be happily balanced between sometimes contradictory demands. Though the frontier now flies

British flags and harbors hostile Indians, we can nonetheless glimpse the creation of a new colonial hero who will not be awed by either – indeed, one who is bold enough to encroach upon both by transcending the contradictions and arrogating for himself the supreme mantle of innocence through a claim to "native" sovereignty. The identities and ideological premises of Freneau's poem, such as the pro-British rhetorical claims, have been substantially revised since 1771. The frontier has been given a political configuration in this poem that will serve to define just where the new nation begins, and how powerfully and in what directions its conquerors feel impelled to move.

Despite history's manifest sanction, Freneau is never fully comfortable with the traditional British argument for the settlement of a continent contested by a complex array of nations and races. Cultural and racial struggles (particularly with the Indians) and geopolitical struggles (with European rivals) converge problematically at the southern, western, and northern borders. Americans, for lack of a better strategy, are forced into parroting British justifications. But those rationalizations could theoretically hold true for any other European empire (besides Spain). Consequently, in his handling of histories of the pre-Columbian New World as well as recent histories of British America, Freneau strikes an equipoise between the nationalist and the culturally chauvinist (pro-European/ Anglo-Saxon). The equipoise is a critical moment in the evolution of frontier thinking as it begins to discern a neocolonial, New World provenance in addition to more direct western claims on North America.

At the point in the 1786 poem when the historical emphasis shifts to account for the British presence on the North American continent, the strained quality of the equipoise is heightened. The poem justifies British claims against North American Indians, but also rationalizes a prospective American empire in contradistinction to the British. Americans will regenerate in the New World the degenerate republican strains of British empire, turning Britain rhetorically against itself. Acasto urges Eugenio to tell what drove their "fathers first / To visit climes unknown" and to "adorn that soil / Which never felt the industrious swain before" ("RGA" 1786, 47). Eugenio obliges Acasto by describing the Pilgrims' "sacerdotal rage," which made them seek "liberty in *faith*" far from "Europe's hostile

34

shores"(47). They also found "men, alike unknowing and un-known," who were ripe for the enlightenment of contract law; Eugenio adroitly considers the appropriation of Indian lands in terms of the legal justification. Hence, William Penn is the first in a continuing tradition of colonial legal lords who have imparted as Britons, and will continue to impart as Americans, rights-based liberty to a frontier occupied by historically and legally illegitimate interlopers – the Indians, the French, the Spanish, and, now in 1786, the British. Note that the wealth of the colonies is later to be "envied" – presumably by any European power but especially the British – and that American colonial virtue stands in distinction to all others European and native.

> Hence, by the care of each advent'rous *chief*
> New governments (their wealth unenvied yet)
> Were form'd on liberty and virtue's plan.
> *These* searching out uncultivated tracts
> Conceiv'd new plans of towns, and capitals,
> And spacious provinces – Why should I name
> Thee, Penn, the Solon of our western lands . . .
> ("RGA" 1786, 48)

In this key passage, Vattel's reasoning blends with the anti-British note of "envy" to constitute a subtly different, British, and yet unprecedented imperial justification.

We have already seen, with regard to the French and Indian War especially, that British history, and in "RGA" 1786 those stories which are preserved as appropriately pre-American, always need a dose of the Black Legend as a tonic of justification. A particularly interesting example of this occurs in the changes wrought by Freneau in the pantheon of pre-Independence war heroes. In articulating these changes, Acasto underscores the way nationalist and colonial histories can create uncomfortable identities and the way that discomfort can be negotiated by historical revisions. The following sequence from "RGA" 1786 is important because, as in "RGA" 1771, which is still overwhelmingly bound up in the obligations of British identity, Freneau finds it necessary to bring in the Spanish, who are still useful and now more than ever are an important New World, imperial rival. (As of the Treaty of 1783, two-thirds of North America was Spanish territory.) In other words, the ideology and tactics of Anglo empire replicate themselves in spite of substantive, imperial revisions to national strategy.

Acasto counters Leander's celebration of General Wolfe's heroism in the French and Indian War by offering Washington as the most worthy epic hero of that conflict.[25] Acasto dismisses British heroes and, in effect, the mandates of a less and less relevant British tradition:

> The dead, Leander, are but empty names,
> And they who fall to-day the same to us
> As they who fell ten centuries ago – !
> Lost are they all that shin'd on earth before;
> Rome's boldest champions in the dust are laid,
> Ajax and great Achilles are no more,
> And *Philip's* warlike son, an empty shade! –
> A *Washington* among our sons of fame
> We boast conspicuous as the morning star
> Among the inferior lights –
> To distant wilds Virginia sent him forth –   [1755]
> With her brave sons he gallantly opposed
> The bold invaders of his country's rights. . . .
>   ("RGA" 1786, 49)

And yet Freneau is eager to avoid the political implications of Britain's imperial war, in which Americans now appear to have been the bravest of dupes. He quickly reverts to Washington's accomplishments as a winner of the frontier, the land itself becoming more important than a French-British quarrel over territories. Even "rights," a term that resonated strongly within the discourse surrounding American taxation and representation, seems a code word to trigger anti-British sentiment. In order to move the argument away from the embarrassments of British history toward a more expansive colonial destiny, Freneau makes the frontier virtues of Washington's conquests foremost. Washington's heroism is metonymically allied with pastoral virtues and the majesty of the frontier; Freneau cannot restrain his enthusiasm for the silent hero of his national epic – the land itself.

> Where wild *Ohio* pours the mazy flood,
> And mighty meadows skirt his subject streams,
> But now delighting his elm tree's shade,

> Where deep *Potowmac* laves the enchanting shore,
> He prunes the tender vine, or bids the soil
> Luxuriant harvest to the sun display.
> ("RGA" 1786, 49)

In contrast to the British flag "awing the subject host," we now have the Ohio River with "subject streams." Washington has won this land because he has a unique covenant with a frontier that is itself inherently sovereign, not because he possesses essentially British virtues. Kingly "subjection" is given a new context and, therefore, a new connotation. Washington's role in this new "subjection" is no longer that of the colonial dupe, but that of one who has a sovereign relationship to a frontier that seemingly transcends the political and the imperial. The implicit meaning of "America" acquires in the movement toward the frontier a geographical resonance, though after having been refigured by revisionary political uses. Ostensibly artless political nationalism, suggested over and over again by the borders of contested colonial domains, is thus superseded by a more efficacious organic, property-based nationalism that figures the land as almost beckoning its perfect conquerors. The prospect of ever-available tillage for one who knew its inherent virtues bolstered the Jeffersonian's self-image as different from (and more worthy than) the British imperialist, and so too cleansed him of the nastier imperial implications of such prospects.

True to form, the invocation of the frontier and the implied jab at Britain prompts a return to the Black Legend, as Acasto contrasts the far bloodier frontier politics at work in Latin America:

> Behold a different scene – not thus employed
> Where *Cortez*, and *Pizarro*, pride of Spain,
> Whom blood and murder only satisfied,
> And all to glut ambition!
> ("RGA" 1786, 49)

The oscillation between pro- and anti-British sentiments continues as Eugenio explains that this is what happens when, as with the European, "the soul / Humane is wanting." In the corresponding sequence of the 1771 poem, Freneau limits the offending conquerors to the Spanish. Here in "RGA" 1786 though, he expands the category to "Europeans."

> . . . but we boast no feats
> Of cruelty like Europe's murdering breed –
> Our milder epithet is merciful,
> And each American, true hearted, learns
> To conquer and to spare; for coward souls
> Alone seek vengeance on a vanquish'd foe.
>
> ("RGA" 1786, 49–50)

Again, the attack on Britain (which at the time was exercising a brand of post-Revolutionary vengeance along the western frontier) implied by this expansion of the category of evil empires prompts the necessary Spanish litany, the cultural backtracking that we have seen become so predictable and so relentless. In a particularly emblematic display of the tenuousness of the work of justification, Eugenio declaims yet again the crimes of conquest committed by "Spain's rapacious tribe" in the quest for "[g]old, fatal gold." In a time of contested sovereignty, a period of internal political uncertainty, treaty-making, and low-intensity conflict with multiple enemies, Freneau must carefully balance his savagism and his anti-Spanish legends with the needs of a multivocal nationalism that bespeaks, above all, the hybridized logic of the expanding frontier.

"Native Innocence"?: The Visionary Epic

When almost two-thirds of the poem have been devoted to the various genealogies of New World glory and shame, the moment arrives for Leander to penetrate "mystic scenes of dark Futurity" and ask "what empires yet must rise" ("RGA" 1786, 53). The rhetoric of the poem is now firmly injunctive: what must rise, and who must fall. In the process, Freneau completes the elision of the dangerous or limiting implications of the past. The visionary mode is saturated with the ordaining energies of historical greatness and the undeniable potential of geographical prospects, while it attempts to erase racial identifications that might blur the ideal new American now coming into focus. Any "misrecognitions" are seemingly corrected.

Leander envisions a time when the American empire will claim territory that is not bounded by fears of European power, and when the Indians are no longer a consideration. Indeed, the American Indian, so crucial to the nation's prehistory, is absent from the nation's "futurity."

> And time anticipates, when we shall spread
> Dominion from the north, and south, and west,
> Far from the Atlantic to Pacific shores,
> And shackle half the convex of the main! –
> A Glorious theme! – but how shall mortals dare
> To pierce the dark events of future years
> And scenes unravel, only known to fate?
> ("RGA" 1786, 53–4)

The American continents north and south, despite the presence of the British, the French, and the Spanish, seem to be his goal. The Spanish, having savagely destroyed the civilization of architecture and agriculture in South America, have ceded their claim to guardianship of the continent. Freneau's New World identity, which has emerged by understanding itself in distinction to European powers and lesser native Americans, stakes out the Western Hemisphere ("half the convex of the main") as its destined empire. This destiny, posited almost half a century before the Monroe Doctrine, sanctions a neocolonial hemispheric horizon in addition to the colonial annexationist future of the North American territories.

Acasto's question in the preceding passage interrogates the ideological work of the poem itself. For if this is but a "theme," then how does it determine the imaginative distance of true empire? The answer resides in a biblical prolepsis that gives voice to national ambitions; the poetic voice has acquired the quality of divine nomination, prophetic and geopolitically aware.

> This might we do, if warm'd by that bright coal
> Snatch'd from the altar of cherubic fire
> Which touch'd Isaiah's lips – or of the spirit
> Of Jeremy and Amos, prophets old,
> Might swell the heaving breast – I see, I see
> A thousand kingdoms rais'd, cities, and men,
> Numerous as sand upon the ocean shore! –
> The *Ohio* soon shall glide by many a town
> Of note; and where the *Missisippi* [*sic*] stream,

> By forests shaded, now runs sweeping on,
> Nations shall grow, and STATES . . .
> ("RGA" 1786, 54)

This passage amply articulates the political mythology that results from the ideological, nation-mapping work of the poem, indicating just how seriously Freneau takes the themes of his hypostatized frontier poetry. The success of the empire is dependent upon the fullness of his vision. Accordingly, the passage articulates the determining contours of American geography with a view to agriculture and commerce; geography, a spatial construct that allows the free play of commercial and therefore internationally astute energies, overdetermines the future. The two main axes of American agricultural and commercial power on the continent, the Ohio and Mississippi, suggest the natural license of prospective expansions. These rivers, moreover, flow east-west and north-south, suggesting the future vindication of Eugenio's call to a truly New World, Pan-American empire without borders, spreading "north, and south, and west." The Columbian epic delivers the republican empire because Jeffersonian ideology so effortlessly delivers a salutary brand of conquest according to commerce, natural law, and the material facts of geography.

Finally, the two versions of "The Rising Glory of America" are substantially different in the mood of their conclusions. In 1771 the uncertainties of what would result as America rose are overwhelming, even for the clarifying power of the epic vision. In spite of the poets' best effort to describe a new entity that would carry on the heliotropic course of European progress, the last lines sound the notes of apocalypse.

> Till all those glorious orbs of light on high
> The rolling wonders that surround the ball,
> Drop from their spheres extinguish'd and consum'd;
> When final ruin with her fiery car
> Rides o'er creation, and nature's works
> Are lost in chaos and the womb of night.
> ("RGA" 1771, 27)

Alternatively, this can be read as a millennialist gesture that optimistically bodes the rebirth of Revolutionary nationhood out of "the womb of night." In either case, the future is still too confounding for an as yet undefined poetic voice trying to sing its ambiguous nation. The innocent nation, a neutral product of "nature's works," is consumed by uncertainties and vague threats.

By contrast, Acasto ends the 1786 poem by returning us to the Miltonic register of rebeginning.

> . . . Paradise anew
> Shall flourish, by no second Adam lost.
> No dangerous tree with deadly fruit shall grow,
> No tempting serpent to allure the soul
> From native innocence.
>
> ("RGA" 1786, 57)

Native innocence is here dependent on the superior agricultural talents of republican farmers who will allow no dangerous outcroppings – Indian, British, Spanish, French – to impede the progress of the redeeming nation. The phrase "Paradise anew" reminds us that American visions of empire suggest in their utopian promise historical precedents both sacred and secular. The exile's genealogy of difference (suggestive as well of humanity's Edenic alienation) operates in the present at the moment of epic closure as a typological affirmation of the Jeffersonian agricultural ideal. Religious energies, however, override the implications of the parallel genealogies of the historical epic; thus, the Indian – north and south – is rendered finally invisible, as the Anglo-American stands sovereign over the historically reconditioned hemisphere.

But the parallel genealogies also allow for the instantiation of a new identity that partakes of the claims of the Indian and the justifications of the colonizing European. By way of displacing the South American ideal and rendering the North American Indian invisible to the destiny of the empire, Freneau puns on the word "native," implying both the adjective and noun.[26] In the cunning conflation of the essential noun and the less racially connotative adjective, a new identity is suggested. In this new subjectivity, the republican cannot be tempted by the "serpentine" confusion of national guilt or a bordered, British-New World-American identity. For all its obsession with the borders of the past, we begin to see an identity oriented toward a borderless future, where the commercial dissolves territories of difference (the "barbaric" or "semicivilized") into zones of improvement or reclamation. In the work of the poem – transforming religious and legendary types into the self-serving and unlimited terms of American progress – Freneau incarnates the American with the most useful identity of all, that of "native," primevally "innocent" of the sins of international politics and illegal usurpations.[27]

Complicating Civilization: Other New World Poems

Lest it appear that Freneau's poetry is too easily summarized as the sublimation of a handy legend of history into a language of innocence, I would hasten to point to the frustration that that legend caused, and indeed, the doubts that came with the emergence of an imperial ideal in Freneau's work. Freneau continued to struggle with the themes of ancient America, discovery, and conquest in other poems, written throughout his life, carrying on a varied and often fractious conversation with himself about the possibilities and sins of empire. Indeed, many of these pieces ultimately express the difficulty of squaring literary nationalism with political nationalism.

One such piece, written shortly after his graduation in 1772, is "Discovery," a less equivocal attack on Spanish depravity and a forthright panegyric on Columbian genius. It is also arguably his first really accomplished poem, displaying the virtuosity of his best poetic propaganda. The poem is successful because Freneau has retreated from the ambitions of the epic. This formal retreat paradoxically creates a more comfortable poetic space in which to express opinions; in contrast to "The Rising Glory of America," there is a more absolute questioning of imperialism, specifically about the morality of Indian removal in both North and South America. We get here no argument for salutary conquest, only an argument for what a proper conquest is not.

> What charm is seen thro' Europe's realms of strife
> That adds new blessings to the savage life? –
> On them warm suns with equal splendor shine,
> And each domestic pleasure equals thine,
> Their native groves a happier bloom display,
> As self-contented roll their lives away,
> And the gay soul, in fancy's visions blest,
> Leaves to the care of chance her heaven of rest.
> What are these arts that rise on reason's plan

> But arts destructive to the bliss of man?
> What are these wars, where'er the tracks you trace,
> But the sad records of our world's disgrace?
>
> (*The Poems*, 62)

Freneau recommends "leav[ing] religion and thy laws at home, / Leave the free native to enjoy his store"(63). In other words, the *translatio studii* should be abandoned. We get in its place a kind of suspended savagism, and we are left anticipating the inevitable praise of the progress of civilization and its greater good. Essentially, savagism without the *translatio*, as we have it here, is anti-imperialist. But Freneau soon escapes from this restrictive injunction (imperial identity being so crucial to burgeoning national identity) by resorting to more politically expedient prejudices. The other shoe drops, but it is not the positive praise of Anglo conquest we might have expected, only the negative poetics of the Black Legend.

> Born to be wretched, search this globe around,
> Dupes to a few the race of man is found:
> Seek some new world in some new climate . . .
> . . . .
> Though men decay the monarch never dies!
> Howe'er the groves, howe'er gardens bloom,
> A *Monarch* and a *Priest* is still their doom.
>
> (*The Poems*, 63)

The Catholic nations and those who still are ruled by royalty are the most responsible for the despoiling of the New World. Discovery is redeemed, however barely, by this resort to the Black Legend. The tenuousness of this attitude seems to echo a similar tension in Whig (and later radical republican) notions of liberty, where property and wealth too often in history have led to corruption and the decline of empires. But to proscribe liberty (i.e., the freedom to expand and discover) is to go against the fundamental creed of republicanism itself: to wit, civil liberty as a function of the right to property.

The troubling contradictions regarding Native Americans generated by New World, British, and American identities prompted Freneau many times to try to reformulate a congenial savagism. These attempts were often poetic failures. What they suggest ultimately is the familiar double discourse of savagism, coupling guilty lamentation and the sense that, in any case, imperial expansion is important for the prospects of the nation and the good of humanity at large. An example is the poem "The Prophecy of King Tammany," a passage from which graced the illustrated frontispiece of the 1782 edition of his poems:

> The Indian chief who, fam'd of yore,
>   Saw Europe's sons advent'ring here,
> Look'd sorrowing to the crowded shore,
>   And sighing dropt a tear!
> He saw them half his world explore,
> He saw them draw the shining blade,
> He saw their hostile ranks display'd,
> And cannons blazing through that shade
> Where only peace was known before.
>
> (*The Poems*, 308)

This is of course a reversal of the New World epic familiar to us from "The Rising Glory of America"; it is the Native American who now prophesies from a privileged vantage point. The rest of the poem gives Chief Tammany's view of present and past troubles for both Anglo society and his own; but Tammany is primarily being used to narrate the Revolution, offering it almost as a parallel to the conquest suffered by his own. Amazingly, despite sadness over the conquest of his world, he proposes as a remedy for domestic strife in the new nation the settlement of America's "gardens in the west," even going so far as offering to lead the way. Of course, his sadness is a typically savagist resignation, a graceful bowing to superior civil society. Fittingly, Tammany at the end of the poem makes his funeral pyre and seeks yet another "world unknown," ceding the world he presently occupies and moving on to the only world now available to his kind.

Such faux-"redskin" performances were a favorite satirical technique for the proto-romantic patriot like Freneau. One of the more remarkable instances of this is a prose piece titled "The Voyage of Timberoo-Tabo-Eede, an Otaheite Indian." The piece purports to be a translation of "hierogliphical records" that are essentially a parody of any number of explorers' letters to their monarch. In this defamiliarization of the discourse of discovery and conquest, Freneau critiques empire. The king, speaking the scientific language of civilization, instructs Timberoo in the methods of discovery and conquest:

> All lands that you shall discover, and which, upon investigation, shall appear to be inhabited by barbarians and savages, we do hereby authorize you to take possession of in our royal name, and for our use, as appendages to this our royal government; and be particularly careful to bring us an inhabitant of every new country you discover, by way of specimen of the make, manners and language of the tribe or nation to which he belongs. (*The Miscellaneous Works*, 205)

This is a truly absolving inversion of the Columbian story, however, since the discovered lands of Otaheite are deemed to serve "no good purpose, and would only tend to corrupt the pure religion and decent system of manners and morals we have received from our ancestors." Freneau's view of difference, and conquest in particular, is typical of Whig anxieties over the degradations of empire: discovery redounds upon the discoverer in the corruptions of imperialism. Whether it represents a cautionary rhetoric or a polemic against new imperial appetites is an open question.

Freneau's "The Pictures of Columbus" is another in his continuing meditations on the degradations of imperial power. Columbus is here portrayed as an almost Newtonian figure who resolves the conflicts between Art and Nature, transcending the political schemes of his base sponsors.

Picture I.

Columbus *making* maps.

> As o'er his charts Columbus ran,
> Such disproportion he survey'd,
> He thought he saw in art's mean plan
> Blunders that Nature never made.
> (*The Miscellaneous Works*, 1)

Columbus's transcendence is so extreme that he is pictured conjuring the future in the "cell of an inchantress." Freneau excuses Columbus's indulgence in witchcraft both by implying Columbus's distance from the politics of the Black Legend (even as he exploits the Black Legend convention of Catholic superstition) and by his-

toricizing in a footnote: "The fifteenth century was, like many of
the preceding, an age of superstition, credulity and ignorance.
When this circumstance therefore is brought into view, the mixture
of truth and fiction will not appear altogether absurd or unnatural" (*The Miscellaneous Works*, 3). Freneau adds a final sentence to
this footnote that addresses the premises behind his own poetic for-
mulations of Columbus: "At any rate, it has ever been tolerated in
this species of poetry." It would seem Freneau is theorizing about
the ways in which poetry has supplanted magic in the modern
world, and especially the New World. The only difference between
magic, which mixes truth and fiction, and poetry like "The Pictures of Columbus," which does likewise, is that poetry is historically conscious. He is, I would argue, making the argument for the
necessity of myth.

The final picture attempts to redeem and fulfill the myth that
started with superstition and now ends with poetic valedictions. Columbus declaims at Valladolid, disgraced and ruined after his four
voyages:

> The winds blow high: one other world remains;
> Once more without a guide I find the way;
> In the dark tomb to slumber with my chains –
> Prais'd by no poet on my funeral day,
> Nor even allow'd one dearly purchas'd claim –
> My new found world not honour'd with my name.

> Yet, in this joyless gloom while I repose,
> Some comfort will attend my pensive shade,
> When memory paints, and golden fancy shows
> My toils rewarded, and my woes repaid;
> When empires rise where lonely forests grew,
> Where Freedom shall her generous plans pursue.

> To shadowy forms, and ghosts and sleepy things,
> Columbus, now with dauntless heart repair;
> You liv'd to find new worlds for thankless kings,
> Write this upon my tomb – yes – tell it there –
> Tell of those chains that sullied all my glory –
> Not mine but their's – ah, tell the shameful story.
>
> (*The Miscellaneous Works*, 29–30)

Two important aspects of New World myth are exemplified. First, Freneau establishes himself in the role of poetic amanuensis in Columbus's behalf; and second, he finds the most salient facet of his story to be the swift movement from glorious discovery – when Art and Nature were in harmony – to the "shameful story" of conquest, the Black Legend. For Freneau to assume this story in the role of poetic and political myth-maker is to see himself as redeemer of not just Columbus's legend, but the slavery of conquered Incas and Aztecs – "Tell of those chains that sullied all my glory – / Not mine but theirs." Indeed the world-altering voices of both men are fused here, as Freneau straddles the modern narrative of national ambitions and the premodern narratives of myth – a frontier moment where Columbus, Incas, and Aztecs all mirror hybrid components of "American" identity for the republican poet. His New World identity is merged, more or less successfully, with his republican identity in the quasi-"magical" operations of the identifying potential of frontiers within the national imaginary.

Naming America

The very title of 1771's "The Rising Glory of America" raises problems for a reading that is sensitive to the demands of nationalism upon the word "America." For if Freneau and Brackenridge are merely re-sounding a familiar British American colonial slogan, then a new reading is not necessary; the poem will yield only minor variations on a discourse of commercial empire (*imperium pelagi* – empire of the seas) that had become common by the second half of the eighteenth century. To understand the "America" of the title as something other than a British possession, however – to see the term as the possibility of a new mode of national thinking – is to begin to sense a subtle change in the discourses surrounding a burgeoning national concept.

To be sure, the original version of the poem bears a variety of encomiums to Britain, and the authors try to be unambiguous about presenting themselves as British subjects. But I would argue that the poem fails to find a stable British identity for its authors. Here I am taking issue with Lewis Leary, who argues with regard to "RGA" 1771:

The collegians of 1771 were loyal British subjects. As colonials they were careless of duties and jealous of liberties; yet there is little in their poem to foreshadow the events of the next ten years. Though both young authors had undoubtedly joined in discussions and demonstrations against British colonial policy, their poem was traditional in allegiance, in form, and in manner – *except for the vision of America*. ("Philip Freneau," in Everett Emerson, ed., *Major Writers of Early American Literature*, 35, my emphasis)

Also downplaying the political effects of cultural declarations is Benjamin Spencer, who writes in *The Quest for Nationality*: "Undoubtedly before 1776, the sense of nationality, of cultural divergence from the mother country, was far more pervasive and insistent than the desire for 'nationhood,' for political divergence" (2). While it is difficult to dispute the loyalist nature of the authors and their poem, Leary for his part seems to be somewhat at odds with himself. He dismisses the nationalism of the poem even as he celebrates the exceptional character of its national vision. Spencer likewise seems to underestimate the subterranean political value of cultural declarations.

It is rather more telling to understand the poem as a source of – and a kind of experiment in – the early discourses of national sovereignty. To my mind, Philip Marsh writes a more sensitive and holistic account of the meaning of these orations than Leary's:

> The theme of "Rising Glory" grew more popular after the Stamp Act, with growing confidence in the national destiny . . . At Yale, John Trumbull orated on it in the poem, "A Prospect of Our Future Glory," and the decline of Britain; he sounded a prelude to American independence . . . The double theme – liberty and the American future – became increasingly popular. In 1771 Brackenridge and Freneau, with Trumbull, were among the earliest colonials to use it. The French-Indian War was over; Canada was now British; the West was being settled; and young America, flexing her muscles, was getting really irritated by parental controls and unwelcome taxes. (*Philip Freneau*, 24–5)

This quality of "prelude," this experimental aspect of the 1771 poem, becomes evident when we see just how the 1786 version mines the earlier work for its ideology of New World empire. Both versions of the poem suggest, and attempt to resolve, the ambivalence of the colonial subject with regard to the problem of empire: how to embody a proud imperial heritage (especially in 1771) and an anti-colonial politics that served more immediate needs. The conundrum for the patriot poet involves resolving loyalties and ambitions, being at once colonist and colonialist, native and invader. British notions of *translatio imperii* (global conquest by Christian empire) and *translatio studii* (the diffusion of civilized life in the form of arts and learning) were not enough to ameliorate the ambiguities and ruptures in colonial identity.

In "The Rising Glory of America" of 1771, manifestations of that nationalist rupture begin to appear when one takes into account the intensifying dissent toward British rule that seems to have spurred the writing of such orations that year. Although it would be over five years until Freneau openly advocated American independence, recall that the Boston Massacre had occurred only a year before, and the rhetoric of colonial anger toward Britain was still strong. In addition, by 1771 resentment had been building over the Americans' heroic defense of the empire in the French and Indian War. Along with the subsequent taxation and economic depression, these burdens soured the colonists on British militarism. When Freneau and Brackenridge make the distinction in their poem between "Brittania's warlike troops" and "America's own sons," they mark a sharpening of the divisions between center and periphery. As Gordon Wood points out in *The Creation of the American Republic, 1776–1787*, one of the major problems the Whig colonists had with Britain was that they gradually recognized themselves not just as the weak partners in an imperial relationship but as the objects of imperial injustice. Britain was an increasingly illegitimate empire, in the tradition of Rome (and, for that matter, Spain); Whigs did not want to be carried along on a degenerate course. The history of empire as a trope and a legend, in both the Old and New Worlds, thereby pointed the way to national identity and the idea of the regenerate republic.

The "America" wielded by young poets in 1771 is, thus, no longer a benign province under the command of British government, nor is it merely another stop in the westward course of the British imagination.[28] At the occasion of Freneau's commencement as literary nationalist, the term "America" begins to augment its geographical denotation, gaining a more historically and politically self-defining connotation. To search for a unique "American" history, as young poets were so determined to do, is to begin to make political demands on the concept of the "American" nation.

Columbus and the pre-Columbians, historical themes upon which an understanding of the entity "America" is contingent, intensify and take on new meanings in such a context. Indeed, the Black Legend offered the figure of Columbus as a pseudo-historical symbol that held unique redemptive promise to anxious colonials like Freneau, both before and after independence. One way to be both colonist and colonialist, both native and invader, both constitutionalist in the best British tradition and dissenter from British rule, was to be, in a sense, Columbian. Columbus, as legend represented him, embodied the anxiety of empire. Thus, Columbus's fabled reaction[29] to what became of his discovery – its "blackness" – stands as a haunting and problematic trope for the colonial imagination, particularly for Freneau.[30] Ultimately, this problematic is converted into a literary idiom of innocence, by identifying with Columbus in all his martyrdom. The Spanish conquest, in turn, performs a dual function that is related to this quest for innocence; it is both a cautionary tale of empire and an emboldening story for Anglo-Americans. In Anglo-American mythology, Columbus, the Aztecs, and the Incas all stand as crucial secular types, the preeminent New World martyrs of corrupt empire.

We see this identity played out over and over in Freneau's poetry on Indians and the spread of civilization in North America. There is a consistent attempt to bring Columbus into the modern fold, and thereby justify the advance of white, politically motivated landholders. The idiom of innocence associated with Columbus and the pre-Columbians, not surprisingly, was a product of the peculiar logic of self-doubt. Freneau told Black Legend stories in order to answer the critical question of whether Americans were good enough to be republicans with imperial aspirations. The positive answer to that question was one of the most tautological and destructive judgments of American exceptionalism: Americans could be the only innocent civilizers of the New World; finding the tropes and precedents within a unique history to talk about such an exceptional identity was an important affirmation of their genius for an emerging republican American culture.

Anne Norton, in her book *Alternative Americas: A Reading of Ante-*

bellum Political Culture, discusses this type of interpretation of early American identity, where a national trope is critical to revising our understanding of political culture.

> Nationality entails not only accordance to certain objective criteria, but also subjective participation in a collective identity . . .
> This subjective nationality has, however, no formal expression. Metaphors . . . reveal the informal, nonquantifiable content of nationality. They provide traits in which nationals can recognize their commonality, symbols and gestures in which they can express it. Metaphors are especially important when nationality is inchoate, nascent, or in flux. In the use of metaphors the speaker likens the unknown, unclear, or ill-defined (in this case national identity), to an object whose traits and political significance are well established.(11)

But the use of a metaphor is never so positivistic and almost never without unintended symbolic consequences. Indeed, something more precarious seems to be playing itself out in the appropriation of Columbus and the Incas and Aztecs of the Black Legend. Here the unclear (American identity) is defined in part by the "known" (the Legend); so too, the "known" is being redefined by the advent of an emerging entity (Americanness). The use of Columbus and, necessarily, the Black Legend is, then, a mode that slips across the New World frontier of difference and identification, which must constantly balance between history and myth, between the long-standing and the politically expedient. Discursive slippage generates self-serving possibilities that enhance the cultural power of terms like "America" and "empire." The appropriation by Whig writers of the key elements that produced this discourse is an incomplete way of trying to understand, under the most difficult of circumstances, the new American in an emerging political order.

2

DIPLOMACY

JOEL BARLOW'S SCRIPTING AND SUBSCRIPTING OF ANCIENT AMERICA

Spanish: Bestow great attention on this, & endeavor to acquire an accurate knolege [*sic*] of it. Our future connections with Spain & Spanish America will render that language a valuable acquisition. The antient history of a great part of America, too, is written in that language.

Thomas Jefferson to Peter Carr, 1787

Our confederacy must be viewed as the nest from which all America, North & South is to be peopled.

Jefferson to Archibald Stuart, 1786

Cosmopolitan Exceptionalism

The legend of Manco Capac's founding of the Inca empire – transmitted to a Columbus who is vindicated by the history he hears – is the originary moment and centralizing myth of Joel Barlow's two poems of an exceptional America: *The Vision of Columbus* (1787) and its more famous, though less enthusiastically pro-Incan, revision, *The Columbiad* (1807). America's genius, Barlow emphatically asserts, is at its source an Indian genius – politically and culturally. Such anomalous geohistory, which goes even further than Freneau in glorifying the "semisavage" as the source of Anglo-American political virtue, would seem a difficult and unlikely starting point for the republican epic of early America.

Nonetheless, I want to suggest that Barlow's cosmopolitanism and republican philosophy of history were an indispensable part of the epic's "Indianized" content. In accordance with the poems' broad latitudes and palpable national ambitions – evinced so well in this chapter's epigraphs from Jefferson, his friend and fellow cosmopolitan – Barlow relied on a notion of political liberty that found no sure limits or rigid axioms within the range of eighteenth-century racial and cultural hierarchies. For Jeffersonian republicans especially, the status of American Indians was notoriously one of contradiction – the noble savage made useful by his very absence, swallowed by the yeoman-tilled soil of civilizing history.[1] In these poems, though, the Inca – the Indian – is one of the great yeoman agents of history; there is both paradox and power in such thematic maneuvering.

Barlow's historical poems not only lead us into unique conceptual problems related to the poetic imprinting of exceptionalism, they also provide a pivotal example of the political usefulness of the historical obsessions I trace from Freneau to Whitman. This chapter may be read as an analysis of the intensifying exhilaration and nervousness of scripting "classical" indigenous history – a scripting so glibly exploited in Freneau's republican poetry, and yet so vexed in William Prescott's nineteenth-century ethnohistories of conquest. Barlow is a solid bridge, in part, because his poetics seem consciously calibrated to alterations in the nation's geopolitical situation. The most important period of Barlow's relationship with Jefferson, when Jefferson was leading the United States into the manifest destinies of the nineteenth century, coincided with the revision of *The Vision of Columbus* into *The Columbiad.* The revision of national policy and power conforms to the reconstructed poetics of Barlow's foundational American poem; the imperial claims that were clarified by national consolidation affected Barlow's affinity for the Incan-American epic.

Between 1787 and 1807 the nebulous condition of post-coloniality condensed into colonial and neocolonial relationships with the Western Hemisphere's Spanish, Spanish Americans, and Indians. Given the overtly diplomatic nature of the poem, this forced a revaluation of the conceptually loose cultural and racial politics that seemed so securely to anchor *The Vision of Columbus* of 1787. By 1807, the conditions that in 1787 called for an American Indian counterhistory to Europe's imperial competitors (France excepted) had changed dramatically, to the point where the national gaze turned more intently west and that mythical In-

53

dian counterhistory became difficult to sustain. The pleasure of
contemplating Inca origins turned to anxiety. As far as the poem's
architecture was concerned, the politics and poetics couldn't be
more stark: Incas are scripted straight into the poem – between
two chapters – in 1787; they are subscripted into an endnote in
1807.

Still, that initial epic placement of the prospective colonized other
at the origins of Columbian American civilization compels more
scrutiny. As post-colonial documents, the two poems rehearse the
nationalist uses of Otherness. Abdul JanMohammed, in attempting
to keep readers of colonial fictions from forgetting power differen-
tials, has characterized such literary appropriations as allegories of
imperialist practice: "Just as imperialists 'administer' the resources
of the conquered country, so colonialist discourse 'commodifies' the
native subject into a stereotyped object and uses him as a 'resource'
for colonialist fiction.''[2] Barlow, by this reckoning, falls rather easily
into the role of symbolic colonialist.

But Barlow is – and one suspects, along with Homi Bhabha, that
this is true of many colonial and colonialist writers – difficult to
render as solely one thing or the other. In Barlow's double situation
as post-colonial/colonialist, the exceptionalism of the very appropriation invites us to ask what ends this complexity might serve. In
keeping with the tricky spread of the clustering categories – administration, commodification, stereotypes, colonialism – Barlow, like
Freneau, seems to affirm and challenge JanMohammed's formula
in a way that may link semicivilized empires to exceptionalist thinking. Rather than yielding discursive confusion, the doubleness yields
coherence in the articulation of America's ordained prerogatives.
Barlow's act of commodification of the native Other is also an in-
ternalization of nativeness, a self-Othering by the imperialist that
brings with it an ethically self-serving dimension. I want to argue
that one of the crucial implications of this identification is to draw
the Americas more absolutely, and, Barlow hopes, more ethically,
into commercial domains; the New World story, with its new stereotypes, was seen by Barlow as the moment for an epic intervention
in history. The New World of historical Indians and contemporary
Columbards entered the domain of commodifiable and commodi-
fying territories.

Narrating Natives into History and Commerce

Barlow's first musings on New World history and destiny came, as with Freneau, in two commencement poems, both of which were read at Yale, the first in 1778 (the year of his own graduation) and the second in 1781. The earlier poem, titled "The Prospect of Peace," is, true to its title, a plea for peace, heralding the dawning of a golden age of reason and piety. An intensely religious work replete with millennial language, the poem ultimately translates Puritan resonances into a secular vision of international peace and prosperity devoid of all notes of apocalypse. The later poem, "A Poem, &c.," written for the occasion of Yale's 1781 commencement, was an important model for *The Vision of Columbus*, which he had begun in 1779. The structure, common to both the 1781 commencement poem and *The Vision of Columbus*, relied on heavenly agents directing an earthly vision. In the 1781 work, an angel, akin to Milton's Raphael, instructs the poet to uplift the people of America. A new empire, founded on the peaceful arts of science, commerce, and poetry, must be celebrated. Note how the Western Hemisphere covets the power, commerce, and science of the other realm.

> Behold, from each far realm, what glories shine!
> Their power, their commerce and their science mine.
> And here, what roving views before them spread!
> Where this new empire lifts her daring head!
> (*Works*, 2:33)

Barlow's career as a cosmopolitan American, one who lifted his "daring head" among timorous Europeans, began several years after his graduation from Yale. In 1787, after completing *The Vision of Columbus*,[3] he set off on the first of his many foreign sojourns with a trip to France to sell overvalued land titles to unsuspecting emigrants. The next seventeen years of his life would be spent as an expatriate, making his way among the markets, salons, and republican gatherings of Britain and France. It is in this spirit of transatlantic return – "return" as a grandiose representative of Columbus – that he dedicates the first edition of *The Vision of Columbus* to Louis XVI, a beneficent monarch who "laid open all parts of the earth to the range of the liberal mind" (*Works*, 2: 103–4).[4]

Not surprisingly, Barlow was beloved in France and became somewhat notorious in England as a feared subversive and fiery enthusiast
of the French Revolution. Along with a deputation of eleven other
Americans, he congratulated the French National Assembly in 1790.
In 1792, he published a famous piece titled "Letter Addressed to
the People of Piedmont on the advantages of the French Revolution
and the necessity of adopting its principles in Italy," which constituted an argument for French annexation of Piedmont and employed the effusive rhetoric of revolutionary republicanism. (This
piece occasioned his nomination for deputy to the Convention from
Savoy; he was defeated in the election.)

My point in providing this background is to underscore the ideological affinities between cosmopolitan, republican adventurism,
and the poetics of empire. In Barlow's poems, the New World, and
especially America, are somewhat turgid expressions of cosmopolitan practice and ideals.[5] *The Vision of Columbus*, in particular, is an
early articulation of American exceptionalism that, if not a conceptual remedy for paradox among hierarchies, can explain the ener-
getic expansions and capacious appetites resulting from the
Inca-Anglo pairing. Amidst the multiple contexts and identities of
early national America – the New World's vertiginously imposing
national and natural resources – Barlow probably saw the issue simply as one of mastery, a variety of JanMohammed's commodification:
Who would speak for "ancient America" and gain the power
accorded by history and the promissory ethics of commercial con-
tractualism? The answer to such a challenge tendered mastery over
the chaotic possibility of new things, ordaining a modern nation
arising from *any* past, even a past that was ambiguously situated in
the received progressive history of republicanism. If it was an
English-speaking American who could master something like a "classical" American past, he could authorize the curve of progress writ
large over Old and New Worlds.

In his attempt to do that, Barlow adopted a British pseudo-history
about ancient America (the Black Legend's idyllic South American
civilizations) and monopolized both the Inca's glory and the figure
of Columbus as martyred hero. Ancient American history in the
poem is a matter of publicity and recognition beyond individual
fame; it is a diplomatic recommendation, making the new American
nation historically identifiable to imperial Europe by rendering it

both familiar and different. Moreover, the act of writing about an origin in the transatlantic sphere denoted the promise of value – value to history and value to potential financial creditors. Barlow's poems, as economic and political emblems, thus exemplify Euro-American political recognition necessitating wide historical and geographical sightlines.

In the recovery of the Inca empire for the delectation of cosmopolitan neoclassicism, Barlow addressed two key aspects of cosmopolitanism: the fetishizing of the New World as a site of utopian legacies and the exotic, and the more general nervous appeal to the authority of antiquity. Barlow's epic announced the European arrival of the American cosmopolitan, that the enlightened world must now take into account the transatlantic intellect founded upon North-South historical origins. For Barlow, the American component of cosmopolitanism was crucial, since America was to be the apotheosis of republican self-determination, and was itself the realization of New World promise originally dreamt of by the Renaissance English, who figured the Incas and Aztecs as people of supreme virtue, defeated only by the outrageous corruption of the Spanish. In short, American cosmopolitanism engendered the need for refining the Black Legend resource and then undertook the reinvention of the exceptional Indian, neither savage nor civilized, but both.

The history still presented problems. Before the Anglo-Inca hybrid could be used to full effect as political indemnification, the martyrdom of Columbus and the conquest of the Incas and Aztecs needed to be addressed. Until that happened, the promise of a republican golden age would be thwarted; without the epic articulation of South America's semicivilization, the history of progress could not be completed. This philosophy of history implied a break with the standard cyclical millennialism of Calvinist Federalism, a move toward "progressive linearism."[6] Though Timothy Dwight (Barlow's fellow Connecticut Wit from his prerepublican phase and coauthor of *The Anarchiad*) is traditionally viewed as Barlow's philosophical opposite, he remarked on America's historical role in progressive, linear terms that Barlow might have found succinct and congenial. The end of the humanist sentence of history, Dwight wittily wrote, is to be found in the New World's new republic: "[In America] human greatness will find a period."[7]

Barlow's progressive history found its historical missing terms and, therefore, grammatical closure in the New World. This, coupled with his evolving anti-nationalist predilections and the savagist terms in which he celebrated Manco Capac's achievement, were enough to make this treatment of ancient America into a somewhat ambivalent poetic project. His notes on the poem, along with the preface and introduction, reveal just how difficult he found this issue of savagist aggrandizement and New World internationalism. While Barlow guards against such "absurdities" as trying to write a panegyric on the Revolution, he also finds himself hard-pressed to provide a coherent rationale for the poem of American origins he has it in mind to write.

Thus the question seems to stick: Why turn to South American civilization for a central myth of republican America? Was it an example of nationalist romanticism, what Homi Bhabha has called "the narcissism of self-generation," where Manco Capac symbolizes for the American optimist the progressive nation springing from the symbolic genius of a politically "modernized" mind? Or was it related to an attempt to articulate a new relationship with Indian America as Anglo-America gained power in the new colonial matrix of the Western Hemisphere? The answer, not surprisingly, is both.

In one of the earliest outlines of *The Vision of Columbus,* dated August 1779, Barlow described making the poem "rather of the philosophic than the epic kind."[8] This would seem an appeal to the Enlightenment ideal of writing histories that are philosophical.[9] But an ambiguity arises out of the literary choices he is left with: What else but the epic could truly culminate with the rising glory of a new nation, in this case America?[10] The literary exceptionalism of his answer – in essence, "this epic *is not* an epic" – accurately echoes the national, racial, and cultural exceptionalism of his Indian paradigm. The best answer Barlow could come up with partook of an exceptionalism that arose out of contested categories of identity – where the literary figure of Columbus and the imperial, native paradigm of Inca civilization as proto-republican served to provide identitarian and ideological cover for a variety of nationalist shortcomings in the transatlantic sphere. Ultimately, his philosophical justification for the project becomes a peculiarly crafted American apology for the tragic origins of New World history, soothingly directed at the notoriously wronged Columbus.

I say "peculiarly" because it embodies both vindication (the American empire redeems Columbus and carries on the genius of the Incas) and condemnation (of racial dominations within the hemisphere perpetrated by the retrograde forces of European exploiters). The global poem of American origins and prospects was invented as an ethical vindication, but was covertly at odds with its own racial and historical hierarchies. It attempted to vindicate the destruction of native peoples by Europe and the imposition of economically oppressive structures that led to the enslavement of Africans. At the same time, it was an implied revelation of the expansive possibility of the exceptional American nation that arose from the rhetorical surfaces and symbolic authority of a nationalist and humanist redemption. In the process of lyrical othering, the nationalist work of repression and transcendence is precisely what made Anglo-Americans singular, neither/nor, mobile, modern.[11]

"Chains for a World": Inca History in The Vision of Columbus

Barlow's 1787 dedication of the *The Vision of Columbus* to Louis XVI is a suggestive statement about where his poem might be placed in the international domain of literary circulation and exchange. The dedication begins by positing the New World's discovery as the origin of all contemporary forces and proceeds to tell the ongoing story of the relationship between America's arts and the transatlantic community.

> In recounting the numerous blessings which have arisen to mankind from the discovery of America, the mind dwells with particular pleasure and gratitude upon those Characters, from whose hands these blessings have immediately flowed. That change in the political face of Europe, that liberality of sentiment, that enlargement of commercial, military and philosophical knowledge, which contrast the present with the fifteenth century, are but so many consequences of this great event; an event which laid open all parts of the earth to the range of the liberal mind. (*Works*, 2: 103–4)

Barlow is here enthralled by the idea of Europe, comparing the notion of political liberalism with a corresponding generosity of empire – *translatio imperii* working reciprocally with *translatio studii.* The liberal mind is articulated in the enlarging global map. Thus, Barlow bears out the latter-day cosmopolitan redemption of a botched and incomplete Renaissance discovery.

Barlow's next tactic grows out of the perception of the generosity of empire. He sycophantically obscures France's political self-interest by declaiming the best of European colonialism; he wisely ignores France's own colonial motives for such expansiveness.

> But it was left to [the first Bourbon's] more glorious Descendant, to accelerate the progress of society, by disregarding the temporary interests and local policies of other Monarchs, reaching the hand of beneficence to another hemisphere, and raising an infant empire, in a few years, to a degree of importance, which several ages were scarcely thought sufficient to produce. (*Works*, 2: 104)

Barlow closes his dedication by invoking the sublime political presence of the poem itself. Poetry and political power are equivalent when in the service of republican America, a nation that represents world-historical advancement in arts and politics; the epic is offered in the spirit of international diplomatic gratitude. The international sublime, a political-aesthetic category that works across history, is in the offing. It is structured by the rhetoric of revolutionary tribute.

> This is the sublime of humanity, to feel for future ages and distant nations; to act those things, as a Monarch, which another can only contemplate as a Philosopher, or image in the flights of poetry. America acknowledges her obligations to the Guardian of her rights; mankind, who survey your conduct, and posterity, for whom you act, will see that the tribute of gratitude is paid. If to patronize the Arts can add to the praise of these more glorious actions, your Majesty's fame in this respect will be ever sacred; as there are none, who can feel the subject so strongly as those who are the particular objects of your royal condescension. (*Works*, 2: 104)

In his gushing about the bestowals of empire, Barlow has begun to lay the groundwork for a synthesis of his political and literary theory. Finally, he recasts historical wrongs within the rectifying political economy of his own poetic production.

The following work, which may be considered in part, as the offspring of those reflections which your Majesty's conduct has
taught me to make, possesses one advantage scarcely to be expected in a Poem written in a foreign language. Your Majesty's
permission, that the unfortunate Columbus may once more enjoy
the protection of a royal benefactor, has added a new obligation
to those I before felt – in common with a grateful country. It is
the policy of wise Princes to encourage the liberal arts among
their subjects; and, as the human race are the objects of your
extended administration, they may all in some measure claim the
privilege of subjects, in seeking your literary as well as political
protection. (*Works*, 2: 105)

Historical themes resonate "liberally" as long as they are understood to function within the unfolding of new imperial realities.
Columbus, thanks to Barlow, "may once more enjoy the protection"
of a king. More importantly, Barlow himself can, on behalf of the
American people, "oblige" the French protector of the American
Revolution with an epic, and thereby repay the debt, even as he
figuratively, and somewhat ironically, increases it by making Louis
the second protector of Columbus and, therefore, new sovereign of
the New World.

The dedication is more than just an excessive display of deference
to patronage. History is redeemed within and, more importantly,
outside the text, as Barlow comes to speak with the authority of
historian *and* actor in national revolutions. The poet is in thrall to
the sublimity of international historical redemptions; the benevolent
old regime is transformed, in turn, by the historical agency of the
poet into a natural, progressive force surpassing the genius of the
individual poet or the limitations of national conservatism.

In spite of this utopian rhetoric, the genre seems to trouble Barlow at some level. In the 1787 Preface, his wrestling with the Columbian theme and the American form of epic poetry continues in its
awkward and rather hollow justifications for an American epic that
defies all of the traditional categories of the epic. For instance, Barlow prefers not to call *The Vision of Columbus* a patriotic epic; it is,
rather, a representation "in vision."

> The author, at first, formed an idea of attempting a regular
> Epic Poem, on the discovery of America. But on examining the
> nature of that event, he found that the most brilliant subjects

incident to such a plan would arise from the consequences of the discovery, and must be represented in vision. Indeed to have made it a patriotic Poem, by extending the subject to the settlement and revolutions of North America and their probable effect upon the future progress of society at large, would have protracted the vision to such a degree as to render it disproportionate to the rest of the work. (*Works*, 2: 121)

A "protracted vision" would disrupt the most "brilliant subjects" of New World epic; preserving the originary vision's discrete grandiosity is paramount. The first four books of *The Vision of Columbus* are just what the title promises – visions. They are, more specifically and perhaps surprisingly, given the future-oriented, utopian registers of the Columbian call, primarily retrospective visions; they see backward in time and outward from the colonial metropole, compassing the history of the American continents, from their geological formation, to their population, to subsequent conquests, dominations, and slavery (Barlow is powerfully anti-slavery). Along with the story of the Incas, it is Columbus and the consequences of his discovery that provide the frame and syntax for these panoramic visions. One of the "consequences" of America's discovery is not only the poem at hand and the founding of the United States (a potentially distracting vision), but also a revision of the ancient history of America. Given Barlow's ambivalence as an American cosmopolitan about simplistic and warlike patriotism, the reasons for ruling out a focus on the Revolution should be obvious. When one takes into account that Barlow was skeptical of conservative nationalism, and yet that the epic, as Barlow understood it, could not accommodate such an attitude, we begin to hear hesitancy and uncertainty in the extended syntax of the phrasing, "would have protracted the vision to such a degree as to render it disproportionate to the rest of the work."

Even this structural qualification seems insufficient for such an intriguing choice of founding myths. His best justification may be based on formal concerns posited by such eighteenth-century theorists of balance in literary style as Lord Kames. Barlow's worry over the visionary effects of "proportionality" implies a sense of himself as "editor" of a reified vision of the total sweep of history. He seems fearful of overextension even as he attempts an epic of extensive, indeed global, importance. Such linguistic and syntactic stretching

seems to betray the desire to stretch and redefine the formal premises of the poetic justification given the consciously editorial and
commercial view of the relationship between history and author.
Despite the well-documented contradictions in Barlow's thought, it
would seem that, in poetry, Barlow finds the problems of articulating
a clear notion of cosmopolitan nationalism[12] to be frustrating; ultimately, though, it is resolvable by a new sense of stewardship over
history and its uses in the new poetry of nations.[13]

A better understanding of the problems of the Indian theme and
nationalist poetic form may be reached by probing the idea of the
"visionary" even more closely. Uncomfortable with the recent terms
of his national identity and literary options – its warrior origins, its
epic yet hollow patriotism, and its violent prospects – Barlow must
make bold leaps through history, forward and backward, to pick
among fragments and legends. Such a disposition implied a willing-
ness to rewrite the vaunted republican "sentence of history." The
very notion of a "vision," and the fretting over "proportionality"
within it, address an attempt to regulate closely and judiciously
through a representational bind the rhetorical meanings of his historical approach. Barlow's difficulty with temporality within the epic,
and the political implications of poetic forms in general, reflects his
unease with the meanings of more proximate history – "the settlement and revolutions of North America." Barlow's alternative is to
turn his gaze to the historical frontier of Spanish America, to recover
and claim the history of Peru in order to insert himself as "visionary" author and his nation as "visionary" construct; the "visionary,"
in short, required the reified retrospect to provide the animation
for progressive action in the present. In order to truly achieve this,
the visionary, like Columbus's unsettled ghost, has in some sense to
be *outside* history, temporally and spatially. To remove oneself in this
way is to risk form and content to an unlikely identification – New
World Indian civilization.

Columbus is the symbolic bond between the Anglo republican who
feels not only the historical but the *ideological* necessity for vindi-
cating New World ideals and the innately savage civilization that
originated the heretofore lost ideal of American empire. The Introduction to *The Vision of Columbus* offers more clues as to how Columbus and the new story of Inca America will drive the process

of humanistic vindication.[14] The arrival of adequate New World histories is consonant with Columbus's story itself. Barlow's version of Columbus's life, as it is related in the Introduction, is the paradigmatic story of the market driving the course of modern history. After the sale of his idea of a western passage, Columbus's voyages are seen in terms of their individual and intellectual payoffs. Columbus contracts to acquire a portion of the New World for himself (the infamous one-tenth-of-all-profits compact with Isabella and Ferdinand), and, in return, "gives" the New World to Spain and, ultimately, humanity.

As we have seen, the story of this epic-mediated transaction – the political economy of its transatlantic narrative authenticity – is as important as Columbus's material discovery. Barlow includes in the Introduction the story of Columbus's efforts to preserve, indeed "deposit," the tale of discovery. In so doing, Barlow describes the literal treasuring of the Columbian narrative: "He wrote a short account of his voyage and of the discoveries he had made, wrapped it in an oiled cloth, enclosed it in a cake of wax, put it into an empty cask and threw it overboard; in hopes that some accident might preserve a deposit of so much importance to the world" (*Works*, 2: 116). Columbus is portrayed as continually having to set the record straight after subsequent return voyages to Spain; he must counter specious stories circulated by European detractors intent on devaluing and undermining Columbus's legitimate claims.

> [Columbus's enemies] represented his conduct in such a light at court, as to create uneasiness and distrust in the jealous mind of Ferdinand, and made it necessary for Columbus again to return to Spain, in order to counteract their machinations, and to obtain such farther supplies as were necessary to his great political and benevolent purposes. On his arriving at court, and stating with his usual dignity and confidence the whole history of his transactions abroad, every thing wore a favourable appearance. (*Works*, 2: 117)

But the natural gulf between stories that originate in America and the versions circulated in Europe by perfidious Spaniards becomes unmanageable and, finally, unredeemable in Columbus's lifetime. Columbus's authority is subjected to constant doubt, until Ferdinand finally betrays Columbus under the sway of European misrepresentations of colonial American experience. This story of the gap between European and American versions of truth functions as a cautionary allegory, foreshadowing the problems faced by cosmopolitans like Barlow in placing their authorial imprint on New World conditions of sovereignty.

By the end of Barlow's Introduction we see that Columbus has died not so much of a broken heart as of a breached contract. The broken contract was a product of his thwarted ability to tell his own story, to represent the "whole history of his transactions abroad" so as to further "his great political and benevolent purpose."

> [Columbus] did not suddenly abandon himself to despair. He called upon the gratitude and justice of the King: and, in terms of dignity, demanded the fulfillment of his former contract. Notwithstanding his age and infirmities, he even solicited to be farther employed in extending the career of discovery, without a prospect of any other reward but the consciousness of doing good to mankind. But Ferdinand, cold, ungrateful and timid, dared not to comply with a single proposal of this kind, lest he should encrese his own obligations to a man, whose services he thought it dangerous to reward . . . Columbus languished a short time, and gladly resigned a life, which had been worn out in the most essential services perhaps that were ever rendered, by any human character, to an ungrateful world. (*Works*, 2: 120)

In bringing this history – admittedly culled from European and South American sources – to the attention of Europe, and into the tradition of European national myths of origins, Barlow risks many of the same Columbian problems of transatlantic transaction. As with Columbus, Barlow's discovery carries with it the necessity for authenticity and authority – despite the New World's ambiguous record of accurate representation and the ethical problems that result when New World is represented to Old.

The Vision of Columbus begins at Columbus's lowest point, after the fourth voyage, when his deposits of "truthful" underwriting are gone. Isabella is dead, and he is in disgrace. Even worse, Columbus has lost his claims to financial rewards and hence governance of

Spain's New World colonies. The nations of Europe prey on his discoveries, disrupting a presumed new world of nonmonarchical national formations.

> Long had the Sage, the first who dared to brave
> The unknown dangers of the western wave,
> Who taught mankind where future empires lay
> In these fair confines of descending day,
> With cares o'erwhelm'd, in life's distressing gloom,
> Wish'd from a thankless world a peaceful tomb;
> While kings and nations, envious of his name,
> Enjoy'd his toils and triumphed o'er his fame,
> And gave the chief, from promised empire hurl'd,
> Chains for a crown, a prison for a world.
>
> (*Works*, 2: 125)

Commercial language, as we might have expected, guides the historical retrospection. The final line contains two exchanges, both of which are ironic degradations of the contractual expectations of the epic hero. Barlow seems to ask on Columbus's behalf: "What were his 'toils' and even his 'fame' worth?," metaphorically framing the following myth of origins in the language of commercial transaction. The question's answer must be articulated in the most serious terms, for Columbus's doubts speak to the grave betrayals and fatal corruptions of new empire. For Barlow to provide the epic response to Columbus's desponding doubts, he must conjure a reasoned myth that is consistent with a still-unfolding historical process. He finds that in the New World history of the Inca empire and its founding. First Columbus, and then the Incas, allow Barlow to gain a rational purchase on the present and all its post-colonial anxieties of internal and external conflict. The visionary poet – a new epic consciousness, inside and outside history – tethers himself to the foundational ideas of nation, world, and history with the rhetoric of commerce. The American commercial utopia must cohere around the memorialization of the civilized Incas.

Perhaps even more remarkable about the opening lines of *The Vision of Columbus* is, as we have seen with Freneau, their ability to make the past seem entirely present through the invocation of Columbian anxiety. Taking issue with Robert Arner, who holds that Barlow did not "develop a strong sense of the present, a moment in time upon which to base an integrated and integrating American identity" ("The Connecticut Wits," 249), I would suggest that Barlow makes an ingenious attempt to integrate an American identity in the present. To understand this attempt is to understand the concept of the vision simultaneously as historical, destinarian, and commercial;[15] for Barlow, to read ancient American history was to convert these terms into real political advantage. Though most critics, including Arner and William Dowling in his *Poetry and Ideology in Revolutionary Connecticut*, lump Barlow's fascination with the Incas in with his admiration for the classical ideals of Rome and Greece, I would argue that in the essay on Manco Capac, Barlow makes a sophisticated, if indirect, attempt at integrating an American identity by transacting with the stuff of history. For that reason, my emphasis will be primarily on this aspect of both *The Vision of Columbus* and *The Columbiad.*

Barlow's intercalary essay, "A Dissertation on the Genius and Institutions of Manco Capac," provides essential historical contexts for the poetic narrative of the rise of the Inca empire, which he deems the most noble of all ancient civilizations. Having situated the essay between the second and third books, Barlow feels it necessary to interpolate the historical prose within the body of the poem, as if this historiography *must* intervene to stoke the progress of the lyric. It is, in its lugubrious and tendentious political and national theorizing, the symbolic gene of the poem; this essay is the integrating center, setting the combined and recombined terms of promised redemption.[16]

The republican with the authority to move so radically within history, among categories of civilization and race, is on display in at least two levels of the poem: first, in the prose essay embedded within the poem, and second, in the poetic allegory of the unredeemed Columbus (a poetic response to the first). In the essay, Barlow presents Manco as the most successful pioneer in the construction of national identity the world has ever seen.[17] In the poem itself Barlow becomes the benevolent buyer of historical relief for a bereft Columbus; he does so by subjecting the acquisitive logic exhibited in the prose history to the rhetorical discipline of the epic line. The poem's prose acts as an experimental theoretical stage, after which the transactional mode is transported into traditional poetic meter. This, in turn, enables Barlow to view his own symbolic manipulations converted successfully as a poetic legacy of Incan national self-creation. The poem embodies most effective expression of a redeemed and redeeming history.[18]

The dissertation makes clear that Barlow's New World history is one to rival any myth of origins from the Old World. Manco Capac established an empire based on religion, albeit imposed with the aid of "superstition." This foundation was admirably exceptional, for it was religion-based but rational. It consisted of a politically systematized idea of divinity not dissimilar to the "Deity . . . of Socrates or Plato" (*Works*, 2: 177). The bulk of the essay is devoted to showing how Manco Capac measures up to those biblical, classical, and European nation builders "who have been considered as legislators among barbarous nations"(2: 177), including "Moses, Lycurgus . . . Mahomet, and Peter the Great."[19] These empire builders are contrasted with the Inca, based on their success at three principles of empire-building among the "barbarous." First among these principles is that

> his system be such as is capable of reducing the greatest number of men under one jurisdiction. Secondly, that it apply to such principles in human nature for its support, as are universal and permanent. Thirdly, that it admit of improvements correspondent to any advancement in knowledge or variation of circumstances, that may happen to its subjects. (*Works*, 2: 178–9)

Moses and Lycurgus never moved their nations beyond essential barbarism. The "Jews . . . were not only uncivilized . . . they united the manners of servants and savages . . . their national character is a composition of servility and contumacy, ignorance, superstition, filthiness and cruelty" (2: 179). The Spartan Lycurgus "rendered the nation powerful and warlike," but along with Moses did not observe the "third object of legislation . . . providing for the future progress of society"(2: 181). Muhammad, on the other hand, expanded his realm according to a systematized creed, not individual charisma, and did so with the "capital advantage" of "the allurements of pleasure and the promise of a sensual paradise"(2: 182). He falls short, however, on point three, since, according to Barlow, "Arabs" have regressed culturally and intellectually. For his part, Peter was an adaptive genius, selecting institutions to suit his people and allow for great progress.

Above these, though, there seems an irresistible political, and even aesthetic, logic to the Inca's conception of empire and social welfare. Manco Capac, as the first ruler, established himself as embodied emblem of the sun and so converted on Barlow's first principle, while adeptly following the people's "natural predisposition." Just as Barlow is in the process of contriving a national essence in the transactional ethics of the epic, he describes Manco as having crafted an "artfully contrived" public ideology that guided a feudal society, and it was an ideology that was precociously responsive "to the happiness of the people of a greater empire." Barlow acknowledges the Inca's feudalist hierarchy, but hastens to point out that it had more to do with the communal aspects of feudal agriculture than with arbitrary displays of power or greed.

In this regard, the agricultural Inca is the most admirable monarch: "The cultivation of the soil, which in most other countries is considered as one of the lowest employments, was here regarded as a divine art" (2: 185). There was reciprocity between nobles and the populace with regard to labor and social needs. A public spirit (if not sphere), based on maximizing the welfare of a consenting society, was ideally enacted by the Incas. Manco Capac "inculcat[ed] more rational ideas of the Deity" linking the divine with notions of "justice and benevolence," thereby "produc[ing] a greater change in the national character of his people, than any of the laws of Moses" (2: 187).

What really separates Manco Capac from all other famous nation builders is this last supremely rational and social attribute: "Can anything be more astonishing than to view a savage native of the southern wilds of America, rising in an age, void of every trace of learning or refinement, and acquiring by the mere efforts of reason, a sublime and rational idea of the Parent of the universe!" (2: 189). Barlow posits a God of Reason, but He is part of the systematic construction of a cohesive political system and a corresponding national identity.[20] The Inca's symbolic juridical reason produced the galvanizing force of a fixed faith; the rational agency of Manco Capac impelled the nation builder, and thus his people, into "acquiring" an idea of the universe's ultimate power.

Barlow emphasizes this rational faith in the transcendent that can take hold in national identity. This faith was perfectly suited in Capac's nation to the needs of a benevolent empire. Barlow's language borders on the evangelical as he describes Capac's benevolent yet somewhat overly militarized empire. Rational transcendence, a kind of secularized religion, is the difference between the barbaric and the civilized.

> These humane ideas of religion had a sensible operation upon the manners of the nation. They never began an offensive war with their savage neighbors; and, whenever their country was invaded, they made war, not to extirpate, but to civilize. The conquered tribes and those taken captive were adopted into the nation; and, by blending with the conquerors, forgot their former rage and ferocity. (*Works*, 2: 189)

The nation is here an entity that reflects the power of a benign engagement with superstitious symbolism. Religious rationality, as such, can be harnessed to craft a civilized ethos that "operates" upon the populace and leads to smooth international transactions (exemplified by the words "adopted" and "blended"). Manco Capac, we are told, was adept at the politics of conquest – redeeming the vanquished with the benefits of civilization. The civilizing course of history is thus reflected in a powerful nation with a consciously crafted, symbolically derived identity.

To his credit, Barlow's historical perspicuity allows him to see past the more obvious shadows of racist teleologies. His reading of Inca symbology is Machiavellian in its elevation of political need over racial necessity.[21] He suggests the reason the Incas were so easily conquered by the Spanish had less to do with European superiority and more to do with the fact that the legitimate Inca, Huayna Capac, subverted his own authority by marrying outside his immediate family, a royal lineage of the sun's direct descendants. Huayna Capac pursued this move for transparently political motives, intending to unite Quito with the empire. Not only was the fabric of the sacred symbolic "constitution" thereby marred and left open to profound doubt, so too was the time-honored process of ethical empire-building. Huayna Capac foolishly and selfishly cut against the symbolic logic of Incan national identity; the religious identity of the Inca's authority was subverted by the clumsy politics of empty aggrandizement. Barlow's view is unequivocal: had Huayna Capac adhered to the genius of Manco Capac's system, history would have had its greatest empire here, in the New World.

On the whole, it is evident, that the system of Capac is the most surprizing exertion of human genius to be found in the history of mankind. When we consider him as an individual emerging from the midst of a barbarous people, having seen no possible example of the operation of laws in any country, originating a plan of religion and policy never equalled by the sages of antiquity, civilizing an extensive empire, and rendering religion and government subservient to the general happiness of mankind, there is no danger that we grow too warm in his praise, or pronounce too high an eulogium on his character. Had such a genius appeared in Greece or Rome, he had been the subject of universal admiration; had he arisen in the favourite land of Turkey, his praises had filled a thousand pages in the diffusive writings of Voltaire. (*Works,* 2: 191)

Such advocacy is really a transition to literary critique when seen in a nationalist and post-colonial context; as a result of this transition, Barlow positions himself within a difficult historiographical space. Despite his questionable measure of authority, he can nonetheless recognize, just as capably as the great Voltaire, the majesty of a great civilization. Even more importantly, Barlow hypothetically presumes to point to the unwritten "thousand pages" of the European intellectual tradition. Barlow has, in fact, produced a lengthy discourse himself, generated in large part by his exuberant admiration of an obscure Indian king. His anger is an index of his historiographical defensiveness toward European standards of historical and national greatness. There is an ire here that seems to bridle at the compulsion, self-imposed or not, for European literary acceptance; his counter to Voltaire is challenge, plaint, and submission.[22]

The anger generated by the historiographic disregard of ancient America and the ingrained snobbery of European literati is rhetorically assuaged and historically redeemed by the course of the vision. This is especially so at the poem's end. If Manco Capac is the oldest moment of American nation-building currently in view, then the Columbian present, with all its anxiety, is the latest. To return to it is to provide continuity to the course of American destiny.

Just as the neglected history of New World glory is all the more painful for Columbus to consider, it is also distressing for the American who seems unmoored in the absence of a relationship with a semicivilized Other. But the obverse is also true. Barlow's anger vis-à-vis Voltaire accords directly with the relish with which he trumpets Inca civilization and the power he can thus invest in the poem's redeeming progress. The destruction of the Incas is ingeniously valuable to the poet in that the details of their success as a national polity incrementally heighten their grandeur and augment, therefore, the poetic debt paid to Columbus.

In the poem's last lines we find Hesper, Columbus's generous and patient storyteller, imparting to the tragic hero a vision of the Columbian project delivered in the most modern terms. Yet again, we find conflict in the division between the nationalist demands of the epic and the universal implications of Barlow's zealous historicism. Describing the sun, a transcendent symbol to guide the nations, Barlow writes, "A fire elect, in peerless grandeur, shone; / And rising oped the universal cause, / To give each realm its limit and its laws" (*Works*, 2: 357). Here "each realm," each nation, gains from the symbolic rendering of universals – in this case "laws" and "limits." Laws and limits provide the republican world of the future with observable and objective means to conduct international affairs. A kind of commercial empire is envisioned, finally, that converts fully on the terms of a realized republican ideal.[23] As one might have come to expect, Manco Capac's sun symbolism plays into the poem's culminating utopian imagery.

> Bid one great empire, with extensive sway,
> Spread with the sun and bound the walks of day,
> One centred system, one all-ruling soul,
> Live thro' the parts, and regulate the whole.
>
> (*Works*, 2: 357)

The epic ends, finally, after nine books of history, philosophy, and Columbus's (and Barlow's) suspended anxiety, by optimistically blending national hopes with millennial fervor. Columbus's grief is allayed as the myth of his singular heroism is adopted and justified completely. A global vision (derived from the Inca's heliotropic fixation, which Columbus inadvertently helped to destroy) concludes and soothes his historiographic agony.

> Let thy delighted soul no more complain,
> Of dangers braved and griefs endured in vain,

Of courts insidious, envy's poison'd stings,
The loss of empire and the frown of kings;
While these bright scenes thy glowing thoughts compose
To spurn the vengeance of insulting foes;
And all the joys, descending ages gain,
Repay thy labours and remove thy pain.

(*Works,* 2: 358)

Columbus moves with the poem into the modern era of anti-monarchical republicanism: "Let thy delighted soul no more complain, / Of . . . The loss of empire and the frown of kings." The vision that restores the teleology of republican history allows Columbus to compose the terms of his own redemption, the pacifist ideology to satisfy his loss: "thy glowing thoughts compose / To spurn the vengeance of insulting foes."

In an even more general way, the language of the poem's conclusion complements and refers back to the original question that compels the vision. The commercial drive, which seems to thrive on revisiting history with republican optimism in hand, reseals the visionary crisis or rupture. With the redeeming language of commerce – "loss," "gain," and "repay" – the poem can be said to be free of debt. Once Columbus has been reimbursed, the final removal of cosmic disappointment is achieved. Commercialized history in the form of the epic has purchased the New World's freedom from the original sin of native cultural liquidation and imperial perfidy. Barlow as Anglo-American – and final amanuensis for Columbus, author – has written the hemisphere free. *The Vision of Columbus* even prophesies republican-based world government, preeminently scientific and humane, and it is the product of American benevolence. Columbus and Manco Capac, seemingly apt projections of American notions of imperial republicanism, facilitate the entry of the American republican into global history and its corresponding ambitions.[24]

"By Any Latitude of Reasoning": Going Below History in The Columbiad

The application of American international power caught up to the progressive implications of Barlow's utopian and Columbian strains.

73

The Columbiad appeared in 1807, four years after the Louisiana Purchase, at the height of Jefferson's aggressive extension of American power in the name of republican and American ideals. Many of the changes in Barlow's epic, from *The Vision of Columbus* to *The Columbiad*, reflect the consolidation of the Jeffersonian drive to merge commercial appetites with a perceived geographical destiny. In *The Vision of Columbus* it is the historical identity originating in the South American ideal, while in *The Columbiad* it is a militarized identity, secure in its own ability to command political power.[25] This change is of a piece with the ideology of cosmopolitanism and cosmopolitanism's relationship to colonialist modes of thinking.

It is interesting that most critics have identified *The Columbiad* as the true source of the imperial Pan-American imaginary, when *The Vision of Columbus* seems the more compelling text in that regard. For example, John McWilliams writes in *The American Epic* that Barlow figures his patriotism such that it can only be healthy if it is a product of a wide-ranging, cosmopolitan historical consciousness; and that cosmopolitan historical consciousness is, in turn, a function of the geographical contours of the New World itself. More precisely, cosmopolitanism – that European ideal of expansive, border-crossing comfort – seems to project a more sinister appropriativeness in the New World context. McWilliams says of Barlow's Preface that while it

> contends that "*The Columbiad* is a patriotical poem [,] the subject is national and historical" . . . Barlow challenges Americans who define patriotism in terms of political borders. As geographical determinists customarily did, Barlow describes the land before its history . . . Using a perspective best described as a Pan-American pan shot, Barlow first places his reader at the Isthmus of Panama, then draws the reader ever upward until all of North and South America are seen as one land mass ordained by Nature to be one Western Hemisphere, one New World. (*American Epic*, 57)

As in *The Vision of Columbus*, the geography of the New World expands the patriotic possibilities of history and the nation, a crucial move in the process of American decolonization and then articulation of an American colonial worldview. Barlow oversees, along with the likes of Jefferson, the transfer of colonial power to Europe's in-residence image, the United States. *The Vision of Columbus,* despite its indisputable Francophilia, is primarily a way of rectifying an ungrateful European literary tradition (think of Barlow's of resentment of Voltaire), showing that Americans are indeed capable of gestures of contractual fidelity, of the historical or commercial kind.

As McWilliams makes clear, Barlow's perspective seems to be truly Pan-American. But taking McWilliams's point a bit further, we realize that the effect of Barlow's Pan-American gaze is, in an important sense, transatlantic. The New World will reflect its political and earthly riches back on the Old World, dazzling her with new configurations of power and empire. When that happens, the seat of civilization will be located in the West, and the terms of savagism will be reversed. Now the sources of civilization will spring from this moral hemisphere, unsullied by the historical stain of aristocracy.

Dowling points out in *Poetry and Ideology in Revolutionary Connecticut* that all of Barlow's thematic emphases, in both poems, are superseded by the great theme of commerce.

> The implication throughout *The Columbiad,* one already insistently visible in "The Vision of Columbus," is that commerce . . . is the very heartbeat of the historical process, and that to understand why this should be so is to be given a glimpse into the workings of history denied to any previous generation. More than any other major theme in *The Columbiad,* in short, Barlow's portrayal of trade and commerce suggest the degree to which he imagines himself to be looking at history in a radically new way. (96–7)

Dowling is right. Barlow is redefining the authorial function in the context of national identity and the commercial dynamics of history. The commercial spirit saturates the poem, signaling the arrival of a proudly commercial author constructing national identity out of the historical resources at his disposal. What emerged from Barlow's engagement with the ancient history of America was a historical myth designed to suit the emerging republican imperial identity, an identity that increasingly recognized the saliency of commerce to both national and poetic ambitions. Such grandiose revisions of history seemed manifestly justifiable given the global contest over ideology and the stakes involved in America's quest for a sovereign identity. Barlow effuses about a Columbus– and Manco Capac–

inspired universal reign of reason, arising out of new insights into American history, before which the old aristocratic politics of Europe must now yield.[26]

Yet one of *The Columbiad*'s major differences from *The Vision of Columbus* is its enthusiasm for the Incas. In *The Vision of Columbus*, the essay on Manco Capac occupies a place of honor in the text, situated between two books. In *The Columbiad*, the Incas have been de-emphasized, relegated to a footnote, and recounted with noticeably less ardor and admiration. A decade later and Barlow, it seems, is more circumspect about the accuracy of his history – almost embarrassed by his youthful zeal.

Barlow now scales down his magnification of New World history, worries more about his sources, and increases his troping on more direct notions of international power. He doubts the accuracy of his key source for the history of the Incas, the work of Garcilaso de la Vega, a sixteenth-century descendant of Inca royalty; rhetorically, he places Garcilaso between himself and his earlier conception of Inca history. Indeed, Barlow's own "zealous" work of collection and historical didacticism is supplanted, and masked, by his criticism of those very qualities as they are exhibited in the work of the South American historian. The displacement is obvious:

> The honest zeal of Garcilasso de la Vega in collecting these traditions into one body of history, as a probable series of facts, is to be applauded; since he has there presented us with one of the most striking examples of the *beau ideal* in political character, that can be found in the whole range of literature. He treats his subject with more natural simplicity, tho with less talent, than Plutarch or Xenophon, when they undertake a similar task, that of drawing traditional characters to fill up the middle space between fable and history. (*Works*, 2: 797)

Having invoked, via his reconsideration of Garcilaso, this "middle space" between fable and history, Barlow is oddly reluctant to explore this new territory.

> With regard to the true position that the portrait of Manco Capac ought to hold in this middle space, how near it should stand to history and how near to fable, we should find it difficult to say and perhaps useless to inquire. (*Works*, 2: 797)

Barlow's persistent use of the metaphor of a spatialized collection is, however, telling when it comes to the "middle space" of historical representation. The spatial reification of historiographic processes signals the loss of visionary retrospection as a transcendent value. Instead, his discourse evolves out of a more practical form of visual fetishizing – portrait collection. The visionary gives way to collection – fully playing out the logic of commerce (beyond the limits of the merely contractual and ethical). Note how Barlow casts Garcilaso in the role of creative empiricist, collecting and shaping truth in the passively critical accretions of "collecting," rather than exercising the critical modes of "judgment" or "ornamentation":

> [Garcilaso] writes apparently with the most scrupulous regard to truth, with little judgment and no ornament. He discovers a credulous zeal to throw a lustre on his remote ancestor Manco Capac, not by inventing new incidents, but by collecting with great industry all that had been recorded in the annals of the family. (*Works*, 2: 798)[27]

The 1807 Fry and Kammerer edition of *The Columbiad*, with its polished engravings by Bromley (based on paintings by Smirke), is the best example of *The Columbiad* as a representation of Garcilaso's "industrious" collection.[28] Book Six has a long narrative of the murder of Lucinda by the Mohawks – really, according to Barlow, by the British who employed the Indians. An engraving of Lucinda being murdered by two hatchet- and knife-wielding Indians echoes in its structure the imagery of Capac teaching in one of the edition's first plates.

In that first plate (see Figure 1), a group of Incas listens ardently to Capac and Oella. A warrior is seated on the left with his hatchet at his side, while another warrior on the right has his knife safely sheathed. Both are devoting full attention to Capac. But in the later engraving depicting Lucinda's murder, while the iconography is remarkably parallel, the pastoral tone of South American civility is gone. It is as if these two once-pacified Indians had been reduced to natural savagery in the northern continent (see Figure 2). (The Spanish had receptive Indians and, irrationally, mistreated them; we had malevolent Indians and suffered, were martyred, at their hands.)

The logic of potential reversal in the civilized savage is nowhere

Figure 1. The original Inca, Manco Capac, teaching his subjects, from the 1807 edition of *The Columbiad*. Courtesy of the Library Company of Philadelphia.

Figure 2. The drama of savage reversion, from the 1807 edition of *The Columbiad.* Courtesy of the Library Company of Philadelphia.

clearer than in these contrasting illustrations. But content aside, here as elsewhere, the form tells as much about Barlow's shifting historicism. Portraiture that plays into stereotyped American identities attests to the collecting impulse of his historicism. Collecting, rather than envisioning and polemically rehistoricizing the founders – whether of Inca empire or of the American republic – is the new poetics of the Columbian epic. Appropriately, the edition begins, even before the title pages, with a reproduction of all the signatures of the Declaration of Independence (see Figure 3). This iconography of foundational signatures refocuses the constituting national gaze back to North American sources. According to *The Columbiad*'s new collections, patriotism is now possible.

Barlow has backed away from angry polemic against European histories that ignore the glories of American antiquity; Manco Capac is somewhat less credible, less perfect. Barlow acknowledges instead the benefits of the very constructedness of mythic national consolidations, as opposed to those seemingly fabulous and transcendent ideals exalted in *The Vision of Columbus*. Note the appeal to the "real" historical character of Manco:

> The character of Capac, *in regard to its reality,* stands on a parallel with that of the Lycurgus of Plutarch and Cyrus of Xenophon; not purely historical nor purely fabulous, but presented to us as a compendium of those talents and labors which might possibly be crowded into the capacity of one mind and be achieved in one life, but which more probably belong to several generations; the talents and labors that could reduce a great number of ferocious tribes into one peaceable and industrious state. (*Works*, 2: 797–8, my emphasis)

Garcilaso's good intentions yield a portrait of the civilized Inca who embodies not the individual genius of *The Vision* but a cleverly constructed collective national character. He is a collective identity, furthermore, whose very claim to civilization is a product of the collecting and self-interested historian. Garcilaso has, like Barlow, written a colonial counterhistory that, in due course, became an undependable, but instructive, form of hagiography.

Having admonished his sources as well as, by indirection, the excesses of his own Inca fable, Barlow apologizes for the space taken

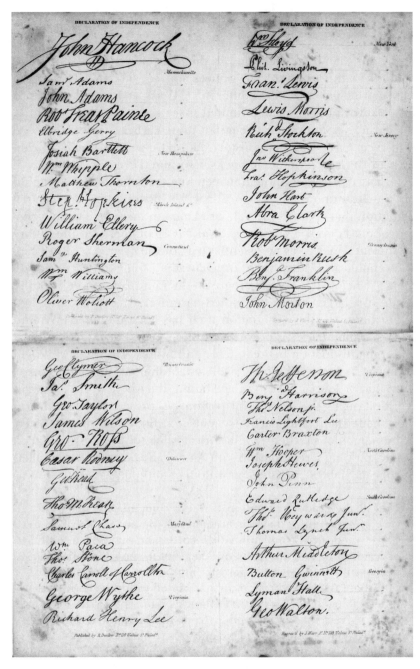

Figure 3. Graphic signatures of nationhood, from the 1807 edition of *The Columbiad.* Courtesy of the Library Company of Philadelphia.

up by this "fabulous tradition" in the foregoing poem: "The space allowed to this episode may appear too considerable in a poem whose principal object is so different" (*Works*, 2: 799). The concern for relative volume within a limited space and context is evident in the earlier version of the poem, but those earlier worries had to do with recent, Revolutionary history. As I have already noted, in contrast to the space between Books Two and Three in *The Vision of Columbus*, it is now endnote nineteen that contains the "Dissertation on the Institutions of Manco Capac," a material and conceptual demotion that reduces the role of Manco to mere artifact in a rhetorical museum. If *The Vision of Columbus* accommodated the history of ancient America as an essential part of the grammar of progressive republican history, then *The Columbiad* is only too eager to submerge it below the line of progress – literally, to footnote it in the sweep of a larger, more surefooted narrative.

Furthermore, the dissertation itself has been modified. We find Barlow scaling back his previous enthusiasm and being circumspect about the distinction between fable and history. His tone, while still admiring, is noticeably cooler: "the establishments of Manco Capac, if we may follow Garcilasso in attributing the whole of the Peruvian constitution to that wonderful personage, present the aspect of a most benevolent and pacific system" (2: 800). Barlow ultimately claims a fabulous rather than historical value for the story of Manco Capac, positing a relationship with American antiquity that parallels European "fables" of Greek and Roman antiquity.

> I recall the reader's attention to these comparisons, not with a view of contending that our accounts of the actions ascribed to Capac are derived from authentic records, and that he is a subject of real history, like Mahomet or Peter; but to show that our channels of information with regard to him being equally respectable with those that have brought us acquainted with the classical and venerable names of Lycurgus, Romulus, Numa and Cyrus, we may be as correct in our reasonings from the modern as from the ancient source of reference, and fancy ourselves treading a ground as sacred on the tomb of the western patriarch, as on those more frequented and less scrutinized in the east, consecrated to the demigods of Sparta, Rome and Persia. (*Works*, 2: 806)

Manco's "authenticity," seen through the channels of "information" that result in "real history," is now explicitly in question. Still, he is useful, in that strikingly apt metaphor, as a subterranean foundation – a "fancied" "sacred tomb" containing a "western patriarch." Barlow has not completely lost the zeal for a revisionary American epic. It has been reexpressed as an argument for a more direct form of national and imperial power. Barlow's new fascination is with the glories of modern warfare, and this emphasis occupies much of his new Introduction to *The Columbiad*. If Barlow's justification for not writing his epic primarily about the Revolution relied on the idea of a religiously derived symbolic Incan politics of empire and conquest in *The Vision of Columbus*, the emphasis on the historicist pacifism of imperial expansion was devalued by the time the poem is rewritten as *The Columbiad*.

Accordingly, there is a new confidence to *The Columbiad*, a mature arrogance of nationalized civilization that before seemed elusive or ideologically distasteful. Barlow seems to have shed his conflict with the received terms of the epic, writing forthrightly in the preface to *The Columbiad* that this "is a patriotic poem; the subject is national and historical" (*Works*, 2: 375), as against 1787's "to have it a patriotic poem" would "render . . . an absurdity." Still, he admits to a residual problem with the form and content of the epic, since America's national origins in the Revolution are "inflexible to the hand of fiction" and so are obviated in favor of the Columbian visionary form: "The poem, therefore, could not with propriety be modelled after that regular epic form which the more splendid works of this kind have taken" (2: 375–6). He goes on to say that he will "enter into no discussion on the nature of the epopea, nor attempt to prove by any latitude of reasoning that I have written an Epic Poem"(2: 376). He instead theorizes the "narrative poem" in his own terms, distinguishing between the "poetical object" and the "moral object" of the work. As he puts it, "The poetical is the fictitious design of the action; the moral is the real design of the poem" (2: 377–8). His prioritization of the political and social effects of the poem, its "real design," forces Barlow to reevaluate such great epic poets as Homer and Lucan.

Among Homer's most egregious sins is that, without the necessary tonic of commercial republicanism, he "inflame[d] the minds of

young readers with an enthusiastic ardor for military fame . . .
teach[ing] both prince and people that military plunder was the
most honorable mode of acquiring property" (2: 378–9). Homer
was thus a destructive agent of history. As a detriment to the history
of civilization, Homer made his fame by exalting the barbaric "plunder" of military acquisitions: "his existence has really proved one
of the signal misfortunes of mankind" (2: 379). So, too, with Virgil,
whose greatest failing was his lack of republican feeling, which led
him "to encourage like Homer the great system of military depre-
dation" (2: 380). Barlow's favored classical poet was Lucan, who
established a connection between national policy and literature, and
maintained a republican philosophy that rescued the poetic failures
of his epics. Barlow only wishes that a poet with Homer's creative
talent and Lucan's political agenda could have provided "a splendid
model for all succeeding ages" and "given a very different turn to
the pursuits of heroes and the policy of nations. Ambition might
then have become an useful passion, instead of a destructive dis-
ease" (2: 381). Barlow expresses this hope in the utopian strains of
Book Ten.

> But now no more the patriotic mind,
> To narrow views and local laws confined,
> Gainst neighboring lands directs the public rage,
> Plods for a clan or counsels for an age;
> But soars to loftier thoughts and reaches far
> Beyond the power, beyond the wish of war;
> For realms and ages forms the general aim,
> Makes patriot views and moral views the same,
> Works with enlighten'd zeal, to see combined
> The strength and happiness of humankind.
>
> (*Works*, 2: 766)

This international poetic ideal is strictly visionary, and is therefore
only partly historically grounded. For now, poetry can rectify national "ambition" by converting martial poetry into commercial poetry.

As such, Barlow's poetical object is the same as in *The Vision of
Columbus* – to soothe the despondent Columbus with the pacifying
effect of new commercial possibilities, while his moral object is more
clearly defined as an adjunct of national policy: "the real object of

the poem embraces a larger scope: it is to inculcate the love of rational liberty, and to discountenance the deleterious passion for violence and war" (2: 382). The corresponding move is made in the poem again in the redeeming Book Ten, when Columbus wonders (almost metafictively) why the poem makes such grand claims for its harmonizing work.

> Or tell if aught more dreadful to my race
> In these dark signs thy heavenly wisdom trace;
> And why the loud discordance melts again
> In the smooth glidings of a tuneful strain.
>   The guardian god replied: Thy fears give o'er;
> War's hosted hounds shall havoc earth no more;
> No sore distress these signal sounds foredoom,
> But give the pledge of peaceful years to come;
> The tongues of nations here their accents blend,
> Till one pure language thro the world extend.
>   (*Works*, 2: 768)

Peace will arrive in the form of the universally apprehendible language of unity. That unity, for the time being, will have to suffice in the more pragmatic connective possibilities of commerce; linguistic unity will have to reside in the well-written poem. As Barlow writes in an extended note appended to Book Ten:

> We should have perceived the real and constant interest that every nation has in the prosperity of its neighbors, instead of their destruction. France would have perceived that the wealth of the English would be beneficial to her, by enabling them to receive and pay for more of her produce. England would have seen the same thing with regard to the French; and such would have been the sentiments of other nations reciprocally and universally.
>
> I know I must be called an extravagant theorist if I insinuate that all these good things would have resulted from having history well written and poetry well conceived. No man will doubt however that such would have been the tendency; nor can we deny that the contrary has resulted, at least in some degree, from the manner in which such writings have been composed. And why should we write at all, if not to benefit mankind? The public mind, as well as the individual mind, receives its propensities; it is equally the creature of habit. (*Works*, 2: 850)

And yet in spite of all these claims, in his revisions to the Introduction Barlow fixates on modern, as opposed to ancient, modes of
warfare as a poetical object. Barlow's moral argument is not so much
with war per se as it is with ancient methods and motivations of war,
and thus ancient poetical praise of war. Modern war is developmentally superior as a moral and poetic object because it is "richer"
and, in the ample "middle space" between history and fable, more
"copious." As such, it is inherently benign, serving above all the
commercial dynamics of history.[29]

> It will occur to most of my readers that the modern modes of
> fighting, as likewise the instruments and terms now used in war,
> are not yet rendered familiar in poetical language. It is doubtless
> from an unwarrantable timidity, or want of confidence in their
> own powers of description, that modern poets have made so little
> use of this kind of riches that lay before them. I confess that I
> imbibed the common prejudice, and remained a long time in the
> error of supposing that the ancients had a poetical advantage over
> us in respect to the dignity of the names of the weapons used in
> war, if not in their number and variety. And when I published a
> sketch of the present poem, under the title of The Vision of Co-
> lumbus, I labored under the embarrassment of that idea. I am
> now convinced that the advantage, at least as to the weapons, is
> on the side of the moderns . . . In short, the modern military
> dictionary is more copious than the ancient, and the words at least
> as poetical. (*Works*, 2: 384–5)

Once again, Barlow seems to have written himself into a tight corner
of the shifting discursive field of the epic. His compulsion to redefine the American epic, as in *The Vision of Columbus* with the glorification of the Incan ideal, once more leads to the fruitful logic of
capital ("the riches that lay before them") and modern empire. In
short, poetry and commerce have been refined into a unitary *civilizing* technique of empire.

New Western Patriarchs

Still, even in *The Columbiad*, Manco Capac is our "western patriarch," laying sacred ground for American empire and martial progress. The paradox undergirding the undivided construction of
poetry and commerce remains. The flaw, the "paradox," in such

thinking centered on a familiar problem with Jeffersonian liberalism: the articulation of a fuller political humanism that might accommodate racial equality. Despite his assertion of liberal claims within geohistory, Barlow devalued competing indigenous and Spanish creole claims to sovereignty within the geopolitics of the New World, basing his neglect on intercolonial prejudice (the Black Legend) and positing *inherent* capabilities that limit rights of self-determination. His refusal or inability to fully hear the ideological content of his own voice redounded upon the nationalist ethos of the epic (even as that muting succeeded as a logical diplomatic strategy). It is the Anglo-American, bearing the discursive markings of the emergent colonialist, who comes to manipulate a crucial history, who above all others speaks to European powers as the best hope for a hemisphere that can trade with the Old World. Given the complex work the poetry was asked to perform – stamping a national identity by negotiating the past of Indian America – it should come as no surprise that there were racial and political instabilities inscribed into its representations of Indian civilization. These instabilities are reflected in the changes Barlow wrought in the poem between 1787 and 1807 which betoken a shifting relationship to New World history and thus in his changing status as a national voice.

It is on the issue of conflict, and its possibility for mediation in the written national imaginary, that I want to focus here at the end of this chapter. Whereas the commercial valuation of the historical construct might seem a rather shallow premise to reconceive the epic, in light of racial difference the discourse was effective for smoothing the crises of sovereignty that attached to specific notions of race in the New World. In the context of colonialism, an acquired tradition functions in the way JanMohammed has explained, as a kind of resource which ignores the colonized subject because that subject has been commodified.

But, as we have seen, Barlow's case problematizes even the most helpful theoretical explanations. Unlike JanMohammed, who regards colonialist fiction as an undifferentiated discursive strategy, positing a Manichean binary between the "barbaric" and "civilization," we see in Barlow's colonialism a more complicated and heterogeneous distribution of orientalist difference. While I agree with the dynamics of the imperialist fiction, it is on the question of difference that Barlow departs from JanMohammed's Manicheanism. Because of the slipperiness of the myriad categories at stake – republicanism, national identity, race, European-American, barbarism, civilization – Barlow wrote with dissonant authority regarding Europe, the republican ideal, the African slave, and the Indian native. To hear that discord is to recognize the self-Othering that made Barlow recoil so oddly in *The Columbiad.*

Barlow was, if nothing else, diplomatic and worldly, wily in the art of publicity and nimble in his national and cultural negotiations. At the same time, one can sense the overwhelming unresolvability of the chaos of race-thinking within the republican narrative of historical progress; confusion and contradiction insistently vexed the question of difference for Barlow, as they had for Jefferson. Barlow's own politicized subjectivity changed with each negotiation and justification, ending finally with the Anglo superimposition over the Spanish and Indian, both within the text and in the territories of the New World. When the militarized subtext eclipsed the Incan, it was really Barlow succumbing to the tensions involved in the glorification of the civilized Indian. A similar dilemma ensnared William Prescott.

Perhaps the best evidence for the magnitude of the post-colonial problem for Barlow – who was, in many ways more than Freneau, a true Pan-American visionary – lies not in his capitulation to the pacifist promise of the technology of warfare, but in his silence on the rights and liberty of the Incas in his own time. The discourse of equality was easier to articulate within history than in the present – in both 1787 and 1807. Equality becomes rhetorically easy to declare, but placement within the epic hierarchies is the true measure of justice. Though he spoke of Incas as historically equal and even superior to European counterparts, their contemporary political plight – as legitimately anti-colonial as the North Americans' (indeed more so) – remained absent from his republican vision. This deep reluctance to acknowledge indigenous struggles as in any way parallel to the republican struggle seems to inhabit both poems and makes Barlow's Inca demotion appear that much more inevitable.

Incas had in fact challenged colonial Spain at nearly the same time as the Anglo-American colonies were rebelling against Britain, and one can assume that the rebellion was noticed by the educated

elite of the Anglo colonies. Just after Barlow had graduated from
Yale, the following report appeared in *The Connecticut Courant and
Weekly Intelligencer* of March 12, 1782. It is typical of revolutionary
North American attitudes toward rebellions against the Spanish em-
pire.[30] The article recounts the uprising of Tupac Amaru, a direct
descendant of the last Inca, against the Spanish.

> the mutinous Indian Joseph Gabriel Tupe Amaro, who attempted
> to have himself proclaimed King of Peru, had been taken and
> beheaded, together with his whole family and the other Caciques
> his allies . . . A considerable number of the revolters had been
> hanged, and others were upon the point of sharing the same fate.
> It is to be hoped these acts of severity will make some impression
> upon the minds of the disaffected, and that the flames of sedition
> will be extinguished . . . Thus, whatever the English may say, we
> shall not see another Boston upon the southern continent.

This attitude demonstrates a prevailing revolutionary concept of the
Anglo colonies' own status within the context of New World political
authority, decreeing just who is justifiably revolutionary, who is capable of historical returns and restorations. Despite the story of the
noble Incas and Anglo-America's deep distrust of the Spanish empire, Anglo-Americans could not allow Indian self-governance or
self-determination, North or South. The Anglo-Americans' own
moderation on the issue was meant as a sign to England, "whatever
they may say," that revolution and national independence were not
maniacally spreading power to the ungovernable – that is, to those
racial Others who resided outside the transatlantic community of
exporters and importers. Barlow's epic shift of focus, from acquisition within the historical realm to the power implicit in military
language, represents perhaps most importantly the constancy of the
commercial logic in spite of the differing views of history. The difference itself is an emblem of the complete fusion of the discourse
of acquisition with diplomacy; this is, in turn, consistent with the
consolidation of the militarily capable nation-state as nascent *pax
Americana.*

Barlow, cosmopolitan revolutionary and upholder of liberation
struggles throughout France and Britain, remained silent throughout his essays and poetry on this crucial issue of colonial injustice.
History, as Barlow figured it, could rescue injustices past, but not

those caught in the diplomatic necessities of the present; history's capital was available only to those who could insert themselves into the discourse of commerce, or who had access to the pacifying possibilities of peace and prosperity brought about by modern military strength.[31] In Jefferson's America, the Spanish were to be taken from, perhaps acquired from, and, when necessary, they were to have their colonial history used against them. Jefferson, ultimately, translated his "nesting" imaginary into designs for the annexation of Spanish territories to the south (Florida, Mexico, and Cuba). When the descendants of a dispossessed New World civilization rebelled, then Spanish hegemony was endorsed by the circumspect American cosmopolitan in Europe; the New World American propagandist was, in certain political and racial configurations, an Old World partisan. In both the poetic and political realms the moral object of historical myths was held narrowly to the demands of national expansion, and to the ever-shifting rationale behind America's colonialist rearticulations; Barlow's ancient America, a bargain in spite of all its difficulties, affirmed Anglo-American destiny in the hemisphere.

3

NOCTOGRAPHY

PRESCOTT'S SKETCHINGS OF AZTECS AND INCAS

Noctograph: A writing frame for a blind person.

OED

[The noctograph's] framework of wires is folded down upon a sheet of paper thoroughly impregnated with a black substance.

George Ticknor, Life of Prescott

Still another difficulty occurred, in the mechanical labor of writing, which I found a severe trial to the eye. This was remedied by means of a writing-case . . . which enabled me to commit my thoughts to paper without the aid of sight, serving me equally well in the dark as in the light. The characters thus formed made a near approach to hieroglyphics.

Prescott, preface to The Conquest of Peru

I am in the capital of Montezuma, staring about at the strange Aztec figures and semi-civilization.

Prescott to Francis Lieber, 1842; written while in the midst of work on The Conquest of Mexico

The historian's work is a blind business.

Prescott to Francis Lieber, 1840

Composition

There is a strong line connecting the nearly blind romantic historian William Prescott, author of the *History of the Conquest of Mexico* (1843) and the *History of the Conquest of Peru* (1847), not only to Joel Barlow, but to Washington Irving, his most imposing American literary predecessor: Prescott, Barlow, and Irving all shared a fascination for the history of Spain and Spanish America.[1] The line connecting them is discernible as well in compositional terms, how they similarly made their unprecedented histories into readable texts.

By way of beginning to understand the sources of Prescott's compositional methods and self-reflexiveness, I offer the following letter Prescott wrote to Irving while working on the Aztec history, dated December 24, 1839. It humorously dramatizes composition: "The whole of that part of the story [pre-conquest Aztec history] is enveloped in twilight – and I fear, I shall, at best, make only moonshine of it – I must hope that it will be good moonshine . . . As I have only half an eye of my own, my progress is, necessarily, no more than a snail's gallop" (*Papers of Prescott*, 153). The possibilities of a narrative enveloped in sensory limitations, emanating at once from author and theme – limitations in body and in history imposed by muteness and darkness – are cavalierly troped (the eyeless snail, oxymoronically galloping) in a way that wryly bespeaks his influences and his method. In its strange imagery, linking blindness to the work of history writing, the passage suggests the intensely self-reflexive quality of his historicism and his mode of composition.[2]

But we must go back earlier to understand Prescott's calling as historian of the mute civilizations of pre-Columbian South America and his vocation's relation to his own physical impairment. Soon after resolving to devote his intellect to producing histories of Spanish colonialism in the tradition of Irving, Prescott wrote to Alexander Hill Everett, Irving's predecessor as U.S. Ambassador to Spain. The letter is dated December 26, 1826.

> Johnson in his life of Milton says that no man can compile a history who is blind. But . . . if my ears are spared me, I will disprove the assertion. Although I should lose the use of my vision altogether . . . my chronicle, whatever other demerits it may have, shall not be wanting in accuracy and research. If my health continues thus, I shall necessarily be debarred from many of the convivial, not to say, social pleasures of life, and consequently must look to these literary pursuits as the principal and permanent source of future enjoyment. (*Literary Memoranda*, 49)

History writing is here a surrogate social pleasure, a substitute for full immersion in the world of the senses. Such motivation, encompassing the lure of sensual pleasure and a necessary orality, must have been powerful in the face of Dr. Johnson's daunting admonition. The passage to which Prescott refers expresses Johnson's skepticism of blind men engaging in the business of writing history: "To compile a history from various authors, when they can only be consulted by other eyes, is not easy, nor possible, but with more skillful and attentive help than can be commonly obtained; and it was probably the difficulty of consulting and comparing that stopped Milton's narrative at the Conquest."[3] For Prescott, a mediation between the oral and the printed, requiring "more skillful and attentive help than can be commonly obtained," was a necessity. That mediation shaped his imaginative encounter with civilizations like the Incas, which had themselves produced a significant mediation between physical symbol-making and orality. After all, though capable of reading in limited amounts, Prescott was always dependent on a succession of secretaries: George Lunt, Hamilton Parker, James Lloyd English, Edmund Burke Otis, Robert Carter, John Foster Kirk, Henry Cheever Simonds, Elijah Dwight Williams, and especially George Frederick Ware – all took dictation and read to him.[4] To read a biography of Prescott is to read a chronicle of his determination to write history in spite of his eyes.

Nonetheless, he encountered and represented history visually. As I have suggested, Prescott took inspiration from the sensational directions for historical writing pioneered by Irving.[5] Irving, who had cornered the Spanish American history market in North America, made Prescott's New World possible; thematically and professionally, Irving is the prologue to Prescott. Irving writes in "The Voyage" (the *Sketch-Book*'s opening piece), "The vast space of waters that separates the hemispheres is like a blank page in existence" (17); he thereby invites the sketching of a textual bridge that would at once span an international, intellectual passage, and fill an internal ontological void. For Irving, international distances seem to quietly redound upon individual fulfillment. Prescott's own language regarding his literary aims is consonant with Irving's: "I have made a book illustrating an unexplored and important period . . . As a plain, veracious record of facts, the work . . . will fill up a gap in literature" (Ticknor, *Life of Prescott*, 98). It is the literature of Irving's Spanish

93

colonial histories and later works by Prescott that would supply the characters for the hemispheric and existential "empty pages."

The Irving-Prescott bond that asks us to probe the visible presence of prose textuality went back to the very beginning of Prescott's career. Prescott was a founding member of a literary group at Harvard that published *The Club Room Magazine*, in which his first efforts appeared. Two of those pieces, according to William Charvat and Michael Kraus (early twentieth-century proponents of Prescott's literary reevaluation), were "sentimental story-essays in the *Sketch-Book* manner, the third an editorial in which he took pains to deny that the magazine was an imitation of Irving's *Salmagundi*, although his denial reproduced the facetious tone of that periodical" (Charvat and Kraus, *Prescott: Representative Selections*, xxv). That sense of literary obligation and emulation continued well into Prescott's career. In 1839, as he was about to begin the histories of Mexico and Peru, Prescott wrote to Irving, in typically visual terms: "Though I cannot see you bodily . . . I am sitting under the light of your countenance – for you are ranged above me, (your immortal part) in a goodly row of octavos, – not in the homespun garb, but in the nice costume of Albermarle and Burlington Streets" (*Papers of Prescott*, 153).[6] Prescott took up Irving's prescription for historical fiction in America, to "fill up the blank pages of existence" and array them not in the mundane fabric of everyday New England life, but rather in the more exotic, print-bound "costume of Albermarle and Burlington Streets."[7] The comment is telling in its portrayal of the sensual presence of the literary as an influence on Prescott.

I am suggesting that Irving imparted to Prescott not just a theme, but the alluring problem of first perceiving Otherness and then inscribing it into the national literary project. Irving's influence encouraged an obsession with pictorial "costume" and the exotic in the historical narrative. Literary language itself was a kind of vaguely foreign picture, a visually readable emblem of the awkwardness of national progress. The visual, visible, and therefore literary, history was Irving's real legacy to Prescott.[8]

Such influence is, as we have seen, present in Prescott's characterizations of his own method. When Prescott wrote of his experience with noctographic writing – that "the characters thus formed made a near approach to hieroglyphics" – he names an aspect of com-

94

position that speaks volumes about the nation's blank, undecorated pages. The hieroglyph, or any other kind of historical decoration (like architecture) – any visible example of philological and literary hierarchies – is crucial to an understanding of Prescott's cultural poetics. The presence or absence of "picture writing" in the civilizations he studied determined Prescott's representations of them, shaping ambivalent attempts to decorate the pages of interhemispheric literary history. The ambivalence, in turn, was part of the problem of envisioning a U.S. national imaginary that was not susceptible to uncomfortable analogies to civilizations bred for imperial conquest or anti-individualist autocracy.[9]

While it was Irving who suggested to Prescott the romantic scenes of Spanish American history, Prescott's introduction to hieroglyphics could have come from any number of sources that appeared just as he began his career. One source must have been his friend Edward Everett, who wrote a review in 1831 for the *North American Review* of J. G. H. Greppo's *Essay on the Hieroglyphic System of M. Champollion, Jr.* Everett's piece is representative of the hold hieroglyphics had on the literary imagination, a topic that has been comprehensively addressed by John Irwin's *American Hieroglyph* (1980). Irwin's summary of the general meaning of the hieroglyph for men like Everett is incisive: "The movement from a writing made up entirely of figurative signs capable of presenting only simple, concrete ideas to a writing composed largely of phonetic signs capable of presenting the most complex, abstract ideas demonstrated both evolution and progress" (7).[10]

Everett, however, complicates this demonstrative progression. Concluding his essay with a fascinating turn, he betrays a dissonance between his notion of progress (as it relates to hieroglyphic interpretation) and his savagist idea of the limitations of lesser civilizations. Specifically, Everett acknowledges that in Champollion's translations – this new insight into the origin of civilizations – may reside the possibility of a superlanguage, an alloy of the hieroglyphic and alphabetic. Everett advocates a kind of progressive regression, an enlightened recuperation of a cultural form that has long since gone out of use:

> We cannot but hazard the remark, that for contemporary use, it
> is by no means certain that such an intermixture of figurative with

alphabetical signs, is not a more lively and impressive system of writing than the exclusively alphabetical. If, for instance, most sensible objects, the names of which occur in a written discourse, were represented by a picture of those objects, in a simple but easily recognized form, we are by no means sure, that it would not have its advantages. If the conception of a more compendious system of language . . . be ever realized, there is no way in which it is more likely to take place than by a partial recurrence to picture writing, – taken as an illustration of the other modes of expressing thought. ("Review of *Essay on the Hieroglyphic*," 124)

Out of this arises speculation on the meaning of Mexican hieroglyphs and on the historical work still to be done, work that unfortunately cannot be addressed in Everett's own article.

The perfection, to which the art of picture writing was brought by the Mexicans, a people exceedingly low in the scale of civilization, and the rapidity with which they communicated through this medium, may teach us to what uses it might be applied, as a supplement to other methods. We had intended, at the commencement of our article, to describe the Mexican system of picture writing, and compare it with the Egyptian hieroglyphics, but our remarks have already been protracted to a length, which warns us to draw them to a close. ("Review of *Essay on the Hieroglyphic*," 124–5)

Everett seems to ask the reader to complete his speculations. Just as Prescott took up Irving's Latin romanticism and its visible wonders, I would suggest that Prescott answered Everett's call to rethink composition within the context of philology, to complete this speculative project on what "the art of picture writing . . . may teach us" and "to what uses it might be applied, as a supplement to other methods."[11]

Everett's remarkable speculation invites us as well to recast Prescott's self-critique – "the characters thus formed made a near approach to hieroglyphics" – into a surprising and rich context. Is Prescott merely being glib, evaluating his writing from the standpoint of penmanship? Or is he implying something more ambitious – a graphic superlanguage, a hybridized historical method incorporating ancient, semibarbaric methods of composition? Or, equally possible, is he reflecting the insecurities of his national identity, devaluing in the process his work as historian writing from within an empire that itself stood in an anxious relation to the civilized and the barbaric – and perhaps most anxiously in relation to race?[12]

There are, of course, no certain answers to these questions. As I hope to show, Prescott seems to be taking part, consciously and unconsciously, in the possibility of making novel truth-claims; Prescott probes the limits and capabilities of composition given Everett's incomplete speculations. Rhetorically, Prescott desired the oil painting of romance narrative and scorned the sketchings of the hieroglyphic; but in important ways – perhaps deriving from Everett's exhortation – his desires ran counter (a snail's gallop?) to the implications of his compositional hermeneutics. The history as written oil painting was, after all, something of a hieroglyph itself – narrative "reduced" to a vivid, pictorial grammar. Because he was aware of this, Prescott made of his own troubled process an ideologically useful, but necessarily conflicted, methodology.

That is, again and again we see Prescott attempting to limit the impressive effects of strange civilizations with the philological dimensions of racial differences. Prescott's writing provided the means to understand and thereby hierarchize nations and races as though they were textual emblems. Incas and Aztecs were "characters" to be interpreted and then refigured by the very contingent process of his iconographic composition. The layered paradox of his compositional method threatened to decompose his narrative of progress, then limitation, and finally salutary but awful conquest. His sympathetic identification with Aztecs and Incas, a reflection emanating from the core of his self-abasing expression, persists in spite of the terms of progress.

Composition, seen through the concept of noctography and the interpretive issues of historicism within the emergent American empire, is, then, the problem that drives this chapter. Several mediations and issues, hinted at in my epigraphs, are subject to critical rescripting: author, racial representations, and writing cultures (hieroglyphics, noctography, quipus); and author and empire (America, Spain, Mexico). My hope, as it was with Freneau and Barlow, is to come to a renewed understanding of exceptionalism, especially for a U.S. historian of the 1840s.[13] For Prescott continues the story of exceptionalism requiring New World others to emulate and then revile. To write about the Aztecs and Incas in Prescott's self-reflexive literary mode, as we will see, is to portray the United States as insecure civilization and ambivalent empire always confounded, and yet always served in its national imaginings, by sensational, racially shadowed writing.

"The Characters Thus Formed": The Conquest of Mexico

I focus first on the ethnographic nature of *The Conquest of Mexico*, embodied primarily in the critically neglected first book of the history.[14] The ethnographic sketch begins with a note of anxiety over the need to decipher an entire civilization and thereby embark on a composition of historical coherence. Prescott seems truly disturbed by the unreliability of surviving literature about the Aztecs. A "true" vision of the race is obscured behind a kind of palimpsest – the "dubious language of hieroglyphics," covered over by the inaccuracies of the Spanish interpreters and their linguistic and conceptual faults. Prescott struggles to distance himself from the deficiencies of accuracy and detail appearing first in the hieroglyphic record and then in the Spanish chronicles. The first chapter of Book One ends with an important caveat:

> How much is the difficulty [of gleaning accurate information] increased . . . where this information, first recorded in the dubious language of hieroglyphics, was interpreted in another language, with which the Spanish chroniclers were imperfectly acquainted, while it related to institutions of which their past experience enabled them to form no adequate conception! Amidst such uncertain lights, it is in vain to expect nice accuracy of detail. All that can be done is, to attempt an outline of the more prominent features, that a correct impression, so far as it goes, may be produced on the mind of the reader. (*History of the Conquest of Mexico and History of the Conquest of Peru*, 32–3)

Prescott hopes for a sketchy but effective translation, where in lieu of a "nice accuracy of detail," an "outline of the more prominent features" will have to suffice to effect "a correct impression, so far as it goes . . . on the mind of the reader." The edgy language of his description of the source materials, Spanish and hieroglyphic, seems an advance apology for the obscuring confinement of his own literary effects. At the same time, there is reason to be hopeful about alternative means of representing the past, for Prescott has apparently succumbed to the very dubious language he indicts. With that final expression of "all that can be done," Prescott metaphorically sees himself "impressing" his noctographic stylus immediately upon the reader's imagination, suggesting the fortunate hieroglyphic directness imparted by the "uncertain light" of the historical palimpsest. Out of the morass of historical evidence will emerge a raft of pictorial and analogic resemblances as well as phonetic chronicles that promise new light. As he quipped to Irving: While the source materials boded moonshine, it was good moonshine.

Prescott's discussion of the hieroglyph – a dubious technology of *self*-representation – reveals his simultaneous admiration for, and condescension toward, Aztec civilization. The fourth chapter of Book One, titled "Mexican Hieroglyphics – Manuscripts – Arithmetic – Chronology – Astronomy," explores the process of hieroglyphic interpretation; and it is, necessarily, a meditation on accurately perceiving the past by means of visible emblems. In recognizing the hieroglyphics of the Aztecs as representative of a complex manipulation of ideas, Prescott claims for them the beginnings of a "literary" impulse, and, thus, civilized life. Such beginnings indicate, moreover, the glimmerings of limited, but noticeably integrated and individualistic, historical consciousness.

> To describe actions and events by delineating visible objects seems to be a natural suggestion, and is practised, after a certain fashion, by the rudest savages . . . But to paint intelligibly a consecutive series of these actions . . . requires a combination of ideas, that amounts to a positively intellectual effort. Yet further, when the object of the painter, instead of being limited to the present, is, to penetrate the past, and to gather from its dark recesses lessons of instruction for coming generations, we see the dawnings of a literary culture, – and recognize the proof of a decided civilization in the attempt itself, however imperfectly it may be executed. (*History*, 55)

Yet despite the credit he accords them for a nascent historical consciousness, distinctions in communicative capabilities must be drawn. Therefore, Prescott delineates three levels of hieroglyphic writing: (1) representative – or direct pictorial representation; (2) symbolic – which is analogical and metaphorical, often arbitrarily so;

and (3) phonetic – the most like the alphabet, though still subsumed under the figurative (a footnote calls the awareness of "the
phonetic property of hieroglyphics, – the great literary discovery of
our age"). The representative, or strictly figurative, is the lowest
order of the hieroglyphic, and it is this mode that Aztecs employed
most frequently. The Egyptians, on the other hand, used the phonetic system: "The Egyptians were at the top of the scale, the Aztecs
at the bottom" (56). Nonetheless, and perhaps most surprising, the
Aztecs were familiar with all forms of writing.[15]

Prescott goes on to imagine a sort of double reading: A Mexican
hieroglyphic text is "read" based on Prescott's reading of Gama's
Descripcion Histórica y Cronológica de las Dos Piedras. The passage is remarkable for scrupulously maintaining the fiction of an unmediated
relation to the figures, of the author inspecting the hieroglyphic
manuscript as if with his own eyes:

> In casting the eye over a Mexican manuscript, or map . . . one is
> struck with the grotesque caricatures it exhibits of the human
> figure; monstrous, overgrown heads, on puny, misshapen bodies,
> which are themselves hard and angular in their outlines, and with-
> out the least skill in composition. On closer inspection, however,
> it is obvious that it is not so much a rude attempt to delineate
> nature, as a conventional symbol to express the idea in the most
> clear and forcible manner . . . Those parts of the figure are most
> distinctly traced, which are the most important. So, also, the col-
> oring, instead of the delicate gradations of nature, exhibits only
> gaudy and violent contrasts, such as may produce the most vivid
> impression. "For even colors," Gama observes, "speak in the Az-
> tec hieroglyphs." (*History*, 56)

In its monstrous symbolism, these hieroglyphs announce the
achievement of cogent representation and artifice. The Aztecs succeeded in overcoming witless crudity by caricaturing their way to the
greater meaning embodied in the rational symbol. Even colors,
which were excessively vivid, approach the level of an intelligible
code. In their not-so-subtle departure from realism – a facile mir-
roring of the natural world – the Aztecs achieved an advance up the
hieroglyphic scale, beginning to display literary, and thus self-
conscious, capabilities.[16]

But the advance was modest. For Prescott, the Aztecs were developmentally peculiar in their grotesque mix of the civilized and the barbaric. So the gnawing question remains: Why did they fail to progress along the teleological line of philology? Prescott spends a great deal of energy addressing this problematic of ethnographic characterization. Before he proceeds to an analysis of other types of cultural evidence left behind by the Aztecs, Prescott first attempts to locate them in a world-historical context of analogues encompassed by barbarism and civilization. From his advantageous point in history, with the ancient world of both hemispheres now in view, Prescott can render an accurate evaluation of the Aztec's "claim" to civilization.[17] Microcosms may now be taken for totalities – the fully revealed modern world is a completed scene of comparable nations, and history may be read as civilizing progress signifying the disclosure of that world. To make comparisons between nations necessitated reading them as fixed teleological "characters" to ascertain the microcosmic, potentially individualizable, figure of identity – the national character.[18]

To begin this mode of reading, Prescott compares the Aztec and Tezcuco civilizations favorably with North American tribes, an unsurprising move derived from the Black Legend and one we have seen in Freneau and Barlow. Prescott rates the Aztecs on a par with Anglo-Saxon civilization under King Alfred. But the most useful historical analogy is, of course, to the ancient Egyptians. That ancient civilization is, after all, the standard – a culture seemingly embalmed for the very purpose of scientifically gauging the mysteries of progress.

> Enough has been said, however, to show that the Aztec and Tezcucan races were advanced in civilization very far beyond the wandering tribes of North America . . . In respect to the nature of it, they may be better compared with the Egyptians; and the examination of their social relations and culture may suggest still stronger points of resemblance to the ancient people. (*History*, 32–3)

Prescott then considers the effects of conquest and subsequent domination upon the descendants of the liquidated Aztec civilization. Prescott is writing history conscious of the contemporary status of his historical subjects; the modern character is teleologically continuous with developments in the past. Once again, the Aztec/Egyptian analogue persists as an all-purpose cross-reading loaded with historically salient relics.

> Those familiar with the modern Mexicans will find it difficult to conceive that the nation should ever have been capable of devising the enlightened polity which we have been considering. But they should remember that in the Mexicans of our day they see only a conquered race, as different from their ancestors as are the modern Egyptians from those who built, – I will not say, the tasteless pyramids, – but the temples and palaces, whose magnificent wrecks strew the borders of the Nile, at Luxor and Karnac. (*History*, 33)

Prescott's attempt at reading the past through the present and the reconstituted interhemispheric picture, leads him to familiar denigrations of the conquered. Left with the singular fact of a "conquered race" (both Mexicans and Egyptians here) who still inhabit, uncomprehendingly, the ruins of their ancestors, Prescott can only lament the disparate fortunes that history bestows. The disparity is clarified in the following passage by moving from the image of architectural ruins to images contained in now obscure literary "monuments." Literary impulses are rendered mute by history's worldly progress and they now lie inert, awaiting keener intellectual capabilities.

> The difference [between the Aztec and the modern Mexican] is not so great as between the ancient Greek, and his degenerate descendant, lounging among the masterpieces of art which he has scarcely taste enough to admire, – speaking the language of those still more imperishable monuments of literature which he has hardly capacity to comprehend. Yet he breathes the same atmosphere, is warmed by the same sun, nourished by the same scenes, as those who fell at Marathon, and won the trophies of Olympic Pisa. The same blood flows in his veins that flowed in theirs. But ages of tyranny have passed over him; he belongs to a conquered race. (*History*, 33–4)

The positioning of the modern Mexican within the panoramic history of civilizations can be read most tellingly in the word "belong." Though he seems to argue for a strictly historical construction of individual achievement (some cultures may be civilized at certain points in history, others barbaric, depending on circumstance), the racial discourse ultimately undercuts this. For the modern Mexican cannot claim the *heritage* of a civilization – the imaginative and material achievements of a people; instead, he belongs to genealogical bloodlines. Another way of putting it: the Mexican is claimed by his race. He is the living trace of a "degenerating" race, and for Prescott this belonging is appropriate, since it carries the force of judgment related to the work of fully substantiated readings of historically confirmable hierarchies. The Mexican belongs because, in light of his subsequent disinheritance from the achievements of his forebears, that is where he *must* be in Prescott's hermeneutics of natural faculties. Tyranny has passed *over* him, not through; thus it has not changed his bodily inheritances.

This passage is followed immediately by further evaluation of the New World aboriginal seen as genealogical type. But something important has happened in the course of Prescott's ethnography. A technique has been established that will now shape the reading of the "racial character" as comprising both individual bodies and national monuments. By consigning the Indian to static racial categories marked by notable limits on rational expressiveness, Prescott works hard to cleave the individual Indian – past *and* present – from the semicivilization to which he might legitimately lay claim.

> The American Indian has something peculiarly sensitive in his nature. He shrinks instinctively from the rude touch of a foreign hand. Even when this foreign influence comes in the form of civilization, he seems to sink and pine away beneath it. (*History*, 34)

The sentimental, feminizing language – "sensitive," "shrinking," "sinking," "pining" – he uses to describe the Indian (North and South here) discursively posits a productive tension in the relationship between the Indian and the civilizing force of reason. For Prescott, there is a gap between the individual Indian and the social and cultural forms he participated in. Though the evidence of those forms may be called civilized, as in the case of the Aztecs, the individual Aztec remained incapable of recognizing it as such; therefore, he was subordinate to the civilizing "touch" of reason in his own life. Indeed, in the New World, reason seemed discretely "foreign" to the Indians who sometimes feebly exercised it, but never enough to turn reason's power on its own self-description. A "masculine" civilization, capable of unsentimental deeds of rational assertion, would presumably destroy the veil of sensation that made this self-insulation possible and thus activate the final telos of reason's modern domination.

The gauzy fabric that constituted the social formations of the American Indian (especially the Mexican), though woven with moderately instrumental logic, nevertheless bound its subjects into a debilitating lack of individual agency. Supernatural fantasy withheld the Indian from the power of individual self-recognitions, not to mention rational and expressive conceptions of social organization or progressive history. Inherently ruled by this wondrous effeminacy, the Indian was captive to his own irrationality. In a spectacular paradox, the lack of rational faculty was the very precondition of his maintenance of an outwardly civilized polity.

Of course, the paradox of the uncomprehending participant in the civilized is the logic of the hieroglyphic form itself: the rational resides somewhere within characters. Such characters are the emblems of a collective intellect that cannot shake the hold of sensory representation and thereby see itself through to more individuated, flexible, and complex semiotic systems. This interpretation is an extension of classic savagism, where Indians always speak metaphorically, employing a stultifying eloquence that never moves beyond sentiment, unwittingly displaying language's beautiful and dominating landscapes. The logic of hieroglyphs does not allow the cultures who use it to surpass the seductions of analogical representation and so move on to the purely arbitrary, nonpictorial, phonetic alphabet. Though there is a grammatical logic to the supernatural aesthetic, it keeps its practitioners from advanced writing's mature, individualized freedoms.[19] Because of this, the hieroglyphic form is necessarily a dead end in the development of language tools for those who realize it without benefit of reading backward through more advanced forms – presumably readers such as Prescott.

The hieroglyphic logic readily extends into a historical theory. According to the tautological historicism of this sophisticated rendition of savagism,[20] reason continues to be inaccessible to the Indian *because* he has been conquered. The weakening, crushing facts of conquest together with his effeminate, fantastic tendencies have annulled the promising legacies of his blood – his capacity for a kind of degraded civilization – and tipped the balance to retrogression. The bodies of the race – the undistinguished elements of its constituting character – tell the whole story as they succumb fully to their deindividualizing weaknesses. At the same time, the architectural and figural monuments of the race – pyramids and hieroglyphs – endure.

This embodying figuration culminates the interpretation of historical nations. Ethnography is transformed in this essentializing discourse into ethnogeny, the study of ethnic origins. In ethnogenetic thinking, figuring origins is tantamount to conceiving a convenient historical space in which race overtakes the relativizing work of cultural interpretation. An ethnogenetically derived origin produces a free, prior realm within interpretive historicism, where absolute reductions essentialize and prejudice all subsequent racial characterizations. Origins are thus the site of teleological ascriptions, where othering is made prophetic and inevitable; such origins signify the end of nondeterministic interpretation.[21]

In Prescott's ethnogeny, the narrative of inevitable loss is easy to spot:

> Under the Spanish domination, [the Mexicans'] numbers have silently melted away. Their energies are broken. They no longer tread their mountain plains with the conscious independence of their ancestors. In their faltering step, and meek and melancholy aspect, we read the sad characters of the conquered race. The cause of humanity, indeed, has gained. They live under a better system of laws, a more assured tranquility, a purer faith. But all does not avail. Their civilization was of the hardy character which belongs to the wilderness. (*History*, 34)

The sentence beginning "In their faltering step" enacts the kind of interpretation I have been talking about in its most conspicuous form. In spite of the "conscious independence" of the Mexicans' ancestors, they are still "characters" without discretion. Prescott begins to use the term "character" as a symbolic nexus that binds the individuals of the race to that race's historical significance, its national futures and pasts. As an ethnographer of exclusively *textual* representations (Prescott, in a kind of noctographic parallel, never made it to South or Central America), he "reads" the singular body of a "wretched" descendant of the Aztecs, as if indeed it were a living embodiment of the hieroglyphic character. The term "character" precisely acknowledges and transforms the individual elements of the "sad" conquered race.

One of the implications of Prescott's excessive yet careful "characterization" is that the achievements of Aztec civilization were not the result of creative invention driven by rational individual agency. Rather, they were a product of the extraordinary conditions of location: "Their civilization was of the hardy character which belongs to the wilderness." This environmental logic (an old European way of thinking about New World phenomena), coupled with the ethnogenetic reading, provides Prescott with the ethical grounds for Spanish conquest and colonization. Aztec civilization has fortunately been superseded by a superior regime of self-representation (Europe's and ultimately Prescott's); the Indian remains melancholy in spite of his better condition because he was, from the beginning (i.e., preconquest), limited by his technologies of self-representation.[22] The civilization's "hardy character" belongs to the subartifice of wilderness landscapes, rather than animated self-consciousness. Here the civilization is divorced from the Aztec who "belongs" to his "race"; the civilization, less feminine in its sturdy hardiness, belongs instead to the "wilderness."

The hieroglyph thus characterized and historically explained the semicivilized Indians' essential inferiority. It bore out their mute history – the ineffaceable mystery of the conquered – and reported the reasons for their demise. For men like Everett, Greppo, and Prescott the hieroglyph was a narrative in itself, a plot of history that might be read to retroactively foretell imperial triumph, native glory and its degeneration. As an implement of the blind historian, Prescott had seized the figure and attempted to make it a revealing object of his own language.

Three years after the original publication of the *History of the Conquest of Mexico*, Prescott supplemented the original section on Aztec origins with an essay titled "Origin of the Mexican Civilization – Analogies with the Old World." He thus furthered the already critical application of the emblematized, analogic reasoning of the hieroglyph to the historical standing of particular civilizations. This ethnographic annex was conscious of the limited effectiveness of the original text. Insofar as he asks the reader to recompose a picture of the semicivilized world based on yet more analogues, Prescott is still anxious about the accuracy of the picture rendered in Book One.

Such analogic reasoning rested on a theory of New World origins that held that there was pre-Columbian interhemispheric contact, that a relationship existed between ancient civilizations of the Old and New Worlds. The following sets up this theory by suggesting the possibility of reading for trace resemblances and thereby "establishing the fact of a positive communication with the other hemisphere."

> But this work would be incomplete, without affording the reader the means of judging for himself as to the true sources of the peculiar civilization already described, by exhibiting to him the alleged points of resemblance with the ancient continent. (*History*, 692)

Ultimately, it is evidence of intellectual resemblance that advances the identitarian argument for the Asiatic origins of Aztec civilization. These resemblances rely, however, on essentially unexamined and unreliable linguistic forms. The most trustworthy evidence available is the Palenque drawings and hieroglyphs, which in their outward form resemble, or at least correspond to, those of the East: "More positive proofs of communication with the East might be looked for in their sculpture, and in the conventional forms of their hieroglyphics" (708). Prescott believes it is probably the hieroglyph that holds the key to the origins of the New World peoples: "The walls . . . are covered with figures and hieroglyphics, which, on the American, as on the Egyptian, may be designed, perhaps, to record the laws and historical annals of the nation" (708).

Unfortunately, the Palenque drawings present an impenetrable linguistic mystery to the scientific-historical decipherer. Therefore, an accurate reading is impossible; a narrative of origins, promised by the material presence of the hieroglyph, cannot be deciphered.

> That [the Palenque hieroglyphs'] mysterious import will ever be deciphered is scarcely to be expected. The language of the race who employed it, the race itself, is unknown. And it is not likely that another Rosetta stone will be found, with its trilingual inscription, to supply the means of comparison, and to guide the American Champollion in the path of discovery. (*History*, 709)

In light of this scarcity of explicit intelligibility, Prescott can only work analogically, deriving impressions from national characters already established and the formal characteristics of the legible remains. He must work from outward forms that are ineffaceable, but also inherently limited in their capacity for offering (self-)representation. Prescott is compelled to conclude his inquiry in equivocal, deliberately sketchy terms, and, revealingly, with a note of "embarrassment."

> The consideration of these and similar difficulties has led some writers to regard the antique American civilization as purely indigenous. Whichever way we turn, the subject is full of embarrassment. It is easy, indeed, by fastening the attentions on one portion of it, to come to a conclusion. In this way, while some feel little hesitation in pronouncing the American civilization original; others, no less certainly, discern in it a Hebrew, or an Egyptian, or a Chinese, or a Tartar origin, as their eyes are attracted by the light of analogy too exclusively to this or the other quarter. The number of contradictory lights, of itself, perplexes the judgment, and prevents us from arriving at a precise and positive inference. (*History*, 713–14)

This somewhat agnostic view of the genealogy of ancient American civilizations is markedly different from that of Freneau who worked more firmly within the tradition of the Black Legend and therefore credited certain pre-Columbians with an Old World genealogy. In Prescott, on the other hand, we read ancient America analogically in the context of philological and literary hierarchies that do not allow for such comforting affiliations. While his ability to apply his techniques of reading Aztec civilization is magnificently sharp in that it allows for narrative judgments on the political morality of conquest, it brings with it a host of self-critical conundrums.

As Prescott writes in Book One, the Aztecs' national character is discernible primarily in their refusal to merge, "engraft," become hybrid; though the moral inner representations are invisible, and so absent, he may yet be able to see through to their "individuality as a race":

> The fierce virtues of the Aztec were all his own. They refused to submit to European culture, – to be engrafted on a foreign stock. His outward form, his complexion, his lineaments, are substantially the same. But the moral characteristics of the nation, all that

constituted its individuality as a race, are effaced for ever. (*History,* 34)

It may seem Prescott is deeply pessimistic about the effaced characteristics, particularly those ideologically and racially loaded "moral" forms, of a race surviving for the historian's interpretation. But I would suggest a reclamation is occurring here, a recuperation of the outward *moral* form of the Aztecs, seen retrospectively at the edge of their destruction within the narrative. As one might have already guessed, Prescott believes in the readability of outward forms more than he is willing to admit. Indeed, moral judgment of the Aztecs, derived explicitly from richly textualized characters and characteristics, is one of the central devices of his narrative; it is precisely the outward form of moral characteristics (sacrifice, for example), seen through his authorial filter, that drives the tragic but necessary narrative of Aztec destruction.

While the Aztecs, with a kind of dumb nobility, deny a pragmatic and perhaps saving identification with their conquerors, Prescott does not deny himself the pleasure of a certain aggrandizing identification with the conquering heroes of his narrative.[23] But another identification that arises out of his hieroglyphic stylistics is more vexed – he is Aztec. Prescott is then both author-Cortés and Aztec priest-scribe; like Cortés on his horse, Prescott too can envision, emulate, and refigure – translate – what he would take such agonistic, authorial pride in destroying. In short, an ambivalent moral poetics that is intimately connected to sensual figuration is constitutive of his history. As he playfully yet tellingly wrote to Dickens while composing *The Conquest of Mexico*: "I am hammering away on my old Aztecs, and have nearly knocked their capital about their ears. They die game, certainly, and one can't help feeling a sympathy for them, though they did occasionally fricassee a Christian or two" (Prescott, *The Correspondence of William Hickling Prescott, 1833–1847*, 329).[24]

The narrative part of the history is riddled with such moralistic justifications (delivered in a considerably more sober tone) of his Cortésian narratological destruction. We might want to read his analyses of Cortés, therefore, as a self-critique that points up the links between narrative vision, narrative ethics, and political morality. For instance, the following indictment of Cortés's powers of observation might also be read as a critique of the Cortésian ways in which Prescott's own descriptive capabilities are deceptively enhanced: "The truth is, that Cortés, like Columbus, saw objects through the warm medium of his own fond imagination, giving them a higher tone of coloring and larger dimensions than were strictly warranted by the fact" (*History*, 253).[25] (This imagination is not unlike the overly vivid colorings and exaggerated dimensions of Aztec hieroglyphics.) Though he may fancy himself exempt from the odd tints of his own vision, there is enough evidence to suggest that Prescott is all too aware of the problems of envisioning history with any degree of representational accuracy, free of progress's philological determinations.

This conflation of the composing character of Prescott, author, with the destructive nature of Cortés, historical character, leads us back once again to the compositional effects of contemplating "barbaric" self-representation – whether as Cortés (authorial destroyer as agent of history's inevitable plots) or as Aztecan scribe (priest figuratively, indeed hieroglyphically, emblematizing history for the reader-believer). His zealous desire to deflect historical error into the all-devouring category of "barbarousness" – to place blame by an act of (paradoxically) self-alienating displacement – is present even in the Preface:

> I may reasonably ask the reader's indulgence. Owing to the state of my eyes, I have been obliged to use a writing-case made for the blind, which does not permit the writer to see his own manuscript. Nor have I ever corrected, or even read, my own original draft. As the chirography, under these disadvantages, has been too often careless and obscure, occasional errors, even with the utmost care of my secretary, must have necessarily occurred in the transcription, increased by the *barbarous phraseology imported from my Mexican authorities.* (*History*, 6, my emphasis)

While the noctograph produced a kind of hieroglyphic print, its ultimate compositional effect can be conceived of more broadly as a romantic narrativization of barbaric forms. Prescott indulged in an excess of pictorial depiction that seemed to suggest an even more subtle infusion of hieroglyphic technique into the narrative methodology of romantic history. That blending took the stylistic tone of ambivalence, disavowing Otherness by fixing once and for all its logical and historical affiliations (hieroglyphic reasoning applied to determine what was "civilized") and flirting with it by identifying with Cortés and the figure of the Aztec priest-scribe. Though an ever-present moral qualification seeks to keep the barbaric in view, drown out self-subversion, and distinguish his own visual limitations from that of his textual competitors (the Spanish chroniclers and the Aztec priests), it is not enough. The figure of the hieroglyph seems both to haunt him and to imbue his design, delineating his ability to locate a civilized American identity for himself as well as his ability to identify, by any process of finding samenesses, that which is so barbaric, so different.

Prescott concludes an infamous sacrifice scene with a passage that exemplifies what I mean. He praises the conquering Spanish for "dispelling those dark forms of horror" that evinced the grotesqueries of barbaric rituals and the cultural forms embedded in a semi-civilization:

> The debasing institutions of the Aztecs furnish the best apology for their conquest. It is true, the conquerors brought along with them the Inquisition. But they also brought Christianity, whose benign radiance would still survive, when the fierce flames of fanaticism should be extinguished; dispelling those dark forms of horror which had so long brooded over the fair regions of Anahuac. (*History*, 52)

The elaborately staged scene that provokes such civilized indignation demonstrates the meta-critical core of Prescott's hieroglyphic writing. Here is the conqueror-priest-author with all his ambivalence about the hieroglyph as an adequate method of representation.

> As the sad procession wound up the sides of the pyramid, the unhappy victim threw away his gay chaplets of flowers, and broke in pieces the musical instruments with which he had solaced the hours of captivity. On the summit he was received by six priests, whose long and matted locks flowed disorderly from their sable robes, covered with hieroglyphic scrolls of mystic import. They led him to the sacrificial stone, a huge block of jasper, with its upper surface somewhat convex. On this the prisoner was stretched ... The tragic story of this prisoner was expounded by the priests as the type of human destiny, which, brilliant in its commencement, too often closes in sorrow and disaster.
> ... It should be remarked, however, that such tortures were

not the spontaneous suggestions of cruelty, as with the North American Indians; but were all rigorously prescribed in the Aztec ritual, and doubtless were often inflicted with the same compunctious visitings which a devout familiar of the Holy Office might at times experience in executing its stern decrees. (*History*, 47)[26]

As I have suggested, the scene is a metafiction. With its iconic panorama of pyramids and hieroglyphic robes of "mystic import," it culminates in the priestly invocation of a "type" of human destiny that embodies disaster. But even here, at the height of the transcendent conceit, the poet as priest is complicated by the cultural politics evident in the historical narrative. The Aztec priest *and Prescott* preside over a history that necessitates the textual dispatching of the sacrificial victim. This, then, is the scene of composition, at once seductive and repugnant, facing the new historian. "Priests" of his sort – keepers, moralists, and decipherers of the hieroglyphics of history – are confronted with tragic destinies that might frighten those who are ignorant of the compositional work of history writing itself. Prescott must discern the seductions of such writerly sacrifices and avoid the sorrow of the doomed. He must remain priestly, transcendent, cultivating the beautiful "hieroglyphs" of his literary costume, his "sable robes"; he must resist the emotional, angry dangers of the bloody facts. The body of the Aztecs' victim, like the bodies of Aztecs at the hands of Cortés, are sacrificed to the demands of self-justifying representation.

This analogous conception of the artificer is clearly visible in the figure of the priest as repositor of historical knowledge.

> But, although the Aztec mythology gathered nothing from the beautiful inventions of the poet, nor from the refinements of philosophy, it was much indebted, as I have noticed, to the priests, who endeavoured to dazzle the imagination of the people by the most formal and pompous ceremonial. The influence of the priesthood must be greatest in an imperfect state of civilization, where it engrosses all the scanty science of the time in its own body. (*History*, 42)

Once again, the body (a figurative expression of the collective priesthood) contains and limits character, language, and action. It is as if science's free momentum (the rational agency so lacking in the Aztecs' unfree world) cannot escape the "engrossing" gravity of the corporeal figure.

In Prescott's discussion of the relationship between Aztec oral tradition and hieroglyphic composition, there is yet another point of identification.

> In order to estimate aright the picture-writing of the Aztecs, one must regard it in connection with oral tradition, to which it was auxiliary. In the colleges of the priests the youth were instructed in astronomy, history, mythology . . . and those who were to follow the profession of hieroglyphical painting were taught the application of the characters appropriated to each of these branches. In an historical work, one had charge of the chronology, another of the events. Every part of the labor was thus mechanically distributed. . . . The hieroglyphics served as a sort of stenography, a collection of notes, suggesting to the initiated much more than could be conveyed by a literal interpretation. This combination of the written and the oral comprehended what may be called the literature of the Aztecs. (*History*, 58)

Prescott's role as priestly artificer is strikingly similar to that of the Aztec in its unique admixture of orality and pictorialism achieved through mechanistic compositional devices; he too is a conveyor of "more than literal interpretation." Those who understand the subtleties of this methodology are called "initiates," the imaginative elite who can perceive, through the work of composition, analogues and resemblances beyond scientific facts. The analogue speaks to the presumed literariness of Prescott's own composition; he implies that in the strange combination there is an original source of literary value to be found on either side of the barbarism/civilization binary. Authors of this sort thus seem to transcend an essential New World problem.

The figure of the priest has yet other analogues with provocative implications for Prescott. Developmentally, we are told the Aztecs resemble the ancient Greeks in their religious mythology. But more significantly, Aztec religious thought resembles ancient surviving Asian religions such as Hinduism, with its monstrous gods.

> The Mexican religion . . . although little affected by poetical influences, had received a peculiar complexion from the priests, who had digested as thorough and burdensome a ceremonial, as ever

existed in any nation. They had, moreover, thrown the veil of allegory over early tradition, and invested their deities with attributes, savoring much more of the grotesque conceptions of the eastern nations in the Old World, than of the lighter fictions of Greek mythology, in which the features of humanity, however exaggerated, were never wholly abandoned. (*History*, 37)

In similar fashion, Prescott's ethnography *cum* ethnogeny is invested with the priestly work of awe-inspiring allegory. For instance, his description of the Aztec royal household elaborately portrays the architecture's minute details and so undoes the Aztec "veil of allegory" by reinscribing his own ethnogenetic allegory. Prescott proceeds to decipher the spectacular residence and the meanings those details and structures encoded, contrasting his own priestly reading with the interpretations tendered by Cortés and his fellow chronicler-conquistadors: "The rude followers of Cortés did not trouble themselves with such refined speculations. They gazed on the spectacle with a vague curiosity not unmixed with awe" (*History*, 320).

The same sort of interpretive power play against Cortés is at work in the following passage describing the Aztecan version of the pyramid, the *teocalli*. The "veil of allegory" – inadequately perceived by Cortés and generations of scholars – takes the form of the microcosmic religious translation of the hybrid and complex codes of Aztec social life. The "microcosm"[27] is, in its massive symbolic outline, a kind of allegorized hieroglyph, fantastically self-reflexive without provoking self-knowledge, a miniature representation of a society both "barbaric" and "civilized." And whereas the Spanish saw only barbarism, he sees an intricately grand combination of barbarism and civilization:

It was a microcosm of itself, a city within a city; and, according to the assertion of Cortés, embraced a tract of ground large enough for five hundred houses. It presented in this brief compass the extremes of barbarism, blended with a certain civilization, altogether characteristic of the Aztecs. The rude Conquerors saw only the evidence of the former. In the fantastic and symbolical features of the deities, they beheld the literal lineaments of Satan; in the rites and frivolous ceremonial, his own especial code of damnation; and in the modest deportment and careful nurture of the inmates of seminaries, the snares by which he was to beguile his deluded victims! Before a century had elapsed, the descendants of these same Spaniards discerned in the mysteries of the Aztec religion the features, obscured and defaced, indeed, of the Jewish and Christian revelations! Such were the opposite conclusions of the unlettered soldier and of the scholar. A philosopher, untouched by superstition, might well doubt which of the two was the most extraordinary. (*History*, 338)

That reference to the objective "philosopher" is another strategy to remain immune to textual awe, from succumbing to the spectacular semicivilization of *both* the "unlettered" and scholarly conquerors-interpreters who have preceded him. Both interpretive traditions yield equally "extraordinary" results, and yet both serve his own lurid and sensational reinscription.

Finally, the most dramatic part of the narrative, the climax of the fall of Tenochtitlan, is subjected to this skeptical, circumscribing style, which casts its microcosmic, hieroglyphic textuality in terms of the "pages" of romance and history. The hieroglyph, as a graphic representation of visible stories, closely guides and conjoins the ethnographic and romantic impulses. The discourse of graphic textuality encounters, in perhaps its most revealing moment, the claims of literature and the events of history.

> The events recorded in this chapter are certainly some of the most extraordinary on the page of history. That a small body of men, like the Spaniards, should have entered the palace of a mighty prince, have seized his person in the midst of his vassals, have borne him off a captive to their quarters, – that they should have put to an ignominious death before his face his high officers, for executing, probably, his own commands, and have crowned the whole by putting the monarch in irons like a common malefactor, – that this should have been done, not to a drivelling dotard in the decay of his fortunes, but to a proud monarch in the plenitude of his power, in the very heart of his capital, surrounded by thousands and tens of thousands, who trembled at his nod, and would have poured out their blood like water in his defence, – that all this should have been done by a mere handful of adventurers, is a thing too extravagant, altogether too improbable, for the pages of romance! It is, nevertheless, literally true. (*History*, 349)[28]

His appeal to "literal" truth is an oblique admission not only of the fictional qualities of written history, but of the vain powers of the artificer who struggles to illuminate the improbable and the heterogeneous. It is, ultimately, a circular, recursive justification, as the page of his romance has, in one containing sentence, presented the conquest of Montezuma's empire as unbelievable history – as scenic, moralizing romance. Yet there it is, in the microcosmic markings on the page, cataloging events of the scenic history, painting *and* sketching a unique form of "literal truth." At such moments Prescott's history is conscious of its own strange reflections and carvings, its grotesque and picturesque outlines, saturated and made accessible by the very barbarisms they seek to contain.

The Conquest of Peru

Shortly after the *History of the Conquest of Mexico* was published in 1843, Prescott began his Peruvian history, famously saying he would "work the mine" until it gave no more. Fortunately, the documentary materials regarding the conquest of the Incas were more ample and authoritative than those on Mexico, despite the fact that the Incas left no preconquest written records.[29] Accordingly, the obsession with the textuality of historical materials relating to South American Indians is part of a tenacious, ongoing methodology for Prescott. In his preface to the *History of the Conquest of Peru* (1847), Prescott writes grandiosely of the mutual importance of the two histories, Inca and Aztec:

> The most brilliant passages in the history of Spanish adventure in the New World are undoubtedly afforded by the conquests of Mexico and Peru – the two states which combined with the largest extent of empire a refined social polity, and considerable progress in the arts of civilization. Indeed, so prominently do they stand out on the great canvas of history, that the name of the one, notwithstanding the contrast they exhibit in their respective institutions, most naturally suggests that of the other. (*History*, 725)

The invocation here of a kind of pictorial naturalism in the reciprocal intelligibility of the histories is significant. The natural positioning of Incas and Aztecs upon "the canvas of history" affords easy narrative movement from Aztecs to Incas, as well as a graphic illustration of analogic progressions. Regarding his historiographic predecessors, he acknowledges the work of Robertson, while emphasizing again texts filling blank "space," the "characteristic features of the Conquest," and "the coloring of life" in his effort to provide coherence and spirit.

> [Robertson's] masterly sketch occupies its due space in his great work on America. It has been my object to exhibit this same story, in all its romantic details; not merely to portray the characteristic features of the Conquest, but to fill up the outline with the coloring of life, so as to present a minute and faithful picture of the times. (*History*, 728)

He goes on to say that Robertson's theory of historical writing and research, while aspiring to be scientific (he leaves the "scaffolding" of his history for all to view in the form of copious footnotes), allows for the uncertainty of truth – the essential figurativeness of the historical past. Prescott adds to this evaluation by discussing the contingencies of vision one encounters within the textual turmoil of the historical past:

> The actor, engaged in the heat of the strife, finds his view bounded by the circle around him, and his vision blinded by the smoke and dust of the conflict; while the spectator, whose eye ranges over the ground from a more distant and elevated point, though the individual objects may lose somewhat of their vividness, takes in at a glance all the operations of the field. (*History*, 729)

The Peruvian field is, nevertheless, cluttered by too many spectators, obscuring even a panoramic view of the operations of the field. Suggesting again light and spectacle, Prescott explains that the primary documents pertaining to Peru are far more copious than those of Mexico.

> But, whatever be the cause, the collection of manuscript materials in reference to Peru is fuller and more complete than that which relates to Mexico; so that there is scarcely a nook or corner so obscure, in the path of the adventurer, that some light has not been thrown on it by the written correspondence of the period. The historian has rather had occasion to complain of the *embarras des richesses*; for, in the multiplicity of contradictory testimony, it is not always easy to detect the truth, as the multiplicity of cross-lights is apt to dazzle and bewilder the eye of the spectator. (*History*, 727)[30]

The problem confronting the historian is opposite to the case of Mexico: too much evidence dazzles the interpreter. The graphic imprint of the mass of evidence is almost overwhelming in its wealth, registering a shameful desire on Prescott's part. The result of that spectacle of evidence, however, is similar in certain respects to Prescott's Mexican narrative poetics.

Still, there are significant differences that must be acknowledged between the Mexican and Peruvian situations, differences that go beyond the quantity of compositional resources. While the Aztec story provided the ideal of the romantic plot, where all tends to a climactic surrender, the Peruvian story is less satisfactory – the denouement arrives almost immediately with Atahualpa's capture on the plains of Cajamarca. This requires the reader to take a longer view: "we must look beyond the immediate overthrow of the Indian empire" and "by fixing the eye on this remoter point, the successive steps of the narrative will be found leading to one great result" (*History*, 727). That quality of narrative insufficiency, that lack of a natural splendor that leads so nicely to stately narrative satisfaction, requiring the reader to "look beyond" the immediate, corresponds to a peculiar lack of written sophistication on the part of the Incas. The ingenious Inca form of symbolic communication, like the hieroglyph, challenged Prescott's own interpretive and expressive capabilities as a writer and forced him into a series of perhaps even more tendentious comparisons of national character than we see with the Aztecs.

Prescott's "Introduction: View of the Civilization of the Incas" contrasts Inca society favorably against the Aztec: "if their history shall be found to present less strange anomalies and striking contrasts than that of the Aztecs, it may interest us quite as much by the pleasing picture it offers of a well-regulated government and sober habits of industry under the patriarchal sway of the Incas" (*History*, 733). Indeed, Prescott finds the contrast a study in the "opposite directions" taken by the human mind in "its struggle to emerge from darkness into the light of civilization" (815). We are told at this point that the best Incan "resemblance" is to civilizations of the East – to the Chinese and, especially, the Hindus.

Indeed, after a generally approving chapter on the character of the Inca state, Prescott concludes that the Incas could not have been more different from their neighbors the Aztecs. And yet their demise was, if not identical, at least teleologically consistent.

> What a contrast to the condition of the Aztec monarchy, on the neighboring continent, which, composed of the like heterogeneous materials, without any internal principle of cohesion, was only held together by the stern pressure, from without, of physical force! – Why the Peruvian monarchy should have fared no better than its rival, in its conflict with European civilization, will appear in the following pages. (*History*, 775)

Unlike the Aztecs, whose cohesion was based on the fear of sacrifice from above, the Incas present a problem in that their cohesion seemed to have a peculiarly self-evident rational basis. And so hierarchical analogues are tested. In addition to this analogical pressure, the Incas present the other major problematic concerning parallels with the process of Prescott's own composition – noctographic writing coupled with the research and oral dictation provided by reader-secretaries. The Peruvians combined an encrypted system of "pseudo-writing" based on the quipu with an oral tradition embodied in the priestlike person of the *amauta*. The quipu furnished the closest thing to a written linguistic system, but it was mostly a device for recording rhetorical cues used in spoken arts. Prescott describes the system:

> The quipu was a cord about two feet long, composed of different colored threads tightly twisted together, from which a quantity of smaller threads were suspended in the manner of a fringe. The threads were of different colors and were tied into knots. The word quipu, indeed, signifies a knot.
> ... the mysterious science of the *quipus* ... supplied the Peruvians with the means of communicating their ideas to one another, and of transmitting them to future generations. .... For, independently of the direct representation of simple objects, and even of abstract ideas, to a very limited extent ... it afforded great help to the memory by way of association. The peculiar knot or color, in this way, suggested what it could not venture to represent; in the same manner – to borrow the homely illustration of an old writer – as the number of the Commandment calls to mind the Commandment itself. The quipus, thus used, might be regarded as the Peruvian system of mnemonics. (*History*, 792–3)

Yet this system of "writing," for all its remarkable symbolic economy, was insufficient for the purposes of sophisticated ideation and artifice. Though ideal for mathematical computations, the quipu could not be said to obtain the figurative qualities necessary for real linguistic, self-expressive abstraction; the quipu was all suggestion and cabalistic association, an exotic variety of third-level hieroglyph that never achieved the generative mutability of an advanced grammar:

> But, although the quipus sufficed for all the purposes of arithmetical computation demanded by the Peruvians, they were incompetent to represent the manifold ideas and images which are expressed by writing. Even here, however, the invention was not without its use. (*History*, 793)

As part of ritualized oral history, mnemonics did much of the work of continuous historical memory. The system combined the quipu and ritual orality to chronicle raw "data" – the great deeds of the empire, presumably devoid of ideological commentary or descriptive flourish. A state-run system for the production of historical annals made use of this crude method; the Incas presented a civilized polity based on historical memory oddly devoid of true graphic representation.

> Annalists were appointed in each of the principal communities, whose business it was to record the most important events which occurred in them. Other functionaries of a higher character, usually the *amautas*, were intrusted with the history of the empire, and were selected to chronicle the great deeds of the reigning Inca, or of his ancestors. The narrative, thus concocted, could be communicated only by oral tradition; but the quipus served the chronicler to arrange the incidents with method, and to refresh his memory. The story, once treasured up in the mind, was indelibly impressed there by frequent repetition. It was repeated by the amauta to his pupils, and in this way history, conveyed partly by oral tradition, and partly by arbitrary signs was handed down from generation to generation, with sufficient discrepancy of details, but with a general conformity of outline to the truth. (*History*, 794)

That narrative of history, treasured up in the mind by oral and symbolic repetitions, was Prescott's own method. As if recognizing the unsettling analogy, Prescott launches into an encomium on the superiority of the written alphabet and even the hieroglyphs of the

Aztecs, as against the subhieroglyphic mode of the Incas. The ideological weight of philology is heavily brought to bear.

> The Peruvian quipus were . . . a wretched substitute for that beautiful contrivance, the alphabet, which, employing a few simple characters as the representatives of sounds, instead of ideas, is able to convey the most delicate shades of thought . . . The Peruvian invention, indeed, was far below that of the hieroglyphics, even below the rude picture-writing of the Aztecs; for the latter art, however incompetent to convey abstract ideas, could depict sensible objects with tolerable accuracy. It is evidence of the total ignorance in which the two nations remained of each other, that the Peruvians should have borrowed nothing of the hieroglyphical system of the Mexicans, and this, notwithstanding that the existence of maguey plant, *agave*, in South America might have furnished them with the very material used by the Aztecs for the construction of their maps. (*History*, 793-4)

Prescott views the Incas as ignoring the materials for civilized advancement at their ready disposal. For some reason, which Prescott never fully articulates, the Incas were blocked from realizing the benefits of international interchange and a nascent written culture, expressed in its most developed form by the making of maps.

Yet the silent, or rather coded, reason for this imperial sealing off of relatively civilized polities is, once again, reducible to race as it is read through philology. Both Incas and Aztecs are regrettably limited, as any "reading" of the bodies of their modern descendants or the documents exposing their problems with representation will attest. In the world of the progressive historian, it is the relatively civilized polities is, once again, reducible to race as it is read through philology. Both Incas modern nation, forever interpreting and duly sanctioned by history to represent, that is the true yardstick of human development.

Prescott is, in this centralizing mode of measurement, not a historical relativist. Indeed, his characterization of the Incas and Aztecs prevents his ethnographic accounts from interpretation outside the category of race. The ability of a people's written culture to disseminate the thoughts of individuals through time and over geographical space is the true gauge of that people.

> It is impossible to contemplate without interest the struggles made by different nations, as they emerge from barbarism, to supply

themselves with some visible symbols of thought, – that mysterious agency by which the mind of the individual may be put in communication with the minds of a whole community. The want of such a symbol is itself the greatest impediment to the progress of civilization. For what is it but to imprison the thought, which has the elements of immortality, within the bosom of its author, or of the small circle who come in contact with him, instead of sending it abroad to give light to thousands, and to generations yet unborn! Not only is such a symbol an essential element of civilization, but it may be assumed as the very criterion of civilization; for the intellectual advancement of a people will keep pace pretty nearly with its facilities for intellectual communication. (*History*, 793)

The preceding passage demonstrates a rather intricate apportioning of rational, liberating faculties along the scale of civilization. Prescott once again finds an axiomatic correspondence between evidence of symbolic disseminations, immutable capacity of intellect, and achievement of civilization. Despite this algorithm, Prescott has compunctions that arise, interestingly, from the more material aspects of actual composition.

Yet we must be careful not to underrate the real value of the Peruvian system; nor to suppose that the quipus were as awkward an instrument, in the hand of a practised native, as they would be in ours. We know the effect of habit in all mechanical operations, and the Spaniards bear constant testimony to the adroitness and accuracy of the Peruvians in this. Their skill is not more surprising than the facility with which habit enables us to master the contents of a printed page, comprehending thousands of separate characters, by a single glance, as it were, though each character must require a distinct recognition by the eye, and that, too, without breaking the chain of thought in the reader's mind. We must not hold the invention of the quipus too lightly, when we reflect that they supplied the means of calculation demanded for the affairs of a great nation, and that, however insufficient, they afforded no little help to what aspired to the credit of literary composition. (*History*, 794)

He thus allows for a certain admiration of the Incas' ability to read their symbols with "adroitness." As an experienced user of a mechanical facility in the process of symbolic interpretation and production, Prescott knew better than most "the effect of habit in all mechanical operations."

So too, Prescott knew well the uses of orality in the process of annalistic thinking. But Prescott is keen to distinguish the poetic orality of the "rude" Incas, presumably transcribed in the immediate wake of conquest by the Spanish, from the poetic inclinations of the romantic historian – Scott or Irving, for instance.

> Yet history may be thought not to gain much by this alliance with poetry; for the domain of the poet extends over an ideal realm peopled with shadowy forms of fancy, that bear little resemblance to the rude realities of life. The Peruvian annals may be deemed to show somewhat of the effects of this union, since there is a tinge of the marvellous spread over them down to the very latest period, which, like a mist before the reader's eye, makes it difficult to distinguish them between fact and fiction. (*History*, 795)

Once again, the mist before the reader's eye cannot be finally dismissed from the novelistic qualities of Prescott's own engagement with "rude" facts. Whether that smudging of the difference between fact and fiction arises from poetic or novelistic influences, the metaphorical invocation of the eye returns the conceptual puzzle to Prescott's own method.

Civilization's correlation with written progress was even more of a problem in the Incas' case. Though they lacked hieroglyphic writing, in almost every way the Incas possessed a more rational and peaceful state than that of the Aztecs.

> Strange that they should have fallen so far below their rivals in their efforts after a higher intellectual culture, in astronomical science, more especially, and in the art of communicating thought by visible symbols. When we consider the greater refinement of the Incas, their inferiority to the Aztecs in these particulars can be explained only by the fact, that the latter . . . were indebted for their science to the race who preceded them in the land, – that shadowy race whose origin and whose end are alike veiled from the eye of the inquirer . . . It is with this more polished race, to whom the Peruvians seem to have borne some resemblance in their mental and moral organization, that they should be compared. (*History*, 815)

Prescott posits a prior origin for Inca civilization, as he had with the Aztecs, that is now inaccessible to the historian's probing eye and circumscribing hand, and serves to ethnogenetically determine racial limits as well as achievements. It is that mystery race which is to "blame" for the Incas' hindered intellectual accomplishment, though it is credited too for their legacy of "polish" and "organization."

Prescott wants us to draw comparisons retrospectively with this "mystery" race; but his subsequent subsequent national comparisons are perhaps more telling in regard to what he really thinks of the Inca state and its accomplishments. As with the Aztecs, he thereby implies a narrative puzzle to be solved by the progress of history itself. The secret of the destruction of the Incas cannot be explained by an outline of the society as a formal, ascripted entity, as in the Aztecs' case. Only a kind of radical philological exceptionalism can explain the Incas. So Prescott draws on the terms of U.S. exceptionalism to make his distinction. A moral poetics accompanies this narrative too, derived from representation of the individual in a disconcertingly federalized state not unlike the United States.

Prescott initiates his final evaluation of the Incas and their faults by setting up a plausible but jaundiced picture: "a philosopher of a later time, warmed by the contemplation of the picture – which his own fancy had colored – of public prosperity and private happiness under the rule of the Incas, pronounces 'the *moral* man in Peru far superior to the European' " (*History*, 819). Prescott revises this picture with the type of savagism we have already seen in his account of the Aztecs' paradoxical cultural expressions of rationality. The Incas seem to evidence an *excess* of the rational: "The defects of this government were those of over-refinement in legislation, – the last defects to have been looked for, certainly, in the American aborigines" (820). Their overly refined juridical state did not of course correspond to a healthy written culture. As with the Aztecs, the individual character of the Incas defines the imaginative limits of their empire. Indeed, their lack of liberty was linked to a familiar absence of self-will. This ultimately implies a contrast with the nation that had elevated that nexus between individual power and liberty to the level of constitutional textual authority, the United States.

Yet such results are scarcely reconcilable with the theory of the government I have attempted to analyze. Where there is no free agency, there can be no morality . . . Where the routine is rigorously prescribed by law, the law, and not the man, must have the credit of the conduct. If that government is the best, which is felt the least, which encroaches on the natural liberty of the subject only so far as is essential to civil subordination, then of all governments devised by man the Peruvian has the least real claim to our admiration. (*History*, 819)

In short, Prescott deems the Incan state totalitarian, with its immoderation of symbolically crude juridical disciplines upon the individual. This is in contrast to his North American apotheosis of regulated disorder: U.S. civilization is his ideal of the systematized libertarian state, represented by a transcendent authorizing text, the Constitution. Prescott concludes this section by explaining that there is no need for a comparativist appendage to this history, as there was with the Aztecs. This is partly because the best emblems provided by the Incas are their political institutions, not hieroglyphs or quipus, and partly because the most useful national comparison – even if it serves to downgrade in the comparison – is to the United States.

It is not easy to comprehend the genius and the full import of institutions so opposite to those of our own free republic, where every man, however humble his condition, may aspire to the highest honors of the state . . . where consciousness of independence gives a feeling of self-reliance unknown to the timid subjects of a despotism; where, in short, the government is made for man, – not as in Peru, where man seemed to be made only for the government. (*History*, 819)

Prescott is, as we have seen, particularly fond of comparing the Incas to the Aztecs, and, as in *The Conquest of Mexico*, analogies to the Egyptians persist in this work; the section on architectural resemblances draws heavily on the Incas, Aztecs, and Egyptians. What is striking about his attempt to evaluate the Incas comparatively is that, especially here, the poetics of this history is shot through with a nationalist, self-consciously constructed binary that, above all others, explicitly reads between two competing New World empires: the superior United States and the historically upstart Incas. Indeed, the Peruvian state is remarkable in Prescott's anxious assessment for the challenge it presents to the exceptionalism of the United States within the history of political orders in the New World.[31]

> The New World is the theatre in which these two political systems, so opposite in their character, have been carried into operation. The empire of the Incas has passed away and left no trace. The other great experiment is still going on, – the experiment which is to solve the problem, so long contested in the Old World, of the capacity of man for self-government. Alas for humanity, if it should fail. (*History*, 819–20)

The basic difference between Incas and U.S. citizens – unlike any possible difference between Aztecs and U.S. citizens (they are never compared) – resides in the character of government, which once again can be traced back to an ethnography of racial difference. A superiority of "traces," of the visible emblems of difference that endure in history, assures Prescott of success in spite of a palpable anxiety that could engulf both the experiment and, in a moment of romantic high drama, history itself.

As such, the necessity for finding these "traces" in manifestly resolvable ways is paramount for allaying imperial discomfort. Something, in lieu of the evidence of sophisticated self-representation, must be found as a trace that justifies his nervous comparison of the Inca empire with the United States. When it comes to the way representation or the "mechanical arts" sketches and, ultimately, reflects the degree of civilization, Prescott makes a change from *The Conquest of Mexico*. No longer is it the hieroglyph (it is clearly not the quipu, either) that indexes and encodes achievement, but rather architecture.[32]

> But the surest test of the civilization of a people – at least, as sure as any – afforded by mechanical art is to be found in their architecture, which presents so noble a field for the display of the grand and the beautiful, and which, at the same time, is so intimately connected with the essential comforts of life . . . The monuments of China, of Hindostan, and of Central America are all indicative of an immature period, in which the imagination has not been disciplined by study, and which, therefore, in its best results, betrays only the ill-regulated aspirations after the beauti-

ful, that belong to a semi-civilized people. The Peruvian architecture, bearing also the general characteristics of an imperfect state of refinement, had still its peculiar character; and so uniform was that character, that the edifices throughout the country seem to have been all cast in the same mould. (*History*, 811)

According to Prescott, it is unfortunate that the Incas, unlike the Aztecs, were not committed to pictorial splendor that aspired to the beautiful. Inca architecture, while magnificent and awesome, reflects nothing so much as the oppressive anti-individualism embedded in their national and racial character. We see once again that the cultural artifact is read in Prescott's ethnography to underscore preordained judgments related to the inevitable tragedy of conquest; tragic, because the flaws are so visibly obvious. The flaws are also ethnogenetically traceable.

Even more so than Mexico, the case of Peru is fraught – politically and even emotionally. Though Prescott is certainly singular, the poetics of historical self-doubt and the fear of a topos of self-conquest that reside in the very logic of national identity are evident in the other authors discussed in my study. Melville may be the one author, though, who looks at South America and its histories and manages a critical reassessment of American identity. It is a similar sense of the tragic – but with a more critically nimble and self-aware inquiry into the problematics of representation and an unfolding critique of humanist discourse – that would inform Melville's political lamentations of South American demise and vexed historical self-expression.

Conceded or Assumed?

Prescott wrote to Angel Calderón de la Barca during the composition of *The Conquest of Mexico*: "This half civilization breed makes a sort of mystification like twilight in which things appear as big again as they are, and all distorted from the truth" (*Correspondence*, 115). What is most striking here is the very persistence of this way of thinking. Once again, Prescott transforms the "halfness" of civilization into a perspectival metaphor where truth is stretched to the horizon of an ideal vision. What elicits such mystifying vision – this "half civilization breed" – challenges the historical narrative of the sober North American. As I have suggested, the cultural politics of these kinds of visual characterizations are multiply inflected by national, racial, and religious accents.

As Charvat and Kraus have shown, Eurocentric and Christian biases course through and shape his histories. Arabs, for instance, must lose out to the Spanish in spite of their laudable contributions to civilization. So too with the Incas and Aztecs. The Spanish, as a more liberal and theistically congenial people, necessarily had to supplant indigenous South American empires. Aztec and Inca leaders were worthy men but their peoples were terrorized, through such unwritten cultural practices as sacrifice and superstition, into compliance with a social contract. Incas were notably progressive and more civilized, but of course they lacked the supreme virtue of individualism, which made them vulnerable to the peculiarly Catholic, self-conscious advance of the Spanish. And yet, Spain, and Catholicism in particular, represented retrograde forms of civilizing Christianity. Catholicism was a hopelessly sensual religion, while Protestantism inhabited a higher mental plane; it was more conducive to abstraction and broad secular patterns of intellectual accomplishment, rather than the gaudy symbolism and Inquisitorial societies of colonial Spanish America.

Prescott affirmed the differential conquest theory implicit in the Black Legend, essentially absolving Anglo-Saxon imperialism. (Anglo-American colonizers sought political freedom as opposed to the Spanish, who sought only gold.) Such an endorsement spoke to his own authority vis-à-vis rival historians in South America. He criticized the Spanish chronicler Juan Sarmiento for overpraise of the Incas: "It is not improbable, that, astonished by the vestiges it afforded of an original civilization, [Sarmiento] became enamored of his subject, and thus exhibited it in colors somewhat too glowing to the eye of the European" (*History*, 822) (but importantly, not too effulgent for the eye of the North American). Similar criticism was offered of other South American chroniclers – Prescott was critical of the nationalist and sectarian chroniclers of a too proximate conquest.[33]

Such historiographic placement implied a tangibly imperial arrogance of historical coherence suggested, in turn, by the prerogatives of national power. For Prescott, the semicivilized South Americans are the United States' own encoded, ancient civilization in need of decipherment, paralleling Europe's (France's, in particular) relationship with Egypt – an imperialism that implied the necessary rearticulation of historical logic. That historical logic resided in the hieroglyphic remnants of mute civilizations (Incas and Aztecs) and in the archival documents of a nation like Spain whose international power had receded tremendously. The ethnogenetic mystery, embodied in such faulty wonders as hieroglyphic script, the Spanish chronicle, and the quipu, invited the revision of New World geopolitical space in a contemporary context. The Spanish American realm became a quasi-scientific romantic project, subject to empiricist figurations and the great allure of rendered textual pleasures; Spain was no longer a geopolitical rival, but a discursive archive that could help to produce the narrative authority of Federalist escapism. Prescott's historical hieroglyphics constituted a form of orientalism, a romantic signature placed upon history itself. At a time when the new republics of post-colonial Spanish America wished to forget, if not negate, their conquistador past, Prescott made a name for himself and American historiography based on retelling, in all its spectacle, that ignominious story.[34]

If the Incas compel Prescott to nationalist comparisons, we might ask an obvious question: What was Prescott's view of the United States as empire, and how was it related to his conception of history and the text?[35] In a review of George Bancroft's *History of the United States* (Volume III),[36] Prescott writes of America's "mission" as a civilizing force, agent of individualism, commerce, peace, and so on. Four years later he added a footnote to his review (which was reprinted in his *Miscellanies*) that is a harsh indictment of illegal territorial acquisitions:

> The preceding cheering remarks on the auspicious destinies of our country were written more than four years ago; and it is not now as many days since we have received the melancholy tidings that the project for the *Annexation of Texas* has been sanctioned by Congress. The remarks in the text on "the extent of empire" had reference only to that legitimate extent which might grow out of the peaceful settlement and civilization of a territory, sufficiently ample certainly, that already belongs to us. The craving for foreign acquisitions has ever been a most fatal symptom in the history of republics; but when these acquisitions are made, as in the present instance, in contempt of constitutional law, and in disregard of the great principles of international justice, the evil

assumes a tenfold magnitude; for it flows not so much from the single act as from the principle on which it rests, and which may open the way to the indefinite perpetration of such acts. In glancing my eye over the text at this gloomy moment, and considering its general import, I was unwilling to let it go into the world with my name to it, without entering my protest, in common with so many better and wiser in our country, against a measure which every friend of freedom, both at home and abroad, may justly lament as the most serious shock yet given to the stability of our glorious institutions. (Charvat and Kraus, *Prescott: Representative Selections,* 455–6)

Prescott's objection is a strong one and is surely deeply felt. Still, it is based on a liberal, not necessarily anti-imperialist, principle of self-determination. Here, the constitutionality of imperial conquests is at issue – in other words, an appeal to textual integrity, not to the human suffering or economic oppression they implied. Indeed, given the anxious, slipping moral poetics of his histories, one can imagine Prescott theoretically approving of an enlightened reconquest of Mexico, pursued in accord with an explicit, consensual code of moral progress.[37]

Nonetheless, there was an uncategorically anti-imperialist Prescott who understood the power of certain historiographic interventions. For instance, he makes an astonishing comment on U.S. self-conceptions, and the nominative conceits of nationalist chauvinism, in Chapter Two of *The Conquest of Peru* when he writes:

the natives had no other epithet by which to designate the large collection of tribes and nations who were assembled under the sceptre of the Incas, than that of *Tavantinsuyu,* or "four quarters of the world." This will not surprise a citizen of the United States, who has no other name by which to class himself among nations than what is borrowed from a quarter of the globe. (*History,* 752)

To which he appends the amazing footnote that radically cuts against many of the discourses we have seen operating in his own work: "Yet an *American* may find food for his vanity in the reflection, that the name of a quarter of the globe, inhabited by so many civilized nations, has been exclusively conceded to him. – Was it conceded or assumed?" (752). This comment reflects an awareness of the appropriative nature of the American power to name the hemi-

sphere, but more importantly it questions the assumptions of ex-
emption from the categories of imperial brutality that savagism had
dictated. The distinction between assumption and concession seems
almost too soft to withstand the irony; either way, the American is
a conqueror.[38]

We might also view such tortured attempts to reinscribe savagist
discourse for different imperial needs as an attempt to slip between
the cracks of political morality. The resulting moral and compositional torsion exemplifies a contradiction between the fascination
for imperial conquest and the rational political argument that found
the Mexican War and Texas annexation abhorrent. This tension
points ultimately to a split between the sensible world – mere "facts
of consciousness" like the racialized spectacular bodies of the Aztecs
or the architectocracy of the Incas – and the transcendent mind
that apprehends history morally as a teleological justification of imperial fortunes. Only by positing such a binary could Prescott hope
to transcend it. The issue of transcendence in the purely philosophical, sectarian sense is implicated in disquieting questions of imperial
moral transcendence.[39]

Gardiner writes of Prescott's initial foray into the authors who
have written about preconquest Mexico, quoting him saying that
such authors are deceptively erudite: " 'What alarmed me at a distance, under the appearance of curious erudition turns out for the
most part mere mist – moonshine speculation, – a boundless region
into which my duties as a writer of fact will not carry me' " (*Prescott:
A Biography*, 156). Still, given the objects of his histories, indeter-
minacy was inevitably his, in spite of the terms of duty and fact.
Gardiner quotes him subsequently: " 'I hope my readers will take
more satisfaction than I do in the annals of barbarians' " (157).
Prescott places himself outside the pleasure circuit that was the romantic immersion in barbarism. But the triadic relationship between
text, author, and audience is hard to escape; he is, like it or not, a
pathway to those "barbaric annals." Prescott's desire for transcendence is uniquely text-oriented, seeking to appropriate difference
and subsume it under a federalizing unity of authoritativeness that
abjures satisfaction in the name of objective clarity. The problem of
composition can be read finally as an authorial quest to locate civilizing cultural forms that absolve national audiences from barbaric
behaviors – though not its pleasures.[40]

John Irwin points out that Emerson, in his essay "History," held that "science remains ancillary to metaphysics, that the physical fact [the hieroglyph] serves the spiritual fact" (*American Hieroglyph,* 11), and that Emerson in numerous places sees the world as "a grammar of hieroglyphs."[41] Prescott adds the literary, political, and historical exceptions to that grammar, showing that the hieroglyph is also a metadiscourse of history writing. And as such, the noctographic mode that produced such metaemblems can be seen theoretically to serve in microscopic but structurally significant ways the business of writing the U.S. empire. What Emerson, Whitman, and Thoreau attempted to do for the decipherment of hieroglyph and spirit as it relates to individual moral understanding, Prescott accomplished in practice as a historiographic corollary.

For Prescott, words shadow forth from history,[42] emblematizing in their endurance the work of history on the human mind; the romantic history was thus an expressed *perception* of historical order. Prescott produced a narrative that represented his own search for an intelligible center – a federalized point of vision – mediated by language that was at once barbaric and civilized.[43] His linguistic and narrative apprehensions arose, however, from a national imagination obsessed with such frontier binaries – which seemed to write the present and past as with a noctograph, resisting and relishing what Prescott painstakingly entered, using conventional script, into his diary over a period of three months: "D-A-R-K-N-E-S-S" (Gardiner, *Prescott: A Biography,* 28).

4

MUTATIONS[1]

MELVILLE, REPRESENTATION, AND SOUTH AMERICAN HISTORY

Creating Astonishment

Charles Darwin writes at the end of *The Voyage of the Beagle* as if in a fantasy of panoptic clarity. He envisions the shape and full expanse of the New World, and with it the human problem that had so wickedly vexed Prescott: the disappointing ambiguity of the "barbaric" and the prospect of kinship with the "savage." He is in the Andes, looking out over the now-immiserated descendants of the Incas.

> I remember looking down from the crest of the highest Cordillera; the mind, undisturbed by minute details, was filled by the stupendous dimensions of the surrounding masses.
>
> Of individual objects, perhaps no one is more sure to create astonishment, that in the first sight in his native haunt, of a real barbarian, – of man in his lowest & most savage state. One's mind hurries back over past centuries, & then asks, could our progenitors be such as these? – men, whose very signs and expressions are less intelligible to us than those of the domesticated animals . . . *I do not believe it is possible to describe or paint the difference of savage & civilized man.* (*The Voyage of the Beagle*, 506–7, my emphasis)

Paradox is at the core of such empiricism; the human object of knowledge, while "astonishingly" different, is beyond representation, even as one of the supreme categories of difference – barbarism – is brought to bear. With its awesome foreclosure, its final assessment of the effects of human history, one might well imagine the anxious influence exerted upon a young Melville coming across this passage.

That such a textual encounter happened is not improbable. The genealogy of influence provided by Melville's critical biographers is itself unscientific, but the evidence undeniably suggests that Darwin made an impression. Merton M. Sealts, Jr., writes in *Melville's Reading* that while Melville was "no partisan of science himself, he had nevertheless read Darwin's *Journal* as early as 1847 . . . and drawn on it in Sketch Fourth of 'The Encantadas' in 1854" (122). Mary K. Bercaw claims that it was probably much earlier, more like 1841, when Melville read the account of Darwin's voyage.[2] This earlier date places the occasion probably during Melville's own voyage to the Galápagos aboard the whaler *Acushnet.* John Samson in his book *White Lies* cites Jay Leyda's "catalogue of the ship's library, including Prescott, Darwin, and the Harper's Family Library, seventy-two volumes of histories, travel narratives, and memoirs" (2–3).[3] One might imagine further that Melville himself had similar moments off the coast of South America in which "astonishment" triggered the remarkable surge of a creative vision.

And yet obviously, for Melville, Darwin is an obstacle. Such foreclosure – "I do not believe it is possible to describe or paint the difference of savage & civilized man" – at precisely the site of so much of Melville's best thematic sources would seem to have been a primal challenge. If Melville locates this difference as an emblem of the effects of colonization rather than as a natural given, then he dissents, politically and aesthetically, from a key aspect of Darwin's earliest theory of historical representation. My aim in this chapter is to evaluate this dissent by situating Melville within the thematics of New World colonization and empire, and by locating him quite specifically within geographical contexts. For both Darwin's theory of natural selection and Melville's "fictional" stories of conflict were the very contingent products of a critical New World milieu: the post-colonial South American waters where history had a richly hybrid pedigree, born of mutations and mutings, theories and foreclosures.

Indeed, the coast of South America is one place where New World history, and the discourses that continue to propel it in the mid-nineteenth century, can be creatively encountered for writers critical of American power. It is a semiotically and linguistically charged space, the edge of the last Old World imperial center in the Western Hemisphere, where history takes shape in grief-stricken stories about dangerous composites. Robert C. Young writes in *Colonial Desire* that nineteenth-century Europeans viewed South America in particular as the place where racial hybridity ushered in a reverse history of "decivilization":

> South America was always cited as the prime example of the degenerative results of racial hybridization ("Let any man turn his eyes to the Spanish American dominions, and behold what a vicious, brutal, and degenerate breed of mongrels has been there produced, between Spaniards, Blacks, Indians, and their mixed progeny" remarks Edward Long; "they are a disgrace to human nature," adds [Robert] Knox), blaming the perpetual revolutions of South America on their degenerate racial mixture; observations that are dutifully repeated by Spencer and Hitler. According to Alvar's *Lexica del mistiza en hispanoamérica*, published in 1987, there are 128 words in Spanish for different combinations of mixed races. (175–7)

By contrast, Anglo accounts of the continent tend to reduce the multiplicity of difference to the simple code of either/or barbarism; linguistically naming the variety of miscegenation is not as important as reinscribing the maps and charts of "natural" life.

Melville no doubt recognized in Darwin's work on "natural" life an argument about representation – about the role of history in authorial explanations of race and culture in the present. The discursive power of the new science of nature and the influence of the scientist as creative empiricist are nowhere more evident than in Darwin's account of his voyage. Darwin must have challenged Melville, since Darwin's reinscription of the visionary Columbian moment of New World encounter precludes speculation about difference within the human realm, even as it suggests new interpretive paradigms for encountering and creating histories.[4] Theories of "natural history" thus offered a kind of Old World scientific interlocutor for Melville. As John Samson has put it: "Melville does not merely adopt uncritically the formal and intellectual characteristics evident in his sources; he reacts to them in his representation. He sees the ideological 'facts' of these narratives as less than true and in his own narratives controverts them" (*White Lies*, 8). Darwin's South

America elicited from Melville a controverting theory of his own, and it was a theory that made critical use of the ideologies of silence. As such, I would suggest that Melville's obsessive fictions of pivoting perspectives – gyroscopic narratives on difference and conflict in the human universe – can be read as responses to overdetermined theories of race and origins that claim absolute scientific truth, but disallow truths or descriptions that might threaten imperial thinking. Such scientific theories, promulgated by Charles Lyell and Darwin – with their voracious attention to the unambiguous decipherment of all observable phenomena – represented nothing less than a thorough scientific account of the world. The peak of absolute vision, in which the barbarism/civilization binary remains uninterrogated, took into its imperial epistemology the geographical (both Darwin and Melville read Lyell's *Principles of Geography* on their voyages) and the biotic (Darwin).[5] For Melville, the historical result and expression of the arrogant style of such empiricism was nineteenth-century imperialism.

For his part, and in a quite different way, Darwin seems to have understood the political implications of his South American experience. The full concluding passage from his journal is a perfect declaration of pre-Conradian imperial posturing. Darwin's fascination with the volatile terrain of the New World, his "love of the chase," his passion for the creative impetus of travel, all lead one to filling in the blank spots in geohistorical space, and fully articulating the questing male ego of the colonizing West. Darwin begins by describing the trauma of elemental global structures.

> an active volcano – the overwhelming effects of a violent earthquake. These . . . phenomena perhaps possess for me a higher interest, from their intimate connection with the geological structure of the world. The earthquake must, however, be to everyone a most impressive event; the solid earth, considered from our earliest childhood as the very type of solidity, has oscillated like a thin crust beneath our feet; & in seeing the most beautiful & laboured works of man in a moment overthrown, we feel the insignificance of his boasted power.
>
> It has been said that the love of the chase is an inherent delight in man, – a relic of an instinctive passion: if so, I am sure the pleasure of living in the open air, with the sky for a roof, and the

ground for a table, is part of the same feeling. It is the savage returning to his wild & native habits. I always look back to our boat cruises & my land journeys, when through unfrequented countries, with a kind of extreme delight, which no scenes of civilization could create. I do not doubt every Traveller must remember the glowing sense of happiness, from the simple consciousness of breathing in a foreign clime, where the civilized man has seldom or never trod.

There are several other sources of enjoyment in a long voyage, which are perhaps of a more reasonable nature. The map of the world ceases to be a blank; it becomes a picture full of the most varied & animated figures. Each part assumes its true dimensions . . . Africa, or North & South America, are well-sounding names & easily pronounced, but it is not till having sailed for some weeks along small portions of their coasts, that one is thoroughly convinced, how large a piece of our immense world these names imply.

From seeing the present state, it is impossible not to look forward with high expectation to the future progress of nearly an entire hemisphere . . . (*Voyage of the Beagle,* 507–8)

The spirit of awe before a fully revealed physical world, open and "significant," compels his desire to "chase." Darwin's project, and in different ways Melville's too, is to resolve the authorial gap between "representative" histories of individual experience in exotic locales and the objective reality of life and land in those exotic places; it is, of course, a classic anthropological (and, in slightly different ways, historical) problem. In contemplating the pleasure of human origins – savagery as salutary simplicity – Darwin romanticizes anthropology.

How does this romanticization actually occur? What does this have to do with imperialism? Darwin converts the diminishment of power implied by his recognition of geological trauma into the satisfaction that comes with the new capability of mapping a complete world. Oddly, the thought of earthquakes – global destruction and reformation in spite of any possible human counterefforts – smoothly prompts the idea of the earth's *human* domination. Thus romance and imperialism conjoin, for the inviting physicality of the world is subsumed by the process of naming the world in all its wondrous specificity. Darwin's emphasis on the map's signifying achievement, as opposed to the human and geophysical reality of the map's referent, essentially writes off the possibility, or even desirability, of understanding the human Others roughly designated by the place names on global charts. In the narrative of human history, places can be named adequately, but humans cannot; savage simplicity is, without the empiricism of the imperial project, a precondition to maintaining those blank spaces on maps. Darwin leaves the representation of difference among humans unresolved at the level of culture and race; this undescribable, yet "real," situation of racial inferiority leaves him helpless to narrate. That descriptive absence in the humanist narrative relies not only on objectively surveying the nonhuman, but looking down, with a hint of nostalgia, on certain historically "lost" humans and, ironically, *describing* them, relegating them to an irredeemable state of barbarism.

This is where Melville seems to acknowledge, and then resist, Darwinian thinking. Melville opposes the objective "realness" of racial inferiority and, in so doing, refuses the nostalgic position in historical progress, and declines as well a condescending faith in the virtues of romantic savageness and imperial mapmaking. His post-Darwinian response is then to prove the intriguing narratability of a difference that is not merely an occluded object of knowledge, but has an unrepresented history of physical enslavement and disfigurement. Cultural divisions that the imperial quest of civilization brings into view with maps, along with fantasies of civilized-to-savage reversions and "progressive" panoptic views, are such that they inhibit full articulation on both sides of alterity – the unitary self of the West and the fragmented and dispossessed colonized. Colonized and colonizers share their *limited* ability to describe the difference between. But *narrating* that sad condition, that profoundly ineffable mutual acknowledgment, is Melville's counter to Darwin.[6]

I hope in this chapter to elucidate a Melvillean consciousness of New World history and that history's disquieting effect on the question of difference. The Columbian and Darwinian[7] themes I read for are implicit in the narrative features that guide "Benito Cereno" and "The Encantadas": violence, textuality, and the degree to which history continues to hurt. The experience of creative encounter with history, at the site of global trauma and Otherness – and in which present, past, and future are disorganized – is essential to the explicitly unromanticized moments of encounter in "Benito Cereno" and "The Encantadas." The pace and direction of history in the the Americas determines the pitch of Melville's counter-Darwinian theme. "Benito Cereno," with its underestimated poetics of place, will lead to a less critically discussed story, "The Encantadas," structured and driven as it is by the poetics of surviving human and nonhuman colonies.

Reading Spanish American History in "Benito Cereno"

In his essay " 'Benito Cereno,' and New World Slavery," Eric Sundquist situates the discourse of race and political power within antebellum fears of Caribbean revolt and decolonization. Sundquist's focus on Haiti and Cuba in locating the historical referents of the story's slave rebellion posits a strong moralistic allegory.[8] But this focus on the Caribbean downplays an even more obvious geopolitical denotation of the text: Spanish America's viceroyal domains. The fact of Spanish American imperial influence is of great consequence to Melville. For instance, note that he relocates the trial to the viceroyal capital of Lima, when in Amasa Delano's original account (from which the story was adapted) the trial takes place in Concepción, Chile. The setting of the story off the coast of Chile and its resolution on the territory of Peru – indeed its concluding at the very heart of Spain's viceroyalty in the New World – is a direct engagement with the destructive histories of imperial Spanish America. The relocation allows Melville to intensify a historically "creative center," placing great symbolic pressure on the imperial centrality of the story's racial content.

Indeed, imperial and racial histories are insistently cross-related in "Benito Cereno." Note in the following exchange the web of African, European, and Indian identities that structures colonizing discourses in the New World. Delano is the first speaker, Cereno the second:

> "[I]t were strange, indeed, and not very creditable to us white-skins, if a little of our blood mixed with the African's, should, far from improving the latter's quality, have the sad effect of pouring vitriolic acid into black broth; improving the hue, perhaps, but not the wholesomeness."
> "Doubtless, doubtless, Señor, but" – glancing at Babo – "not

to speak of negroes, your planter's remark I have heard applied to the Spanish and Indian intermixtures in our provinces." (Melville, *Great Short Works*, 284–5)

This concatenation of difference, the echoing fear of composite degenerations, ultimately creates a din in Delano's ear. The tonalities of historical subtlety implied by the shared North-South chaos of mixtures are inaudible to his simpleminded tendency to worry about "wholesomeness" rather than "improved" color. The exchange stands as a perfect example of Delano's consistently glib shunning of the ethnic changes that confound "pure" narratives. Interpretation is always grossly self-serving; an overt articulation by Delano, Cereno, or Babo of the racial and national differences among the three is, throughout the story, muted by a restless shifting of interpretive filters.

But reading the mutations themselves, seeing into the historical narratives of the New World "voyage" as Melville has recrafted them, produces a critique of racial and national superiority. This triangulation of difference – European (Spanish/Anglo), African, and Indian – is constructed by, and propelled by, the lead trope of Columbus the colonizer. He is the figure who semiotically gathers the panoptical gaze of history, brings on one of the great clashes between "barbarism" and progress, and then challenges the full description of the conflict. As such, "Benito Cereno" is the first major revision to the Columbian trope in North American literature. The story posits an ambiguous antihero – the lead slaver – making way for domination, but also for the kind of subsequent postcolonial reversals identified by Sundquist. The Columbian trope of the Black Legend – of Freneau and Barlow – is, like so much else in "Benito Cereno," turned inside out.

One merely has to read the pedigree of the nationalized ships and their imperial lineages to gauge the extent of the inversion. Captain Cereno's ship emblematizes the ebbing Spanish empire, "which, like superannuated Italian palaces, still under a decline of masters, preserved signs of former state" (*Short Works*, 241). Melville refines this mood of Spanish decay, focusing on the ugly richness of the Spanish herald:

But the principal relic of faded grandeur was the ample oval of the shield-like stern-piece, intricately carved with the arms of Castile and Leon, medallioned about by groups of mythological or symbolical devices; uppermost and central of which was a dark satyr in a mask, holding his foot on the prostrate neck of a writhing figure, likewise masked. (*Short Works*, 241)

Obviously this image literally heralds the masked drama to come; but it is important to remember its genealogy: Spanish history in the New World provokes a retrospective animation of the processes of domination that have produced the narrative, indeed the drama, of "Benito Cereno."[9]

Delano's historical basis for judging the vessel is the Black Legend, with its overdetermined and oversimplified national symbolisms. As a symbol of the failed Spanish imperial mission in the hemisphere, the ship evokes a Columbian genealogy – Italian by way of Spain; it is a "principal relic of faded grandeur" with "tenantless balconies [that] hung over the sea as if it were the grand Venetian canal" (*Short Works*, 241). It is

[a] very large, and, in its time, a very fine vessel, such as in those days were at intervals encountered along that main; sometimes superseded Acapulco treasure-ships, or retired frigates of the Spanish king's navy, which, like superannuated Italian palaces, still, under a decline of masters, preserved signs of former state. (*Short Works*, 240–1)

The ship has still more markings and significations that signify the creole Spanish American Other and are notable even before we see the ship in those Columbian tropes of national decline. The *San Dominick* appears first to the narrative gaze as part of a remarkable metaphor that embodies the Latin coquette and, perhaps, "sinister" intent.

With no small interest, Captain Delano continued to watch her – a proceeding not much facilitated by the vapors partly mantling the hull, through which the far matin light from her cabin streamed equivocally enough; much like the sun – by this time hemisphered on the rim of the horizon, and, apparently, in company with the strange ship entering the harbor – which, wimpled by the same low, creeping clouds, showed not unlike a Lima intriguante's one sinister eye peering across the Plaza from the Indian loop-hole of her dusk saya-y-manto. (*Short Works*, 239–40)

Thus piqued by sexual opportunity and the danger of prospective intrigue, Delano launches into his investigation of the historical come-on: Is this ship playing sinister, perhaps flirtatious, games, or is it merely fading into the dusk?[10] As he later thinks, "strange craft; a strange history, too, and strange folks on board. But – nothing more" (*Short Works*, 273).

Appropriately, Delano wants the "whole story" of what happened on the ship, a story only superficially and obliquely provided by the Black Legend's national troping. But Cereno is capable of only a partial, initially dishonest story of the intent of his ship. In similar fashion, the Spanish histories and chronicles, which, we are told, underwrite the narrative, are captive to the inconsistencies of Spanish rule and Spanish language. As such they perpetuate a maddeningly clever flirtation with truth, rendered by Melville throughout the story – a possibility of truth apprehended as if through the loops of the creolized fabric of Indian/Spanish femininity, the *saya-y-manta* (a kind of shawl). The Spanish "black-letter text" – what for Delano is a rearticulation of the luridly suggestive Black Legend, but for Melville is a suggestive trace of repressed truths – for now had best be left with an "open margin."[11]

"Benito Cereno" is about the temptation and the need to resist the Gordian knot ("Undo it, cut it, quick") of historical and historiographic discovery and recovery. The undoing of the pure narrative line demands its redeemer overcome his naïveté about difference, retrieve a story about multiple dominations, and finally recover *from* an inability to decide about difference (the sexual dominant or the disappointed Columbian ship overthrown?). Then the redeemer must describe it to important interlocutors. First, Cereno must recover the ability to describe the difference between slave and master, the "natural" terms of racial power in the New World. But this recovery is of course dependent upon regaining power and – literally as well as symbolically – retrieving the Columbus trope from mutinous slaves. Delano for his part must surmount his inability to be free of his own discursive and interpretive prejudices in order to hear the real history of the *San Dominick* and understand the gaps and mutilations in cross-racial, cross-cultural, transnational engagements.

Apropos of the recuperative thematics of the story, we may view all the characters as analogous to real historical characters; dominant traits seem to resonate forward and backward in time, like the Spanish herald. Cereno thus comes to embody a type of Columbus, representing the exhaustion of the Spanish empire. He is a Columbus of the third voyage, his "national formality dusked by the Saturnine mood of ill-health." Aranda is this third-voyage Columbus brought to his final end. Delano, by contrast, can be viewed as a first-voyage Columbus who maintains an energetically naive faith in the benevolence of his intervention. Accordingly, Babo is, as Sundquist points out, something of a historical replication of any number of colonial revolutionaries – Toussaint, Dessalines, Nat Turner, Cinque, Muré.[12] But he too may be implicated in the reversibility of the Columbian sign, as he is brought under the emblem of his own, originally subversive, rewriting of Columbian direction – "Follow your leader" – at the story's very end.

But Babo's historical prototype is clarified considerably – his "real" leader is followed – when his story is brought to its conclusion in Peru: he has a striking similarity to Tupac Amaru, the notorious Indian rebel who had engineered a spectacular insurrection against the Spanish only a decade and a half previously (c. 1782). Indeed, Amaru's death by dismemberment at the hands of Spanish governors and the glory of his mute stoicism in a plaza of the Inca capital of Cuzco are echoed in Babo's famous defiant silence in the viceroyal capital of Lima. Both Amaru and Babo are reduced to heads without bodies; ironically, their mouths refuse agonized speech.

> Some months after, dragged to the gibbet at the tail of a mule, the black met his voiceless end. The body was burned to ashes; but for many days, the head, that hive of subtlety, fixed on a pole in the Plaza, met, unabashed, the gaze of the whites; and across the Plaza looked toward St. Bartholomew's church, in whose vaults slept then, as now, the recovered bones of Aranda: and across the Rimac bridge looked toward the monastery, on Mount Agonia without; where, three months after being dismissed by the court, Benito Cereno, borne on the bier, did, indeed, follow his leader. (*Short Works*, 315)

Muteness, so memorably captured in this scene, and in the historical legend of Tupac Amaru, invites us to recall the theme of "natural history" with its empirical "limits" on human interpretation. The story ends with the enigma of silence and race and the consequent inability of the North American to comprehend or ascribe history in any adequate way. But his inability is dependent upon Cereno's Darwin-like inability, or perhaps – more charitably, given the context – unwillingness, to relate the terms of his story. That narrative pathway is verboten for Cereno because of the overwhelming admonition that is the secret of race. Delano tries to cheer Cereno by pointing him to the open, empty future:

> "You generalize, Don Benito; and mournfully enough. But the past is passed; why moralize upon it? Forget it. See, yon bright sun has forgotten it all, and the blue sea, and the blue sky; these have turned over new leaves."
> "Because they have no memory," he dejectedly replied; "because they are not human."
> "But these mild trades that now fan your cheek, do they not come with a human-like feeling to you? Warm friends, steadfast friends are the trades."
> "With their steadfastness they but waft me to my tomb, Señor," was the foreboding response.
> "You are saved," cried Captain Delano, more and more astonished and pained; "you are saved: what has caste such a shadow upon you?"
> "The negro." (*Short Works*, 314)

With that differentiation between the human and not-human, Cereno sends the issue of articulating history into a palpably Darwinian context. And it is the negro who sends him, as though he were Darwin contemplating the South American Indian, into silent pessimism regarding the imperial "past" which has so lightly "passed." Muteness, a not-human human quality, reigns over the history of the New World and it is a shared condition between master and slave when violence is its creator. "Benito Cereno" thrusts a North American consciousness into an encounter with hollowed-out, muted symbols that he is incapable of accounting for. The narration is meticulous in its attention to the trope.

> There was silence, while the moody man sat, slowly and unconsciously gathering his mantle about him, as if it were a pall.
> There was no more conversation that day.
> But if the Spaniard's melancholy sometimes ended in muteness

upon topics like the above, there were others upon which he never spoke at all; on which, indeed, all his old reserves were piled. Pass over the worst, and, only to elucidate, let an item or two of these be cited. The dress, so precise and costly, worn by him on the day whole events have been narrated, had not willingly been put on. And that silver-mounted sword, apparent symbol of despotic command, was not, indeed, a sword, but the ghost of one. The scabbard, artificially stiffened, was empty. (*Short Works*, 315)

I would suggest that "The Encantadas" can be read as an attempt to give voice and symbolic volume to the "ghosts" of Cereno's violent past as a Spaniard in the New World. "The Encantadas" refigures the mute resignation that "Benito Cereno," and its inadequate Delanovian consciousness, can only cede (a smart critical move on Melville's part) to the official documents of the Spanish "black letter text."

For Delano even revelation is partly muted. The long-awaited revelatory moment comes only with the ambiguous and still maddeningly interpretable moment of violence. The incoherence is precisely that and nothing more for Delano; but it might also be read as Babo's last great intervention – a disruption of history's presumptive forward progress. The revelation arrives only because the violence extinguishes the difference between "past, present, and future," which is, after all, the very narratability of history. As the narrator says of the moment when the slaves battle their masters: "All this, with what preceded, and what followed, occurred with such involutions of rapidity, that past, present, and future seemed one" (*Short Works*, 294).

The machinery of imperial discipline and racial reversal, in this historically concentrated moment – a stripped gear in modern history – is now the "burden" of North Americans, not Spaniards.[13] The neocolonial domain of independent American states, the Monroe Doctrine's logical result in the wake of Spanish decolonization, is signified by the only written text produced by the subaltern: "Follow your leader." The imperial project of the Americas, along with its burdensome histories, is now Anglo North America's to reinscribe.[14] For Melville's new Columbians, difference and its conflicts are partially narrated in history, but even that qualified success is at a cost – the presumption that history itself is the story of human

improvement; the New World is the site of Darwinian differentiation, *without* evolution toward higher forms of self-expression and
social organization. The end of the story gives us a forward-looking
slogan, but one that enacts a kind of guilty, mournful silence about
what produced its leaderly resonance, and about what can possibly
follow.

Mutating: Spanish American Prehistory from The Confidence Man *to "The Encantadas"*

All profound changes in consciousness, by their very nature,
bring with them characteristic amnesias. Out of such oblivions, in
specific historical circumstances, spring narratives . . . As with
modern persons, so it is with nations. Awareness of being embedded in secular, serial time, with all its implications of continuity,
yet of "forgetting" the experience of this continuity – product of
the ruptures of the late eighteenth century – engenders the need
for a narrative of "identity." (Benedict Anderson, *Imagined Communities*, 205)

This passage from Anderson not only serves as a conceptual
tether between stories – the effects of muteness upon the international space described in Melville's fictions – but it reminds us of
the work of identity formation implicit in scientific explanations.
Melville offers fictions that respond to the repressions enabling national and exploratory narratives. As Samson puts it, Melville seems
to respond ideologically to national narratives and their distorting
imperatives of power:

The white culture's generic ideological security – the self-assured
sense that the historical tale has been told and understood – can
be maintained only if its narratives accept unquestioningly the
generic claim to factuality; to move beyond that point . . . is to
break down that claim . . . Melville calls attention to the unstated
generic, ideological, and narratological premises and thus writes
a deflationary but corrective anti-history. (*White Lies*, 15)

"Facts," in Samson's view of Melville's counter, are forever in need
of ideological correction because of the historical errors involved in
their discovery.

Still, I would argue we should not be too dismissive of the scientific achievements of Darwin and Lyell; humanism is a more varied species than we imagine. Melville, Lyell, and Darwin all "deflate" and "correct," in important ways, the processes and articulations of history that seem to mystify and often dismiss the misfortunes of human history. Methodologically, all three stand on common ground. Each reads the history of mute beings and phenomena – human or nonhuman, organic or inorganic – and interpret their findings in a world disengaging from preferred narratives of religious belief. Their methods involve sounding the effects of the present, extrapolating from signs, and unearthing stories of original force. Their methodological similarities, as part of a humanist project, are not entirely contaminated by their imperial complicity; humanism, one hopes, is greater than the limits placed on it from within.[15]

Melvillean humanism seems to consist in a kind of cosmic rendering of sounds and speech that are always threatening to upend us, but that always confirm our interest in listening. These methods of mapping the knowable world with articulate speech and sound are in abundant evidence throughout Melville's work. This humanist project is, again, not always friendly to its auditors or its human speakers (cf. Cereno, Bartleby, Pip, et al.). In that vein, he dedicates his last novel, *The Confidence Man*, to "victims of the *auto da fé*" – victims, that is, of public torture and inauthentic professions of faith.[16] In fact, such confessions are themselves perverse articulations of silence and a kind of antilanguage.[17] Perhaps it is not surprising then that *The Confidence Man* sent Melville into prolonged novelistic silence.

The beginning of Melville's "end" is in a metaphor involving the founding of the Inca empire, invoked in the very first sentence of *The Confidence Man*. Beginning, in the passive voice (most unlike Ishmael's), with a reference to an original American, the novel seems to be an effervescence of history, a bubble blown into the everyday life of a now ahistorical continent: "At sunrise on a first of April, there appeared, *suddenly as Manco Capac at the lake Titicaca,* a man in cream-colors, at the water-side in the city of St. Louis" (*The Confidence Man,* 1, my emphasis). A manifest destiny is embodied in this Mancoic incarnation; a hybrid metaphor greets the man's surfacing at the heart of geographical America and an outpost of "civilization" on the frontier. He comes from the underworld mute; the chapter heading reads: "A mute goes aboard a boat on the Mississippi."

He is, of course, only feigning muteness. Indeed, all who suffered in the wake of the destruction of Manco's civilization and the consolidation of the Spanish empire – the "victims of the *auto da fe*" to whom Melville has dedicated his novel – are precisely those who are unable to speak with authenticity about their victimization. The pre-Columbian reemergence, as a trope of unlikely appearance and harbinger of authorial disappearance, is of a piece with the thematics of narrative silence and disappearance in "The Encantadas." It places at the forefront of our discussion the way Melville understood his own text to operate in received narratives of silence and potential disappearance; this narrative eruption was, at its origin, indigenously American and hemisphere-wide – at its origin, a "natural" history of the partially civilized "mute."

Melville's "The Encantadas" figures the post-colonial Galápagos as a more relaxed and diffuse counterpoint to the concentrated and tense thematics of "Benito Cereno." Here in "The Encantadas" is a plethora of post-colonial victims and ignominious patterns of history – the strata and polities that are left behind in exploration's wake – its mutes and mutations, victims of auto-da-fé, geophysical enigmas, its strange bodies. Unlike "Benito Cereno," which ends with a descent into narrative silence and then a formless proliferation of legalistic text – in essence, a kind of narratological stare – "The Encantadas" ascends *from* silence. Like Manco and the confidence man, it wells up as if from a volcanic nowhere, with the narrator contemplating those that cannot or will not speak – the land, the reptiles, and Hunilla, the Chola widow.

Darwin was indebted to the tortoises and lizards of coastal South America, for he describes in *Voyage of the Beagle* how the lizards, these "imps of darkness," compelled him to "industriously collect all the animals, plants, insects & reptiles from this Island." The next sentence is oddly resonant: "It will be very interesting to find from future comparison to what district or 'centre of creation' the organized beings of this archipelago must be attached" (*Voyage of the Beagle*, 337). Darwin's strictly scientific fascination with the creative forces evident in the Galápagos is realized anti-scientifically in Melville's revisionary encounter with the "centre of creation" – or more

148

precisely a center of creative destruction – that is "The Encantadas." For Melville, part of what is so compelling about the islands' "organized beings" is their uniform prohibition from articulate sound:

> the Encantadas refuse to harbor even the outcasts of the beasts. Little but reptile life is here found: tortoises, lizards, immense spiders, snakes and that strangest anomaly of outlandish nature, the *iguana.* No voice, no low, no howl is heard; the chief sound of life here is a hiss. (*Short Works,* 100)

The monotonal hiss seems to defy the narratives of description hinted at by the differential volumes of more throaty sounds; Melville's "imps of darkness" (Satanic serpents making *all* of Nature "outlandish" and post-Edenic) are emblems of stories, and indeed of original creative acts, which must remain more ambiguous than scientific narratives can tolerate. The New World's Arcadian hopes are rediscovered as what H. Bruce Franklin calls a "paradise lost."

Melville's "natural" history is representable by the very hiss of the nonhuman exile – its metaphoric and ominous recognition of the biblical narrative. At the same time, nature's thoughtless sounds remain unaware of those "black letter texts" of human history. Yet history must be recognized and the beings that survive it must be, at the very least, acknowledged as natural kin – a humanist recovery of the world *not* split into man and beast and all its implicit dominations. Thus "The Encantadas" seems to radiate passively the themes brought to the scene so eruptively by "Benito Cereno"; Melville makes room for interpretive work and historical reflection that "Benito Cereno" and Delano have to foreclose. For one thing, Melville can now write in more than just the margins of Spanish texts, and he does so, impishly, through the "tarned," "Moorish," "inquisitorial" psuedonym that accompanied the sketches' early publication in Putnam's. (The name was dropped when the sketches were brought together in *The Piazza Tales.*)[18]

No palimpsest associated with "The Encantadas" is more important than "Salvator R. Tarnmoor." It digests the linguistic legacies of the "Black Legend," comically evoking the cultural and racial mixtures that survive in Spanish, New World history. Tarnmoor, the nominal repositor of the Moorish conquest of Spain, which prompted the Reconquista, the unification of Castile and León symbolized on the Spanish herald, and, ultimately the Black Legend conquests of the New World, has an oddly but unmistakably Anglo-American voice – at times derisive, sardonic, admiring, pragmatic. His observations are episodic, sometimes sentimental, sometimes biblically evocative, forming sketches that do not bring the drama to any pitch, but rather illustrate some past grotesque. His historical style calls up the past as if history is part of a geophysical descent. But while the past's stories have gravity, the pull is not relentless: it may be escaped by a simple pivot of the gaze. (This is in contrast to "Benito Cereno," which grips the reader with an unrelenting sense of suspended violence and the nervous poise of black-white reversal; the descent in "Benito Cereno" is always pending.)

The most interesting narrative moments in "The Encantadas" come with its contemplation of two exotic "phenomena" – the tortoises and the Chola widow. In both instances, the Darwinian subtext is most important – in the pervasive residue of conquest history and in the intersection between Spanish American and Anglo-American. At its widest angle, the narrative of enchantment – what that can possibly mean in a "real" world with modern atrocities and modern explanations – seems to distort everything. Tarnmoor comes close to unearthing the mystery of the isles' enchantment but never does say outright what that is. In "fact," mystery and enchantment reside in a history that is muted; the tortoise and the widow are figures of that muted enchantment which resists the narrative imperatives of science.

The tortoise, the widow, indeed the islands themselves, all seem to defy scientific narratives of change. The islands are remarkable because they are both mute and seemingly immutable – silent and timeless: "the special curse . . . of the Encantadas, that which exalts them in desolation above Idumea and the Pole, is that to them change never comes; neither the change of seasons nor of sorrows" (*Short Works,* 99). They are monstrously un-Darwinian relics because they testify to some distant, violently discontinuous historical change: "A group rather of extinct volcanoes than of isles; looking much as the world at large might, after a penal conflagration" (99).

This suggestion of a prison riot should remind us of Melville's persistent fascination with the Spanish and their perfection of disciplinary techniques during the time of the *auto-da-fé.* Now silent volcanoes recall the site of tortured speech just over the horizon, geographically and temporally in sixteenth-century Peru. That trace is also embodied in the oddly premodern word "enchanted," quaintly exoticized in the Spanish place name *Encantadas* but applied then to Melville's text of encounter. Enchantment, for Melville, is a narrative mode that seems to accommodate both legend and empiricism. Just as the Spenserian epigraph guides Tarnmoor into his sketches with a showy antiquarianism, Tarnmoor's sense of the enchanted has a manner of ersatz yet compelling profundity. We are told these islands are enchanted because "wrecked sea-officers" have been transformed into the tortoises now occupying this prehistoric realm.

> Nor would the appellation, enchanted, seem misapplied in still another sense. For concerning the peculiar reptile inhabitant of these wilds – whose presence gives the group its second Spanish name, Gallipagos – concerning the tortoises found here, most mariners have long cherished a superstition, not more frightful than grotesque. They earnestly believe that all wrecked sea-officers, more especially commodores and captains, are at death (and in some cases, before death) transformed into tortoises; thenceforth dwelling upon these hot aridities, sole solitary Lords of Asphaltum. (*Short Works,* 101)

The tortoises are related in their enchanted genealogy not only to humans, but to the land itself. They *are* the topography, which itself is a document of human conflict, of "sorrow and penal hopelessness." The Spanish Inquisition, evoked by the words "condemnation" and "penal," seems to have seeped, with a suggestion of agonized outrage and false confessions, into a static, inexpressive landscape.

> Doubtless so quaintly dolorous a thought was originally inspired by the woe-begone landscape itself, but more particularly, perhaps, by the tortoises. For apart from their strictly physical features, there is something strangely self-condemned in the appearance of these creatures. Lasting sorrow and penal hopelessness are in no animal form so suppliantly expressed as in theirs; while the thought of their wonderful longevity does not fail to enhance the impression. (*Short Works,* 102)

Indeed, the tortoises are liminal texts in and of themselves, haunting figures of the auto-da-fé and its disciplinary expressions of memory and historical confession. Tarnmoor describes the human-to-animal transformative presence as a live memorializing text: "I have drawn the attention of my comrades by my fixed gaze and sudden change of air, as I have seemed to see, slowly emerging from those imagined solitudes and heavily crawling upon the floor, the ghost of a gigantic tortoise, *with 'Memento *****' burning in live letters upon his back*" (103, my emphasis).

Melville sketches Hunilla the Chola widow as a taciturn testament to human endurance; both Hunilla and the tortoises help Melville to express a torturous Spanish history. She embodies in her anomalous, feminine presence historical narratives that can never speak their own stories fully. Neither sentimental nor condescending, his portrait inscribes a female, part-Indian presence among the social world of North American circuits of desire, need, and exchange. She is, in her shunning of inquisitorial Americans, not unlike the "liberated" Cereno. When asked repeatedly by the captain about the exact length of her solitude, she thwarts him over and over – "Señor, ask me not. . . . Ask me not, señor" (*Short Works*, 133). Cereno's feminized muteness – portrayed as a sullen weakness in "Benito Cereno" – is here a kind of dignified withdrawal.

> But no, I will not file this thing complete for scoffing souls to quote, and call it firm proof upon their side. The half shall here remain untold. Those two unnamed events which befell Hunilla on this isle, let them abide between her and her God. In nature, as in law, it may be libelous to speak some truths. (*Short Works,* 133)

Much of her story thus remains occluded, and the narrator, unlike that of "Benito Cereno" ("in law") or Darwin himself ("in nature"), is aware of the self-containment necessary to the act of claiming certain human truths.

Her document of exile is likewise "half effaced, as an alphabet of the blind," and she runs her fingers over a reed, "a dull flute, which played on, gave no sound"(133). Hunilla's silence and stoicism nonetheless unsettle Tarnmoor, who understands them to be bound up in the uniquely "Spanish and Indian grief," arising from "proneness on the rack":

> Hunilla was partly prostrate upon the grave; her dark head bowed, and lost in her long, loosened Indian hair; her hands extended to the cross-foot, with a little brass crucifix worn fea-

tureless, like an ancient graven knocker long plied in vain. She
did not see me, and I made no noise, but slid aside, and left the
spot.

A few moments ere all was ready for our going, she reappeared
among us. I looked into her eyes, but saw no tear. There was
something which seemed strangely haughty in her air, and yet it
was the air of woe. A Spanish and an Indian grief, which would
not visibly lament. Pride's height in vain abased to proneness on
the rack; nature's pride subduing nature's torture. (*Short Works*,
136–7)

Here is the memory of history, for all its wondrous "enchantment,"
experienced as torture. The mixed-race Chola body, a cultural and
phenotypic intersection that can only survive in a tension of visibility
and disappearance, is an articulate way for ethnic hybridity to represent itself to the narrating colonizer. She challenges the Darwinian
mindset even further in her ability to "humanize" nature: we are
told that Hunilla haunts the crew with her ability to make "nature"
– things like islands and tortoises and even Indians – human.[19]

This account of a New World subhistory appears to leave out the
local texts that bear the original history. But Melville somehow employs that missing history and its closest representing texts in a way
that enables the story's peculiar aura and thus encodes, through
"enchantment," a powerful counter-ideology to imperial appropriations and representations. Victor Wolfgang von Hagen's introduction to an illustrated 1940 edition of "The Encantadas"[20] is a useful
critical context for the sketches, since it suggests the importance of
indigenous history for Melville's subtle understanding of the place.
The genealogy of Melville's narrative evolves in this light into a genealogy of inevitably "enchanted" truths regarding a history that
left such odd traces.

Von Hagen's introduction brings the major concerns of this chapter into review: his interest in the biological and geographical facets
of the islands is complemented by his readings into texts that constitute the Hispanicized, Incan "prehistory" of the islands. He
points out that there is a Spanish history to these islands that Tarnmoor seems to neglect:

The curtain is raised on the legends of the Galápagos by the episode involving Fray Tomas de Berlanga, Bishop of Panama. He

153

was bound for Peru from Panama with instructions from the Royal council of the Indies to place limitations on the power of Francisco Pizarro, the recent conqueror of the Incas. Nearing the "line" off the coast of Ecuador the vessel was caught in the equatorial doldrums and floated helplessly for awhile until suddenly it entered a strong current that carried it rapidly from the coast, westward, outward, into the Pacific.

On the tenth of March, 1535, after drifting for two weeks, the ship came to anchor at juts of land the mariners had seen for days. To their horror that the islands were volcanic, uninhabited save for curious animals, the Galápagos so large "that each could carry a man on top of itself." The mad search for water began. ("Introduction," xviii)

We are told that Berlanga made it back to Peru and issued a report about the islands to the King. This report in turn found its way to the Flemish mapmaker Abraham Ortelius, "who placed the islands (in their true relative position) on his map of Peru – Peruvae Ariferae Regionis Typus – which was executed in 1574" (xix). He named them the "Isles de Galapagos, after the report of Tomas de Berlanga that they were inhabited by countless galapagos, a term which in Spanish referred to the fifteenth century tortoise-shaped saddle . . ."(xix).

More importantly, von Hagen's supplementary history shows how the renaming of the islands, the Islas Encantadas, was a direct result of the Spanish politics of conquest in post-Inca Peru. He introduces Captain Diego de Rivadeneira, who ended up in the islands after getting caught in an ocean current. In so doing, von Hagen begins a complicated augmentation to the "prehistory" of enchantment that Tarnmoor never fully gets to. According to von Hagen,

> Rivadeneira was fleeing the civil turmoil of Peru where the rapacious conquistadors, the Brothers Pizarro, were locked in a death grip with the Viceroy. He had set sail for a haven but it was not to be found in islands that remained unanchored and floated around in these mad currents . . . To the sailors it looked as if the islands, and not they, were moving. It is quite understandable why the islands were deemed enchanted.
>
> The legend of the Galápagos took more substantial form when Pedro Sarmiento de Gamboa linked the facts of the voyage of Fray Tomas de Berlanga with tales of Inca gold. He learned that

the great Inca, Tupac Yupanqui [first Inca], while carrying on a war of conquest with the kingdom of the Quitus to the north, came with his hosts to the port of Tumbez, where he encountered several large balsa-rafts returning from a sea-voyage. Inquiry informed him that they had come from the islands Avachumpi (the fire island) and Ninachumpi (the outer island) which, according to these Indian merchants, were rich with gold. The redoubtable Inca, so the legend continues, gathered twenty thousand soldiers and building a fleet of immense balsa-rafts with single sails and great rudders, set off on a voyage of discovery. He remained away a year. When the Inca returned, he had with him "Indian prisoners, black in color, much gold and silver and the hides of animals like horses." ("Introduction," xix–xx)

This "prehistorical" legend, dependent in its imperial coercion upon the silence of Inca sources (who no doubt could confirm or deny these stories), leads to an ill-fated expedition. Note how von Hagen, a biologist by training, invokes scientific information to debunk Sarmiento de Gamboa.

Pedro Sarmiento de Gamboa identified their source with the islands de Berlanga had discovered; he did not stop to consider that as these islands were volcanic there could be no gold, or that the Bishop reported that the islands were uninhabited and incapable of supporting habitation. Sarmiento de Gamboa accepted, apparently without reserve, the legend of the Inca's voyage, for he vowed that the booty brought back by Tupac Yupanqui was preserved for a long time in the fortress of Sacsahuaman in Peru. He persuaded the Viceroy that these islands were outposts of a great continent in the austral ocean and pledged that if he were given two ships with funds sufficient to maintain one hundred and fifty men, he would set off for the glory of Spain (and also of Sarmiento de Gamboa). In 1567 the ships set sail for the Galapagos, or at least for the point where the pilots thought they were. The expedition ended up at the Solomons Islands. ("Introduction," xx–xxi)

I have quoted von Hagen at length because I think it is a critical touchstone for a story that seems, ironically, to insist on a kind of Biblical thoroughness and clarity of perspective.[21] Sketch Fourth, "A Pisgah View from the Rock," rehearses that fantasy of clarity that Darwin began this chapter with: "come and be rewarded by the view from our tower. How we get there, we alone know. If we sought to tell others, what the wiser were they? Suffice it, that here at the summit you and I stand" (*Short Works*, 111). We may from here claim to "sentinel . . . the entire coast of South America" (111). But Melville resists the temptations of Darwinian declaration, of Godlike banishments. Indeed, how could he do otherwise, given what he knows of the expectations of those "others" for a suitably savagist rendering, and of the impossible narratives of pain that put him in such commanding position?

Appropriately, it is a frontier prospect Tarnmoor claims to see, for all about is a "boundless watery Kentucky" where "Daniel Boone would have dwelt content" (*Short Works*, 111).[22] He takes advantage of this imperial view to describe, in spite of the geohistorical withdrawal, all about him – the "silence and solitude" that greet the European discoverer. Melville places the discovery of the Encantadas in the year 1670 by Juan Fernández. (Tarnmoor tells us in a footnote that Fernández left the islands because of "the blues" and became a "very garrulous barber in the city of Lima" [122].) Tarnmoor decides all other possibilities of a prehistory of habitation are forgone: "Though I know of no account as to whether any of them were found inhabited or no, it may be reasonably concluded that they have been immemorial solitudes" (113). Still, it is a light dismissal – a reasonable, though not absolute, preclusion.

By far the more significant issue is that something awful has happened in the islands' past and their present condition is a plausible reminder of that humanly tragic experience. All that von Hagen unearths is somehow expressed through those figures of muteness as post-colonial grief. Though Tarnmoor has missed certain aspects of the history of the Galápagos – indeed, a major facet of Peruvian colonial history – he seems to acknowledge the repression and the difference, racial and cultural, implied by its absence. In his figures of muteness he gives witness to the unfortunate reality that difference does *not* provide perfect legibility to racial and national chauvinists like Delano or Darwin or even, for all his cavalier sensitivities, Salvator Tarnmoor.

Critical interpretation, however, can recover Melville's confronting a sense of absence. Inscribing muteness and mutation with his satire of exploration narratives and his anatomizing of geographical enchantment and melancholy, Melville demonstrates that South America is a historical frontier that poses post-colonial, post-Columbian problems for American expressions of self and nation.

The same ground on which Darwin and Lyell had based their representations of the engines of natural change and differentiation provided, for Melville, the opportunity to portray the "difference between savage and civilized man." And it is the irony of a nearly identical encounter (Columbus, Darwin, Melville – all to some degree New World colonizers) that is so arresting, necessary, and unavoidable in Melville's narrative confrontation with his historical masters. For if natural history is symbolically a part of creatively revising the interpretation and understanding of social and national history, then a Melvillean critique of representation must ironically recall the maps that mediate imperial inscriptions and empiricist foreclosures. Critical language cannot do without the requisite terms: selection and differentiation of both the linguistic and racial sort are present most opportunely (the spurs for "creative astonishment," the "centre of creation") within Spanish America. Melville finds scientific modes of narrating the "barbarian," nonhuman, geological world screened by layered representations of intrinsically human dominations; objects (and subjects) are always bent by the scientific mind's imperial predilections.

Melville's figuration of creative American origins is precisely there, in his disruptive obsession with the way America's imperial New World imposes itself – from Columbus to the conquest to the Monroe Doctrine, from the auto-da-fé to the "metaphysics of Indian-hating"; in short, he is compelled by modern history's lacerating effects and the compulsive need for North Americans to "heal." Melville's reconsiderations of these elusively factual places – the Galápagos and the legalistic Spanish viceroyalty – are always cognizant of cultural discernments that recognize only certain accounts of the "real." He is aware of which people make maps, write their own histories, and subscribe to "facts," and those who cannot – or those who withhold speech and representation as a token of resistance to ongoing historical trauma. Homi Bhabha describes the possibility of a "caesura" in the modern narrative given many of the same discourses Melville was involved in:

At the mid-point of the [nineteenth] century questions concerning the "origin of races" provided modernity with an ontology of
its present and a justification of cultural hierarchy within the West
... In the structure of the discourse, however, there was a recur-
rent ambivalence between the developmental, organic notion of
cultural and racial "indigenism" as the justification of supremacy
and the notion of evolution as abrupt cultural transition, discontinuous progress ... The "subalterns and ex-slaves" who now
seize the spectacular event of modernity do so in a catachrestic
gesture of reinscribing modernity's "caesura" and using it to
transform the locus of thought and writing in their post-colonial
critique. (*The Location of Culture*, 246)

Melville is a writer of post-colonial critique through his self-imposed
sense of the mute: Cereno as the confidence man as Tarnmoor as
Babo as Manco.[23] His humanism is radically disruptive and compas-
sionate: "Humanity, thou strong thing, I worship thee, not in the
laureled victor, but in this vanquished one" (*Short Works*, 132).

Obviously I view Melville as something of a corrective to Freneau,
Barlow, Prescott, and, as we will see in the final chapter, Whitman.
In contrast to the other authors in this study, he never allows the
seductions of the past, of origins, to interfere with his examination
of the role of the artist in the project of forming and revising an
inherited national imaginary. Melville seems to make room for sympathy and love within the frontiers he is always reinheriting. He is
fully aware of the manifold narratives of identity that overlap and
sometimes muffle one another in the American hemisphere. After
the United States has completed an illegal war of usurpation in Mexico and just as it is about to rupture politically in the Civil War,
Melville takes stock of who he is as an "American" writer in the
cross-currents of "American" history; this venture teaches him a
lesson in the uses of silence. Paradoxically, he gives voice to the
victims of *auto-da-fé* – to Babo, Manco Capac, Hunilla, and Tupac
Amaru – in the only way a voice from the empire's peaks really can:
by letting their silence describe their status – that to be deemed
"barbaric" is to preclude self-description and, ultimately, to prede-
termine the limits of *all* human knowledge. Unlike Darwin, who
wished not to represent the barbarian for fear that he would see
himself, Melville wishes to represent the effects of empire so that he

might fathom its historical implications; he thus confesses a "barbaric," dominant America.

Melville testifies that American writers who understand this are exiles, refugees from the mania of the national quest. This exile, as evidenced by his own career, carries no easy comforts, returns, or providential rescues. Melville's problematically enchanted spaces – his interruptions in the forward destiny of America – only provide a haven for, as he writes dolefully toward the end of "The Encantadas," "all sorts of refugees; some of whom too sadly experience the fact, that flight from tyranny does not of itself insure a safe asylum, far less a happy home" (*Short Works,* 148).

5

PASSAGE

TWO RIVULETS AND THE OBSCURITY OF
AMERICAN MAPS

The unconscious is that chapter of my history that is marked
by a blank or occupied by a falsehood . . . But the truth can
be rediscovered; usually it has already been written down elsewhere. Namely: in monuments . . . in archival documents . . .
in semantic evolution . . . in traditions, too, and even in the
legends which . . . bear my history . . . and, lastly, in the traces
that are inevitably preserved by the distortions necessitated
by the linking of the adulterated chapter to the chapters surrounding it, and whose meaning will be reestablished by my
exegesis.

> Jacques Lacan, "The Function and Field of Speech and
> Language in Psychoanalysis," in *Ecrits: A Selection*, 49–50

For genius must realize that, precious as it may be, there is
something far more precious, namely, simple Identity.

> Whitman, from the Preface to *Two Rivulets*

The friendly and flowing savage . . . Who is he?
Is he waiting for civilization or past it and mastering it?

> Whitman, "Song of Myself"

we presume to write . . . upon things that exist not, and travel
by maps yet unmade, and a blank. But the throes of birth are
upon us; and we have something of this advantage in seasons
of strong formations, doubts, suspense . . .

> Whitman, *Democratic Vistas*, in *The Complete Poetry and Prose*

Reading Identity

The epigraph from Lacan is an uncanny reminder of the authorial work of recovery and distortion in the "chaptering" of the national imaginary, both for the authors I have studied and for myself. This chapter stands as a necessary epilogue to finding the exegesis of national identity to be triumphantly Melvillean; it is not, as Martí might also remind us. And yet Martí was also the one who installed Whitman as the poet of "our America," so Whitman is offered here as a good example of the knife-edge precariousness of North-South benevolence. His recognition of the need for democratic change and his desire to expunge the history that brought about that need are the essence of his struggle; unfortunately, Whitman's endeavor to Americanize the world had to be squared first with a history that did not yield appropriate narratives of identity. Indeed, "America" had to be purified of the errors and mystifications that inevitably came with the contemplation of history.[1]

And so I reemphasize the Andersonian notion of "oblivions" engendering continuous "narratives of 'identity' " to stress how deeply historical erasures are set into the formation of American national identity. For Anderson has argued that biography – and its complement, identity – accompanied the advent of the nation-state and that this helped to maintain ontological continuity in the post-religious, post-monarchical world. The self took precedence over the theistic cosmos, the nation supplanted dynastic sovereignty, secular history eclipsed ecclesiastical history. Anderson, and more recently Mitchell Breitwieser and Michael Warner, have pointed to Ben Franklin as a *locus classicus* of this new consciousness.[2]

As a way of beginning to think about Whitman and the national imaginary projected by this New World history, I ask that Whitman be viewed in similar ways. Over a parallel span, about one century after Franklin, Whitman was seminal in the articulation of nationalist identity. The resemblances are striking: both began as newspapermen and went on to pioneer the biography of typifying identity, offering to their nation the cumulative chronicle of representative, self-invented Americans. Franklin and Whitman *are* national identity figured as career: two men of letters crafting a bond between individual identity and grand public narratives, a linkage that arose out of the conceptual possibilities of print culture.

My critical resummoning of Anderson is for more particular facets of his analysis. Anderson emphasizes the necessary role of "amnesia," or the "forgetting of continuities," in the generation of narratives of identity by imagining national communities. For Anderson, as for Whitman, people with national identities are made and then directed by the history they choose to recognize, read, and revise; individually and collectively, we are all living expressions of the work of historical imagination. My first task in this chapter is to show that Whitman makes odd choices about history, for there is a strangely Columbus-like failure to recognize the New World as something geographical and historical, as well as new and different, in his dual constructions of personal identity and national community. This failure is, I argue, symptomatic of a broader cultural loss that is related to the assumption of imperial hegemony on the part of the United States.

But why, even with Anderson's suggestive point about the necessity of omission in nationalist thinking, focus on an absence? Evidence of the imperial imagination is all around in mid-nineteenth-century American culture. (The question obtains for Melville as well.) I answer that Whitman's prolonged "blindness" – constituted by the excision of pre-Columbian civilizations and South and Central American historical geography from the national imaginary – is readable, and it can tell us new things about Whitman's nationalist poetics. It is in the recesses that the absence generates where Whitman is forced to confront the ideological problems of his otherwise ardently inclusive historical and national vision; which is to say that New World history projected for Whitman yet another paradox of the national imaginary. And that paradox is part of the ongoing ideological conundrum that is the legacy of New World thinking.

To describe a blind spot requires an interpretation of the visionary processes that stabilize the conceptual environment I call the imaginary. The national imaginary, as I elaborate it in the Introduction, is a symbolic order that operates at the level of the individual and the community, is founded on material and social relationships, and is dependent on binaristic self-mapping. I would assert then that those blind spots in Whitman's historical vision are a result of his abounding faith in the public sphere that accompanied print culture.[3] That is, for Whitman as for other young democrats, and pro-imperialists of many stripes, print culture worked to linguistically and culturally differentiate frontier competitors (Indian, Mexican, etc.) and thus consolidate opinion about a national will. Such (admittedly contested and imperfect) consolidation necessitated, in turn, the ceaseless redaction of historical accounts.[4]

Blind spots arising from the nationalist effects of print culture reveal Whitman's ambivalent relationship to material accounts of history.[5] To participate in, and often exalt, the material culture of dissemination (Whitman is traditionally seen to be incarnating the poetic voice in the book itself)[6] is not to sing it absolutely; indeed, as Michael Warner has recently put it, Whitman seems to specialize in "making the pragmatics of selfing a mess."[7] He longs for an exceptionalism that will make room for his alluring messiness and ambivalences. In the fused scars of his historical construct – a global geography of charts, rather than professed chants,[8] to be found most richly in "Passage to India" – are signs of this ambivalence. At these moments Whitman, because of his incomplete meditation on a past he wants to incorporate absolutely, nervously trills the binaries of modern subjectivity: subject/object, personal/national, tradition/history, self/other. The problematic points up the potential deconstruction of nationalism, for these binaries represent the conceptual haunting of frontier thinking. The originating problem of the line that divides self and other, civilized and barbarian, is the legacy bestowed upon Whitman's project of democratic identity. And if history is haunted by the binaries upon which American identity is founded, then it is haunted too by absence. The absence underwrites and trails Whitman's democratic American identity and the print culture that charts it.[9]

My method implies a yoking. The linkage I work toward is between historical geography – mapmaking with words, stories about an objective "en masse" – and (inter)subjectively held narratives of identity that are national and individual (the province of Jürgen Habermas's public sphere and Anderson's nation). As I have said, New World history posed problems of introjection as well as projection, implying a critical nexus between inside and outside, the shared territory of identity and nation. For Whitman – as for my own critical inquiry – to explore identity is to explore the objective, material world as well as the subjective, ideal history upon which world, nation, and identity are contingent. Whitman's nationalized public sphere, we will see, projects itself indistinctly and casts many shadows.

Just a glance at his poetry confirms that Whitman was keenly interested in classical antiquity: Greek, Roman, Indian, Egyptian, He-
brew. He was scrupulous in his scholarly ambition to obtain a picture
of classical history; his notebooks, even more than his poetry, reflect
this. So it is somewhat surprising that he tends to ignore the past –
indeed the geographical presence – of ancient South and Central
America; this is in spite of a venerable tradition (such popular literary predecessors as Prescott, Barlow, and Freneau) of writing
about the New World's original empires. For example, in the
"World History" section of Grier's *Notebooks and Unpublished Prose
Manuscripts*, Whitman discusses every continent's history except
South America's. The omission becomes even more curious when
one considers that Whitman, from the very beginning to the literal
end of his career, was obsessed by Columbus, a figure whose legend
is bound up in the tragedy of Inca and Aztec demise – bound up
finally in a traditional conception of ancient American history as
South and Central American.

Late in his life, Whitman himself acknowledged the omission as
a problem. Despite the homogenizing trend of American nationalism, he admitted that America's historical narrative is in fact heterogeneous, very much a product of pre-Columbian and Spanish
American cultural influences as well as "Anglo-Saxon." His acknowledgment implied a rejection of an Anglo-dominant thread he had
begun to weave in his 1856 letter to Emerson. In this retrospective
acknowledgment, Whitman implied that the received traditions are
falsely maintained, that America remains culturally overdetermined
by English legacies that have denied the multivocal fullness of American identity.

There is, in short, a fertile amnesia of which Whitman, at least
belatedly, seems to have gradually become more aware. The hope
of writing on blank maps usually suggests the compelling applica-
bility of his self-invention; but it may also be viewed as self-criticism
and fear. In *Democratic Vistas* (1870) he makes clear his shifting
position regarding the nation's untold stories: "we presume to write
... upon things that exist not, and travel by maps yet unmade, and
a blank. But the throes of birth are upon us; and we have something
of this advantage in seasons of strong formations, doubts, suspense ..." (*Complete Poetry and Prose*, 957). He goes on even more

specifically: "We see the shreds of Hebrews, Romans, Greeks; but where, on her own soil, do we see, in any faithful, highest, proud expression, America herself? I sometimes question whether she has a corner in her own house" (978).

These doubts are aired in spite of a poem like "Salut Au Monde" (1856), perhaps his most blissful enunciation of global identities. The persistent refrains, "I hear" and especially "I see," comprehensively confer recognition and autonomy upon all he names. Included among the voluminous catalogs are South American elements that do not appear in his later great poem of Columbian exposure and South American elision, "Passage to India." Whitman begins his tour of naming by imagining his own embodiment of global proportions; here identity easily accommodates difference, not to mention the much-needed corners in America's own house.

> Within me latitude widens, longitude lengthens,
> Asia, Africa, Europe, are to the east – America is provided for in
>   the west . . .
>
> *(Complete Poetry and Prose, 137)*

The performative voice is here inextricably bound to printed and charted demarcations – latitude and longitude expanding "within" him: Whitman is a print compendium of placeable identities, as well as their embodied chanter. This is perhaps the last expression of political optimism in his poetry, coming before the disappointments of the war and the recognition of the failings of America's imperial appropriations. It was the last time he could happily speak of swelling boundaries without invoking the tragic figure of Columbus, who likewise misread all his own charts.

Erasure of this sort would then seem a peculiarly postwar phenomenon. The difficulties he began to recognize in *Democratic Vistas* regarding the world's boundaries and vexing identities, particularly those of the inter-American variety, can be seen most clearly in his work of the late 1870s and early 1880s. In 1883, Whitman wrote a letter (asked for a poem, he insisted on prose because of the lateness of the request) commemorating the 333d anniversary of the Spanish founding of Santa Fe, New Mexico. This letter contains his most forthright critique of America's self-definition according to Anglo history and its boundaries. His national and literary crankiness might not surprise, since the 1870s were a time of depression for

Whitman. His ideal of American democracy and its exceptional imperialism were being devoured by the incorporating forces of capital; his health was failing.[10] But what strikes the reader of the 1883 letter is its tone of regret and relief, as though he were laying down the burdens of historical fictions he could no longer abide.

> We Americans have yet to really learn our own antecedents, and sort them, to unify them. They will be found ampler than has been supposed, and in widely different sources. Thus far, impress'd by New England writers and schoolmasters, we tacitly abandon ourselves to the notion that our United States have been fashion'd from the British Islands only, and essentially form a second England only – which is a very great mistake . . . The seething materialistic and business vortices of the United States, in their present devouring relations, controlling and belittling everything else, are, in my opinion, but a vast and indispensable stage in the new world's development, and are certainly to be follow'd by something entirely different – at least by immense modifications. (*Complete Poetry and Prose*, 1146–7)

By comparison with *Democratic Vistas* or any of the earlier prose, this letter is unambiguous about the diversity of American identity and history. In this regard, he implicitly admits to a struggle with the political and historical genealogies he inherited. That tension between "sorting" our antecedents and then "unifying" them is crucial to the question of difference that Whitman never succeeded in resolving as a practical political issue.

In this view of history, the democratic attributes of heterogeneity cannot be arrived at unless a reckoning is made with history – with the very personal implications of a perceived American national culture and its political historiography. Whitman patiently asserts, however, that "modifications" to a more inclusive, realistic national identity are severely restricted by the inability of a business-dominated society to understand this; the future will bear out the poverty of historical imagination inherent in capitalist America's withered mind. Indeed, the future will realize a more fulsome development of American civilization, of a "new world" that is "entirely different." He proposes a "composite American" – a multicultural identity rehabilitating Black Legend differences within the individual and the nation.

To that composite American identity of the future, Spanish character will supply some of the needed parts. No stock shows a grander historic retrospect . . . It is time to realize . . . that there will not be found any more cruelty, tyranny, superstition, &c., in the *resume* of past Spanish history than in the corresponding *resume* of Anglo-Norman history. Nay, I think there will not be found so much. (*Complete Poetry and Prose*, 1147)

In addition to being publicly critical, Whitman is self-conscious. This letter represents Whitman's frustrations with cultural and historical heterogeneity in his poetry; he recognizes that the "absorbing"[11] property of the English tongue, much praised by him, could also be predatory and destructive. He, like his imperial nation, was unable to bring Latin America and its pre-Columbian legacies into "American" history and literature without "devouring" or placing them outside the realm of the national/cultural "*resume*" (or memory). Or, as Ernest Renan wrote in 1882, several years after Whitman's letter: "Forgetting, I would even go so far as to say historical error, is a crucial factor in the creation of a nation" (quoted in *Nation and Narration*, 11).[12]

In the final two, somewhat resigned and plaintive, sentences from the above passage, Whitman rejects the Black Legend, a tradition that had undoubtedly informed his poetry and yet would not let him confront the lurking problems of empire and difference.[13] Even his most mournful Columbus poems ("Prayer of Columbus," "Passage to India") are really about heroic *authorship* (the tragically difficult life of writing), not about traditional Black Legend themes such as the redress of historical wrongs to Columbus, or the dispossession, murder, and enslavement of South American Indians.[14] He continues in the Santa Fe letter:

Then another point, relating to American ethnology, past and to come, I will here touch upon at a venture. As to our aboriginal or Indian population – the Aztec in the South, and many a tribe in the North and West – I know it seems to be agreed that they must gradually dwindle as time rolls on, and in a few generations more leave only a reminiscence, a blank. But I am not at all clear about that. As America, from its many far-back sources and current supplies, develops, adapts, entwines, faithfully identifies its own – are we to see it cheerfully accepting and using all the contributions of foreign lands from the whole outside globe – and then reflecting the only ones distinctively its own – the autochthonic ones? (*Complete Poetry and Prose,* 1147)

That concluding question, in its strange questioning of the extent of autochthonous "reflection," fails to make the full accounting he calls for. Thus it would seem that "blank" spots in historical geography were troubling to Whitman's dire quest for an exceptional and "faithfully identifiable" union. So plaguing was this heterogeneity that Whitman failed in his own idiom of fluent assertiveness – the inability, even in a confession, to put it in terms of rectifying certainty. What he had called in *Two Rivulets* (1876) "national identity power" was something to be both individually invented and collectively confronted; here that received collective power overwhelms him.

It is my contention therefore that the Santa Fe letter is crucial to grasping the uncertainties of American identity for Whitman, the nineteenth-century avatar of the printed – exportable and expansive – national identity. "Blank spaces" are objectively identifiable on a map, but so too are they a matter of subjective impairment, an unwillingness or inability to see that which is disruptive to his faithful ideal of American identity. They say as much as all that is declaimed in the name of his aggrandizing, disseminating, some might say monologic, identity.[15]

The primary poem I want to use to exemplify this national obscurity – the text I want to read the 1883 Santa Fe letter *back into* – is the 1876 author's edition of *Two Rivulets*.[16] *Two Rivulets* is a rewriting of, at once, Whitman's biography, U.S. history, and New World history; it consists of elaborate reconsiderations of *Leaves of Grass* (reissued in honor of the nation's centennial) and the textual annexation[17] of "Passage to India." My argument at the end of this book is finally about the role of historical oversight in nationalist narratives, and how American identity, the personal and collective national "power" theorized by Whitman, is affected by heterogeneity. The tension in nationalist thinking regarding heterogeneity is there in the authorial struggle with modernity's progressive binarisms, with the various dual pulls of national thinking that generate internal and external frontiers – between biographically streaking inward and collectively surging outward.

Two Rivulets *as History: The Forms of Water*

To understand how and why New World, pre-Columbian history was devoured by Whitman's poetry, we must listen closely to the nuances of his imagined explorations and connections, activities that must be viewed as products of movements and discoveries within history. In the Preface to *Two Rivulets,* Whitman sets out the schematic trope of the title, inviting a dual, Andersonian reading of the necessary connection between individual and nation: "I have not hesitated to embody in, and run through the Volume, two altogether distinct veins, or strata – Politics for one, and for the other, the pensive thought of immortality" (*Two Rivulets,* 6). Metaphorically calling the author's edition "two rivulets," evoking the fluid and life-giving land of the present, only to modify it soon after with the frozen archaeological language of "veins" and "strata," Whitman immediately conveys a characteristic ambivalence about history and the role of printed texts within that imagined realm.[18] That his own work is dual – alive *and* excavatable, agilely oracular *and* reducible to specimen days – indicates this ambivalence with regard to the disclosing nature of the written text in history. As with his obscure political geography, Whitman's view of the role of textuality in history is never definitive. Both the global geography and the national identity he chooses to excavate are the products of, and are dependent upon, this ambivalence. The map, as it is figured over time, is the conduit and the substance of his poetry.

It is, moreover, poetic language, figurative and performative yet unchanging in its print stasis, that allows Whitman to slip ambivalently through bound imaginaries of history and geography. "Passage to India" is an account of historical *and* written movements in the present; its title economically distributes this duality. "Passage" is both past (that which has completely occurred and been passed *over* in time) and continuous movement[19] to the moment of encounter; "India" is both a place addressed (written to) and a place discovered. *Two Rivulets* linguistically binds two modes and two worlds, just as it exemplifies the identity that conjoins the personal and the collective in the coursing waters of past, present, and future.

As I have noted, the Preface to *Two Rivulets* is essential to understanding "Passage to India." Whitman mulls over the revisionary poem/prose dialectical nature of *Two Rivulets*: "Thus, too, the prose and poetic, the dual forms of the present book" (*Two Rivulets*, 6). Whitman brought out the volume to celebrate the "Centennial of our New World Nationality"(5), to mark the occasion of national revision, in addition to his own; autobiography is constantly made to stand for history on grander scales, from the national to the global.[20]

Whitman begins the obsessive linkages (poetry with prose, individual with nation, water with earth, etc.) at the first suggestion of death. The prospect of personal extinction – of a perfectly stable, unitary identity – compels him to propose the self's endurance over time.[21] The prototype for such endurance is Columbus.[22] When Whitman inscribes a Columbian trope in an extended footnote appended to the phrase "my special chants of Death and Immortality" (*Two Rivulets*, 7), he is writing under the shadow of death, his mother's as well as his own (this was written after his first stroke). Columbus is the mask behind which he plays his own death-defying legend; legend-making, it would seem, is but a premodern form of "self-preservation."

Columbus is an exceptional historical type, and especially apt, since he is figured in American literature as a living, still-disturbed consciousness – the primordial ghost in the American house.[23] The extended allegory of the Preface plays off the conceit of heroic, spoken eloquence, but the object that it attempts to express is the life of writing and the failure to succeed publicly with one's written ventures:

> PASSAGE TO INDIA – As in some ancient legend-play, to close the plot and the hero's career, there is a farewell gathering on ship's deck and on shore, a loosing of hawsers and ties, a spreading of sails to the wind – a starting out on unknown seas, to fetch up no one knows whither – to return no more – And the curtain falls, and there is the end of it – So I have reserv'd that Poem, with its cluster, to finish and explain much that, without them, would not be explain'd, and to take leave, and escape for good, from all that has preceded them. (Then probably *Passage to India*, and its cluster, are but freer vent and fuller expression to what, from the first, and so on throughout, more or less lurks in my writings, underneath every page, every line, everywhere.) (*Two Rivulets*, 5)

Whitman addresses here what is evasive and pervasive in his work, the way the world and the poet mask and deflect one another in the interactions of writing, reading, and being read. Columbus serves to mark the subterfuge in Whitman's own written corpus, initiating in legendary character the enduring conflation of cosmic mapping with personal biography in the New World. This visual and performative apparatus – which focuses on certain objects, and necessarily excludes others from the field of vision – is elaborated on in the footnote's mortal, "personalist" vein:

> I am not sure but the last enclosing sublimation of Race or Poem is, What it thinks of Death . . . After the rest has been comprehended and said, even the grandest – After those contributions to mightiest Nationality, or to sweetest Song, or to the best Personalism, male or female, have been glean'd from the rich and varied themes of tangible life, and have been fully accepted and sung, and the pervading fact of visible existence, with the duty it devolves, is rounded and apparently completed, it still remains to be really completed by suffusing through the whole and several, that other pervading invisible fact, so large a part, (is it not the largest part?) of life here, combining the rest, and furnishing, for Person or State, the only permanent and unitary meaning to all, even the meanest life, consistently with the dignity of the Universe, in Time . . . The physical and the sensuous, in themselves or in their immediate continuations, retain holds upon me which I think are never entirely releas'd; and those holds I have not only not denied, but hardly wish'd to weaken. (*Two Rivulets*, 5–6)

Whitman seems to be struggling to sublimate the difficult concepts at stake: "Nationality," "Poetry," "Personalism," "Race," the "State," "the physical and the sensuous." His luffing style betrays the faith he places in the sublimating movement of "Passage to India" – that the poetry will resolve the issues brought up so windily in the prose. Accordingly, he claims to have placed "Passage to India" at the end as a noble statue, a metaphor for identity publicly, materially, and centrally realized, to give "reference to . . . our identity, this grade of it, and outlet – preparation to another grade" (*Two Rivulets*, 7).

Meanwhile, in the prose text of the Preface, he sets out the contours of historiography even further, attempting to delineate the ways in which the Union – the idea of political and bodily "oneness" – is necessary because it provides the screen upon which the Whitmanian American projects himself: ". . . that the vital political mission of The United States is, to practically solve and settle the problem of two sets of rights – the fusion, thorough compatibility and junction of individual State prerogatives, with the indispensable necessity of centrality and Oneness – the National Identity power" (*Two Rivulets*, 8). This is a oneness that will strain the bounds of temporality and materiality, as exemplified by the interaction between author and reader: "Then I meant LEAVES OF GRASS, as published to be the Poem of Identity, (of *Yours*, whoever you are, now reading these lines)" (10). The work of national identity is the vital mission of Whitman himself, as representative poet. The state and the individual must be able to tell their stories in unison, for the power of self-proclaiming identity is the essential power of the nation. The problem, for the purposes of my inquiry, lies precisely in the words "oneness" and "centrality," terms that tend to exclude difference.

But "the power," for now, is set forth as the answer to a problem posed by "two sets of rights." "Passage to India" can thus be viewed as the settlement of the problem by the exercising of "national identity" power in poetry – a textual response[24] to unsettling binaries. It attempts this resolution in its subjective mapping of geohistory. Whitman wants to chart the contours of geography and global consciousness; at the same time he shapes history and its geography so as to propel the national identity power into the future and a higher (national) "grade," beyond the corporeal limitations of an individual life.

So "Passage to India" concerns itself with objective identifying as well as subjective identity. And surely, in its overt thematics, the poem is vigorously performative as against its printed actuality. Yet, as Whitman himself suggests, another problem lies in the necessary split between objectivity and subjectivity that such an elaborate identifying sojourn – performative and printed – demands. That problem is part of, to use Whitman's word, an "obscurity"; blurred objectivity is at the core of "Passage to India" 's subjective poetics. Much remains obscured and indefinite because that is the consequence, indeed the precondition, of any subjective vision. In addition, I would suggest that the smudged, illegible territories are the products of Whitman's print-oriented metaphysics of contact, eclipse, and release. That metaphysics might also be seen as frontier thinking, which fuses and obscures in its rage to focus and then identify.[25]

> In certain parts, in these flights, or attempting to depict or suggest them, I have not been afraid of the charge of obscurity, either of my Two Volumes – because human thought, poetry or melody, must leave dim escapes and outlets – must possess a certain fluid, aerial character, akin to space itself, obscure to those of little or no imagination, but indispensable to the highest purposes. Poetic style, when address'd to the Soul, is less definite form, outline, sculpture, and becomes vista, music, half-tints, and even less than half-tints. True, it may be architecture; but again it may be the forest wild-wood, or the best effects thereof, at twilight, the waving oaks and cedars in the wind, and the impalpable odors. (*Two Rivulets*, 13)

This sounds rather judicious and it relieves him of the charge of being deliberately "difficult" in his poetic style; the terrain is "difficult," so his account is necessarily arcane. But let us not forget that while Whitman attributes this ineffability to the soul alone, he has already told us that the soul's vitality is coextensive with the life of the nation. Indeed, his Preface has demanded such a fusion. And it is Whitman who says that his obscurities – his inability to be clear about his national identity and its historical sources – have a "purpose" whose role is manifest to those with imagination commensurate with his own "vistas." The soul everywhere stands in for the nation, and vice versa; objective ground is subjective ground. The language he uses to describe this mediation metaphorically through blurring and then diffusion is akin to the nineteenth-century medium of the ether:[26] "human thought, poetry or melody, must leave dim escapes and outlets – must possess a *certain fluid, aerial character, akin to space itself*" (*Two Rivulets*, 13).

His inability to sing the past objectively and definitively (in its full, panoramic vista) is, again, curious, given the ample precedent for locating ancient wonders on the very shores of America, the curiously ethereal New World continents Whitman (and Columbus) was so needful to referentially pass beyond. The following reflects his impatience with being caught in history, of having to account for the realm of death when a passage awaits upon the "deeper waters" of the future. In the spirit of Columbian optimism, our rivulets can soon be oceans:

> Finally, as I have lived in fresh lands, inchoate, and in a revolutionary age, future-founding, I have felt to identify the points of that age, these lands, in my recitatives, altogether, in my own way. Thus my form has strictly grown from my purports and facts, and is the analogy of them . . . Within my time the United States have emerg'd from nebulous vagueness and suspense, to full orbic, (though varied) decision – have done the deeds and achiev'd the triumphs of half a score of centuries – and are henceforth to enter upon their real history – the way being now, (i.e. since the result of the Secession War,) clear'd of death-threatening impedimenta, and the free areas around and ahead of us assured and certain, where were not so before – (the past century being but preparations, trial-voyages and experiments of the Ship, before her starting out upon deep water.) (*Two Rivulets*, 13–14)

Whitman is Columbus encountering lands he both objectively claims and subjectively reinvents for his own purposes. These "fresh" territories germinate a history that is teleological and nationalist, embodied in the apt term "future-founding." We also see that Whitman's own form has "grown from . . . purports and facts, and is the analogy of them," thus explaining the poetics of conflating subjective and objective accounts of national selfhood and national boundaries; he is at once organized by the facts of Columbus's New World and analogous to them, maintaining a contiguous association with the material world that gives rise to a language-bound historical understanding of "identity." Such a relationship, curiously, is not bound by the fixities of print; as an American identity, he is free to establish himself anywhere and call it what he will. What nationality was Columbus, after all? He was for all intents and purposes "American," since he shares this poetics of self-understanding.

After the Preface, Whitman goes on in "Passage to India" to figure himself as a harbinger of modern communication – a telegraphic embodiment of communicative action. Such technologies of contact and self-enunciation contribute to the transformation of the past into passage (in the sense of the written *and* transporting passage) – figuring history as a narrative launch to the complete global identity fully enunciated in the lyric.

From the poem's first lines, the New World is the site of "our modern wonders," including the railroad and telegraph. Whitman vaults from singular experience to the collective in history, from "my days" to "our modernity":

> Singing my days,
> Singing the great achievements of the present,
> Singing the strong light works of engineers,
> Our modern wonders, (the antique ponderous Seven outvied,)
> In the Old World the east the Suez canal,
> The New by its mighty railroad spann'd,
> The seas inlaid with eloquent gentle wires;
> Yet first to sound, and ever sound, the cry with thee O soul,
> The Past! the Past! the Past!
>
> (Leaves of Grass, 411)

The seas that bathe the modern wonder of the telegraph are "inlaid" with the sound of the future *and* the past. The haunting iamb "The Past!" intrudes upon the communion-like passage between continental souls.

> The Past – the dark unfathom'd retrospect!
> The teeming gulf – the sleepers and the shadows!
> The past – the infinite greatness of the past!
> For what is the present after all but a growth out of the
>   past?
> (As a projectile form'd, impell'd, passing a certain line, still
>   keeps on,
> So the present, utterly form'd, impell'd by the past.)
>
> (Leaves of Grass, 411–2)

The future, Whitman admits, is bound up in the book of the past: But it is an empty book. Appropriately enough, the metaphor that subtends this passage is occupied with the narrative abyss presented by historical thinking. He senses a "dark unfathom'd retrospect," a "gulf," an infinite and therefore incomprehensible entity. The "projectile" is offered to clarify the concept of movement through time: a missile is issued with deadly substance (yet invisible to the naked eye), producing a vacuum in its wake due to the speed with which it travels. Correspondingly blank, inexplicable cavities seem to surround Whitman's best attempts to reckon with the past and the heavy specter of death.

Whitman is well into his conversion of the idea of past into "passage," a lyric transformation that affirms the substance of the present's speedy emergence into future. If, for instance, Columbus is the missile that stood on some threshold of history, then the "certain line" cannot and will not stop the inertia of the imperial quest. The past, moreover, is merely another facet of the present, while the movement of the present – passage taken as verb – is the living textual emblem of the past, the proof that it happened at all. To understand that the New World *is* American – in other words, Whitman's tropic territory to map as he wishes – is to accept this etherealized notion, this provisional universality, of the past. New World history, indeed the New World's presence on the global map, is thus exceptional in the science of historical knowledge. Ironically, Whitman reproduces the "devouring" dynamics of the "business vortices" he decries in the Santa Fe letter, but in the name of the nation rather than the corporation. History here on the American continents is not only a necessary blank, but a linguistic and conceptual firmament from which the questing mind may propel itself farther into a territorial world and further into a nationalized, centralized identity.

As I've already mentioned, Whitman's metaphorical maps in "Passage to India" arose out of a lifetime of considering, and then vaporizing, the actual historical and political geographies of the New World. Whitman's memoranda pertaining to the geography and history of forgotten civilizations, those pasts that have "pass[ed] certain lines," are explicitly anti-historical, in a way that is regretful but conclusive. For instance, in memoranda preparatory to *Leaves of Grass* Whitman writes:

> The most immense part of ancient history is altogether unknown. There were busy, populous and powerful nations on all the continents of the earth at intervals through the stretch of time from ten thousand years ago down to twenty-six hundred years ago. Signs and materials of them remain.
> Previous to ten thousand years ago, there were surely empires, cities, states and pastoral tribes and uncivilized hordes upon the earth
> their literature, government, religions, social customs, and general civilization, precise mention – silence; – for no one can now

tell even the names of those nations. They had, in their own way, something corresponding to all the essentials of a modern political power . . .

Sublime characters lived and died and we do not know when or where, full as sublime as any that we now celebrate over the world. Beautiful poems, essays of philosophy, witty replies, excellent histories, works of art and ornament. [Of] their literature, government, religions, social customs and general civilization – silence . . .

Do you suppose that history is complete when the best writers get all they can of the few communities that are known and arrange them clearly in books? . . . No dates, no statistics not a mark nor a figure that is demonstrably so. (*Notebooks and Unpublished Prose Manuscripts*, 5:1924b)[27]

Whitman proceeds to locate the unknown in specific places, allowing himself to name those "blank places," fill up the "vacuity of our letters about them," and thus undo the historical exile of civilizations for which there is "not a mark nor a figure that is demonstrably so" (an important repetition of the phrasing).

Upon America stood many of these vast nations . . . Time, the passage of many thousands of years, the total vacuity of our letters about them, their places blank upon the map, not a mark nor a figure that is demonstrably so. With all this they lived as surely as we do now. They lived upon America and upon Asia, Africa and Europe. In the trance of the healthy brain of man these unknown peoples show afar off dim and filmy in their outlines. Some grand and elaborated, women with graceful faces learned and calm, some naked and savage, some like huge collections of meaningless insects, some engaged in the chase living for generations in the woods and unfenced fields. (*Notebooks*, 5:1926)

This imagination of a "possible savage" is startlingly trite and demeaning: some "women with graceful faces learned and calm," "some like huge collections of meaningless insects." As if to recognize the failure of such speculation, he rules out a true history of the everyday life of common people everywhere. In spite of his regret that there is a vacuum in our letters regarding both forgotten civilizations and the common people of well-documented nations, he declares that history necessarily eludes the narrating appetite.

Nobody can possess a fair idea of the earth without letting his or her mind walk perfectly easy and loose over the past. A few definite points mark deeds and national eras, lists of titles and battles and the like make up very little of the movement of humanity and events at any time. *The best and most important part of history cannot be told. It eludes being examined or printed. It is above even dates and reliable information. It is surer and more reliable, because by far the greatest part of the old statistics of history are only approaches to the truth and are often discrepant and suspicious.* (*Notebooks*, 5:1926, my emphasis)[28]

Whitman's attitude regarding the narratability of the historical past, indeed the science of history, is admirably skeptical, and it springs from a sense that a truly democratic history would be overwhelming and impossible – *Leaves of Grass by everyone*. And yet his pointing to the "blank spots" on the map denies certain nations the ability to assert *their* "national identity power" against the devouring effects of modernity. Indeed, we can sense here the sources of imperial ahistoricism for a man committed to U.S. political hegemony, albeit taking the form of the more generous and salutary – that is, democratic – products of "national identity power." Like Prescott, Whitman is wedded to the notion that history *is* ruins – that we encounter a realm in which origins are traceable and probably glorious – but the enduring artifacts can provide no more than indications of decline. Historical poetry is, thus, the occasion for plaintive nostalgia. The "ruins of North America" are just such an example:

> The Ruins in North America – the copper mines of Lake Superior which have evidently been worked many centuries since – probably more than a thousand years ago, perhaps two or three thousand – the mounds in the valley of the Mississippi – the vast ruins of Central America, Mexico and South America – grand temple walls &c., now overgrown with old trees – all prove beyond cavil the existence, ages since, in the Western World, of powerful, populous and probably civilized nations, whose names, histories and even traditions had been lost long before the discovery of Columbus and Vespucius. (*Notebooks*, 5: 1932)

If one listens carefully, there is an argument in the preceding passages about print culture that may be related to *Two Rivulets* and "Passage to India." The elegiac tone of the prose suggests that, in the absence of a print tradition to authorize a true classical past in the Greek or Roman mode, history writing is practiced in vain and facts in the past can only be posited as articles of faith. Whitman is willing to concede the possibility of civilizations that are objective parts of history, but he is unwilling to name them; it is a naming that would have been easy given the historical sources available to him. Dr. Bucke, who comments on Whitman's memoranda in *Notes and Fragments*, directs us to Whitman's remarkable speculations (in italics) on history writing:

> In the big scrap-book upon which I am now working is pasted some leaves of "Graham's Magazine" (no date – must belong to the fifties) containing an article "Imagination and Fact." The writer says, "We should like to see a history of the campaigns in Greece of Darius, Xerxes, and Mardonius written by Persians." Upon which WW has this note:
> *Yes, an ancient history not written by a Greek or Roman – what a face that would put upon old times.*
> Again the writer says: "The mountains, rivers, forests and the elements that gird them round about would be only blank conditions of matter if the mind did not fling its own divinity around them." WW makes this marginal note:
> *This I think is one of the most indicative sentences I ever read.* (Bucke, *Notes and Fragments*, 77)

Here Whitman toys with the useful possibilities of writing history from unexpected, perhaps subaltern, perspectives (as he would later make emphatic in the Santa Fe letter). And yet, immediately we learn that the material condition of the surrounding world, "mountains, rivers, forests and the elements that gird them round," is entirely dependent upon the centrally placed writer to give them substance. The blank reality of their existence, the mute condition of ancient sources as well as natural phenomena, seems to haunt his desire to write such histories into the world and bring new maps into relief; a vacuum propels the national projectile (United States/Whitman) writing itself into an increasingly voluminous and documented print future. In the case of ancient American sources, there is an ellipsis in history, the lack of a certifiably Aztec or Incan print culture. (Whitman remarks on the writerly power to re-create the past with the phrase "indicative sentence," suggesting just how much faith he places in the authorizing power of printed history. His marginal note commends the referent of the words, its "indication," but also attests to the act of its enunciating reality, its sheer irrefutability as a printed, unredacted "sentence.")

Though a science of history is impossible for Whitman, an increasingly objective purchase on the subject can be gained from the disseminating work of poetry. For instance, a technophile's optimism pervades "Passage to India," exalting the unknown as the necessary propulsion for modern science and, necessarily, the identity of the lyric artificer. The second section names both an old (unscientifically Columbian) and new (nonmythically logical) destination for a New World identity – India. India, as it was for Columbus, is a destination without verifying content; the world before us – India despite the evidence – merely confirms the world desired and sought after.

> Passage O soul to India!
> Eclaircise the myths Asiatic, the primitive fables.
>
> Not you alone proud truths of the world,
> Nor you alone ye facts of modern science,
> But myths and fables of eld, Asia's, Africa's fables,
> —The far-darting beams of the spirit, the unloos'd dreams,
> The deep diving bibles and legends,
> The daring plots of the poets, the elder religions;
> O you temples fairer than lilies pour'd over by the rising sun!
> O you fables spurning the known, eluding the hold of the
>   known, mounting to heaven!
>
> (*Leaves of Grass*, 412)

Whitman's pessimism about, or perhaps devaluation of, the "known" – as against the justly inflated legends of old – is notable. But more interesting is that the process of forgetting is part of a questing, spanning movement – "passage to India." Here fusion, the material conjoiner of global elements, the essential dynamic as well of national identity power in conjoining self and nation, is transcendently glorious. The blanks and legends that cannot *be* History are useful because they are the form and substance of "daring plots"; they make the goal of crossing so much easier and then, happily, they are gone to "heaven."

> Passage to India!
> Lo, soul, seest thou not God's purpose from the first?

The earth to be spann'd, connected by network,
The races, neighbors, to marry and be given in marriage,
The oceans to be cross'd, *the distant brought near,*
The lands to be welded together.

(*Leaves of Grass*, 412, my emphasis)

He continues the geographical survey of modernity's achievements. Section 3 starts by praising the Suez canal, great symbol of Europe's Oriental nexus; it is a mystification that involves romantically submerging the "proud truths" of the politics of "connection." Accordingly, he concludes the section with a parenthetical encomium to Columbus and his martyred memory: "(Ah Genoese thy dream! thy dream! / Centuries after thou art laid in thy grave, / The shore thou foundest verifies thy dream.)" (414).

The enactment of Columbus's dream is carried out in the revisionary map and its verifying poem. History's conflicting voices are quieted, as we have seen with so many other writers in the Black Legend tradition, by Columbus's authoritative anxiety. The "ceaseless thought" of "lands found" and "nations born" runs self-regarding rivulets through history until it is confirmed by the singular "rondure" of Whitman's "accomplished world":

Along all history, down the slopes,
As a rivulet running, sinking now, and now again to the
    surface rising,
A ceaseless thought, a varied train – lo, soul, to thee, thy
    sight, they rise,
The plans, the voyages again, the expeditions;
Again Vasco de Gama sails forth,
Again the knowledge gain'd, the mariner's compass,
Lands found and nations born, thou born America,
For purpose vast, man's long probation fill'd,
Thou rondure of the world at last accomplish'd.

(*Leaves of Grass*, 414)

The shape of the globe is at stake in the memorialization of history. History and geography are connected by the material, embodied "indication" of history, wherein the past is a "varied train," incorporated and incarnated by the poet thinking. He thus scripts movement in real time across the modern geography of nationalist hopes. Section 5 takes this up in more detail, and with some doubt, by asking for global answers to the remaining worry of exploratory desire. Can his plaint against the necessity of loss be soothed by the New World's fullness?

> O vast Rondure, swimming in space,
> Cover'd all over with visible power and beauty,
> Alternate light and day and the teeming spiritual darkness,
> Unspeakable high processions of sun and moon and countless
>   stars above,
> Below, the manifold grass and waters, animals, mountains,
>   trees,
> With inscrutable purpose, some hidden prophetic intention,
> Now first it seems my thought begins to span thee.
> Down from the gardens of Asia descending radiating,
> Adam and Eve appear, then their myriad progeny after them,
> Wandering, yearning, curious, with restless explorations,
> With questions, baffled, formless, feverish, with never-happy
>   hearts,
> With that sad incessant refrain, *Wherefore unsatisfied soul?* and
>   *Whither O mocking life?*

> Ah who shall soothe these feverish children?
> Who justify these restless explorations?
> Who speak the secret of impassive earth?
> Who bind it to us? what is this separate Nature so unnatural?
> What is this earth to our affections? (unloving earth, without a
>   throb to answer ours,
> Cold earth, the place of graves.)
>
>   (*Leaves of Grass*, 414–5)

As I've said, Whitman's New World seems to raise its own questions about its discovery, questions addressed to the finding self. If we find the world now "complete," we should hasten to remember that the world and all its historical meanings are complicit in mortality. As an earthly effect of passage, history is also one of death's methods – "unloving earth, without a throb to answer ours, / Cold earth, the place of graves." This, too, is the case for the Whitmanian text that annuls by omission "secret" and "impassive" histories, and thereby consigns whole regions of the globe to the undifferentiated oblivion of the "national forgotten."

But what the poet takes away, he and his printed text can also

restore. It is the poet who can reconcile crucial aspects of history –
death and difference; so too, the poet extends from the solid matter
of the finite (recall the "rivulet" as frozen "stratum") to the conceptually "looser" imaginary of national identity. After history's
progress has given us a world, then we may begin reconquest of
"the whole . . . impassive, voiceless earth" by poetic action that will
"completely justif[y]" such progress.

> After the seas are all cross'd, (as they seem already cross'd,)
> After the great captains and engineers have accomplish'd their
>   work,
> After the noble inventors, after the scientists, the chemist, the
>   geologist, ethnologist,
> Finally shall come the poet worthy that name,
> The true son of God shall come singing his songs.
>
> Then not your deeds only O voyagers, O scientists and
>   inventors, shall be justified,
> All these hearts as of fretted children shall be sooth'd,
> All affection shall be fully responded to, the secret shall be
>   told,
> All these separations and gaps shall be taken up and hook'd
>   and link'd together,   [line 109]
> The whole earth, this cold, impassive, voiceless earth, shall be
>   completely justified,
> Trinitas divine shall be gloriously accomplish'd and compacted
>   by the true son of God, the poet,
> (He shall indeed pass the straits and conquer the mountains,
> He shall double the cape of Good Hope to some purpose,)
> Nature and Man shall be disjoin'd and diffused no more,
> The true son of God shall absolutely fuse them.
>   (*Leaves of Grass*, 415–6)

A closer look at line 109 is crucial to my argument. In a universe
of separations, Whitman is talking about the suturing of matter and
idea. That suturing is also the final result of his conditional logic of
historical accomplishment which sends him rapturously into a grandiose justification of the whole, voiceless earth. We should not forget
that the New World's discovery too is being redeemed yet again,
and in some sense that the South American gap is seemingly accounted for. I say "seemingly" because it is not accounted for so

much as it is "fused," excised from the map. The disjoined man of Columbian sorrow (sorrow for the demise of a world once Incan and Aztec) should suffer no more in the wake of this fusion. Whitman's geohistorical amnesia, a symptom of which is Columbian sorrow, is alleviated in the logic of the nationalist imaginary that can "absolutely fuse" history into lyrics celebrating false differences.

> Year at whose wide-flung door I sing!
> Year of the purpose accomplish'd!
> Year of the marriage of continents, climates and oceans!
> . . . .
> I see O year in you the vast terraqueous globe given and
>   giving all,
> Europe to Asia, Africa join'd, and they to the New World,
> The lands, geographies, dancing before you, holding a festival
>   garland,
> As brides and bridegrooms hand in hand.
>   (*Leaves of Grass*, 416)

In keeping with the metaphor of celebration, section 6 addresses the year 1492 as the one that brought the "wedding party" into the human narrative. Section 6 asks us to have "the retrospect brought forward," to wrench antiquated stories of conquest and exploration – painstaking in its "Arabian, Chinese, Indian, Persian" specificity, yet vague in its reference to "Central and Southern empires" – into the vatic poetic present; the passage forward promises "Doubts to be solv'd, the map incognita, blanks to be fill'd / The foot of man unstay'd, the hands never at rest, / Thyself O soul that will not brook a challenge" (417). With reference to the filling in of "blank spots" on the "map incognita," Whitman attempts to realize poetically what he had written years earlier with considerably more pessimism, in his notes. Thus section 6 finally offers the possibility of global wholeness augured by the discovery of the New World.

> The mediaeval navigators rise before me,
> The world of 1492, with its awaken'd enterprise,
> Something swelling in humanity now like the sap of the earth
>   in spring,
> The sunset splendor of chivalry declining.

And who art thou sad shade?
Gigantic, visionary, thyself a visionary,
With majestic limbs and pious beaming eyes,
Spreading around with every look of thine a golden world,
Enhuing it with gorgeous hues.

As the chief histrion,
Down to the footlights walks in some great scena,
Dominating the rest I see the Admiral himself,
(History's type of courage, action, faith,)
Behold him sail from Palos leading his little fleet,
His voyage behold, his return, his great fame,
His misfortunes, calumniators, behold him a prisoner, chain'd,
Behold his dejection, poverty, death.

(Curious in time I stand, noting the efforts of heroes,
Is the deferment long? bitter the slander, poverty, death?
Lies the seed unreck'd for centuries in the ground? lo, to God's
    due occasion,
Uprising in the night, it sprouts, blooms,
And fills the earth with use and beauty.)
                                        (*Leaves of Grass*, 417–18)

Whitman's dramatic staging of Columbian anxiety and waylaid potential ("Lies the seed unreck'd for centuries in the ground?") is meant to evoke a sense of pity for the lone author whose job it is to assert new geographies and inhabit a legendary identity. Such "unreck'd seeds" are interred beneath the ground, pathetically impotent to give life, yet inhabiting space and providing firmness. Now figured out and summoned forth, Columbus has appeared center-stage, disinterred at last by the embodiment of New World identity in a poem – his seed blooming into poetic uses that eclipse the tragedy given form by his discovery; he performs on the page-proscenium of history's textual theater. Columbus launched the role of modern identity – this is the most useful discovery here, not the hybrid interconnected globe that is now backstage, dimly lit, mere scenery. Whitman himself is present somewhere in this tableau, perhaps a belated director, as he stands "curious in time, noting the efforts of heroes."

The dramatic moment now recalled, the roles now in view, Whitman can begin *re*direction. The next – and shortest – section beseeches the soul's return to origins. Whitman seeks not just history's origin(s) but the self-reflecting, chart-obsessed Cartesian mind's early paradise; this is an "innocently" "intuitive" moment, before the mind became concerned with plotting the original interface between space and time.

> Passage indeed O soul to primal thought,
> Not lands and seas alone, thy own clear freshness,
> The young maturity of brood and bloom,
> to realms of budding bibles.
>
> O soul, repressless, I with thee and thou with me,
> Thy circumnavigation of the world begin,
> Of man, the voyage of his mind's return,
> To reason's early paradise,
> Back, back to wisdom's birth, to innocent intuitions,
> Again with fair creation.
>
> (*Leaves of Grass,* 418)

Spatial movements are only outward materializations of the more inwardly contained inscription of self-centered identities. The imperial world as site of cross-currents and exchanges has been reduced to a backdrop for the more "innocent" explorations of the soul's interior.

This seemingly innocent sojourn is continued in section 8, which chronicles the passage of the poetic soul enthralled by transcendence, circumscribing and spanning the globe, detached finally from the historical fixities of 1492. Passage is made as a beam of light, through the unresisting medium of the ethereal "transcendent" – "Thou" – at once "fibrous" and "breathing" and invisibly pervasive:

> O Thou transcendent,
> Nameless, the fibre and the breath,
> Light of the light, shedding forth universes, thou centre
>   of them,
> Thou mightier centre of the true, the good, the loving,
> Thou moral, spiritual fountain – affection's source – thou
>   reservoir,
>
> (*Leaves of Grass,* 419)

The center that lies in the pervasive neutrality of a transcendent, global self – a vacuuming identity – sees love at the source of all material, objective things. Love is manifest in prodigal family recognition, Columbian difference and desire for the Other contained in the loving rendezvous of two lost brothers; they "melt" in mutual affection.

> Reckoning ahead O soul, when thou,the time achiev'd,
> The seas all cross'd, weather'd the capes, the voyage done,
> Surrounded, copest, frontest God, yieldest, the aim attain'd,
> As fill'd with friendship, love complete, the Elder Brother found,
> The Younger melts in fondness in his arms.
>
> (*Leaves of Grass*, 419–20)

Whitman's familiarizing of discovery, his centralizing of the web of global human relations, is emblematized by his brothering of humanity; the imagery of succumbing, of melting into such bonds, long forgotten but by no means strange, is a diffusion of the self into the very origin of 1492's imaginary fused New World.[29]

The final section completes the flight from history into emotional essences, the orgasmic escape from boundedness in time and matter, the rage to connect and fuse. Whitman imagines a "passage to *more* than India," a release from the grammar of discovery and progress.

> Passage to you, your shores, ye aged fierce enigmas!
> Passage to you, to mastership of you, ye strangling problems!
> You, strew'd with the wrecks of skeletons, that, living, never
>   reach'd you.
>
> (*Leaves of Grass*, 420)

"You" is the centrifugal soul; all events and objects external to it – explorations of the world that is, as it were, the "not-you" – are enveloped and then dissolved. Metaphorically circumscribing all expansiveness into a trope of self-mastery, Whitman deftly allows, indeed commands, those fatal dispersals to return to his poem. History's explorations are elaborately folded into a solipsistic transcendental journey. Whitman breaks into a chant of puzzling identity, attempting to locate ("shores," the pun "mastership"), name ("you," "your," "ye"), and thereby surpass the "fierce enigmas," "wrecks of skeletons," and "strangling problems" that impede the progress of history and national expansions.

The subsequent lines seem to complete the logic of solipsism and centrifugal troping, devouring the very body and pages that constitute Whitman the corporeal author. History and the body are barriers to "immediate passage."

> Passage, immediate passage! the blood burns in my veins!
> Away O soul! hoist instantly the anchor!
> Cut the hawsers – haul out – shake out every sail!
> Have we not stood here like trees in the ground long enough?
> Have we not grovel'd here long enough, eating and drinking like
>   mere brutes?
> Have we not darken'd and dazed ourselves with books long
>   enough?
>
> (*Leaves of Grass*, 420–1)

The language of these lines is striking in its Godlike commandment, its Mosaic national inquiries, its impatience taking the form of self-disdain. It indicts the work of narrative identity implicit in *Leaves of Grass*, desiring instead the power of an immediate identity that is no longer tied to the territory of the body. And yet, for all of Whitman's desire to reach beyond himself, he seems to come up short. It seems that, like Columbus before him, he has somehow done a representational disservice to the corporeal power of his discovering identity.

The phrase "immediate passage" jumps out because of its absolute refusal of the mediated experience of the mapped world and its material accounts of history. Historical mediation – bookish reliance on the past – is troped as barbaric, "brutish," fortifying cultural stasis and rootedness (Columbus too had to abjure false and limiting charts and legends). True cultural diversity is, Whitman seems to admit, a product of immediacy; it cannot be made "real" in print. Stuck in the culture of print, we are like the discovered "savages," darkened and about to be colonized by our own search for origins. He calls for a new technology of mediation that takes us beyond the binaries of self/other and civilization/barbarism. It would seem Whitman has written himself beyond his faith in print culture and American identity as dual means of incorporating the known world.

Or has he? The logic of print's triumphant power is subtle and quiet, but manifest. I contend that Whitman's poetic imagination – because it relies so strongly on print culture for the articulation of national identity, in spite of all his misgivings and Columbian disappointments – is deliberately figured as metaphysically exceptional, an exile from the binaries that created his national self. He makes a final attempt to do what Columbus could not – abandon the dualistic encounters and awful historicity that condemn the expanding self to uncharted wandering and vagueness. Put another way, he seeks a poetic language in "Passage to India" that is purely national and rigorously anti-historical. And it is here especially that my critical language reaches for concepts like "ether" and words like "surpass" to describe the aesthetic implications of Whitman's dialectical movements. Witness my own necessary vagueness: Whitman's poetry, like American identity, is synthesized out of something more than material facts (land or paper) or pure ideas (the imagination or national boundaries); it is something publicly private, more than objective or subjective – one might say it is something "identifiable" in public space but subject to multiple "passages" that both occlude and consolidate the sovereign territory of the personal and the social. It employs the language of inchoate technologies of representation struggling for self-evidence in an exceptional public space. Distance is the final wish, to move away from the center, to cover ground with water.

> Sail forth – steer for the deep waters only,
> Reckless O soul, exploring, I with thee, and thou with me,
> For we are bound where mariner has not yet dared to go,
> And we will risk the ship, ourselves and all.

> O my brave soul!
> O farther farther sail!
> O daring joy, but safe! are they not all the seas of God?
> O farther, farther, farther sail!
>
> (*Leaves of Grass*, 421)[30]

At the end of this poem, we are not only in an ecstatic geography outside the confines of known maps. We are also in an equally uncharted place: the fused seams of the national imaginary's geohistory, where forgotten histories require the ambiguous residue of print's erasures. What in Melville were critically historicized silences have been transformed by Whitman into moments of positive recoil from the imperial dilemma. When Whitman concluded, in "To a Historian," "I project the history of the future," he slyly announced just such a recoil from paradox that underwrote his lifelong experiment with print and self-transcendence. The final lines illustrate this mode by working against their surface logic and thus refining a didactic national creed. The act of speaking these printed words *figures for the reader* a step outside of a historical mode of conventional, limiting passage through time and space that might cloud the horizon of ceaseless expansion, showing us how to become modular poetic texts in and of ourselves.[31] Historical identities do have a crucial use, but it is a self-contradicting one: they provide us with legends as well as modes of being that demand the denial or grand sublimation of their own historicity and of the very maps that guide us through space and time. As such we become absolutely prospective, our appetites pure in their infinite desire, searching for the encompassing, unbounded world spoken of by the poetic imagination: America with, and without, a past.

NOTES

Introduction

1. José Martí, 11. See the Bibliography for publication facts for all works cited.
2. See Hortense J. Spillers's "Introduction: Who Cuts the Border? Some Readings on 'America,' " in Spillers, ed., *Comparative American Identities: Race, Sex, and Nationality in the Modern Text*. Spillers also uses Martí's provocation to survey the post-colonial terrain of American, and what has increasingly come to be called *Americas*, studies.
3. As I use this term, I have in mind not only Gayatri Spivak, Homi Bhabha, and Franz Fanon, but also José Martí, C. L. R. James, Ramón Saldívar, Eduardo Galeano, and Roberto Fernández Retamar. While I realize the idea of the "post-colonial" may seem out of place in a study of cultural victors, I would argue that post-colonial theory has much to offer a discussion of Anglo-American colonial discourses. I do not claim that Anglo-Americans are post-colonial in the same way as Amerindians or Africans, but rather that the terms of post-coloniality suggest powerful explanations of the dangers of nationalism in general and American imperial ideology in particular.
4. There is a rich body of scholarship, both old and new, on British as well as southern European Renaissance constructions of the New World. Among these works are: Edmundo O'Gorman, *The Invention of America*; Stephen Greenblatt, *Marvelous Possessions*; Jack P. Greene, *The Intellectual Construction of America* (among other works); Peter Hulme, *Colonial Encounters*; and Charles L. Sanford, *The Quest for Paradise: Europe and the American Moral Imagination*.
5. The "imagined empires" of my title is thus meant to be read in both directions of subjective agency – Indian and Anglo-American. That is, I hope that I have preserved the sense that the Incas and Aztecs were not just reified legends. Their empires were also "imagined communities," though certainly of a distinctly different order than Benedict Anderson had in mind.

6. For an exception to this see Helen Carr, *Inventing the American Primitive: Politics, Gender and the Representation of Native American Literary Traditions, 1789–1936*. Another useful collection, though not exclusively focused on colonial literature, is David Mogen, Mark Busby, and Paul Bryant, eds., *The Frontier Experience and the American Dream: Essays on American Literature*.

7. See Homi Bhabha, *The Location of Culture*, 246.

8. David T. Haberly, "Form and Function in the New World Legend," in Gustavo Pérez Firmat, ed., *Do the Americas Have a Common Literature?*, 59. For another important volume treating the literature of the Americas in a comparative political context, see Bell Gale Chevigny and Gari Laguardia, eds., *Reinventing the Americas: Comparative Studies of Literature of the United States and Spanish America*.

9. While my emphasis is on the formal act of excision in the generation of suitably expansive national narratives, this may also be viewed in the context of racial arguments about history arising out of the civilization/barbarism distinction. For an excellent discussion of the use of race in the imperial ideology of nineteenth-century America, see Reginald Horsman, *Race and Manifest Destiny: The Origins of Amerian Racial Anglo-Saxonism*. Also influential has been Thomas R. Hietala's *Manifest Design: Anxious Aggrandizement in Late Jacksonian America*.

10. Also invaluable, considering the inter-American perspective of my work, is Anthony Pagden's *The Fall of Natural Man: The American Indian and the Origins of Comparative Ethnology*.

11. Of those more recent theorists, Benedict Anderson (nationalism as a function of collective imaginings and erasures that arise from social practices, especially print culture) and Edward Said (imperialism as, among other things, a cultural, and specifically literary, discourse) represent two of the most obvious directions this work follows.

   I also draw on a rich tradition of recent Americanist scholarship: Quentin Anderson (the imperial American literary self); the ideological critics of American literature – Myra Jehlen, Giles Gunn, Bercovitch; and more recently the work of Eric Sundquist, Eric Cheyfitz, Michael Warner, David Shields, Carla Mulford, and Cathy Davidson.

12. Unfortunately, this model still dominates American political and popular culture – witness the stunning backlash against a modestly revisionist history, "The West as America," mounted at the Smithsonian in 1991. This is in spite of a venerable critical tradition of frontier myth-debunking. See "Old West, New Twist at the Smithsonian," *The New York Times*, May 26, 1991; and "Vox Populi," *The New York Times*, July 7, 1991. See also Bryan J. Wolff's review, "How the West Was Hung, Or, When I Hear the Word 'Culture' I Take Out My Checkbook," *American Quarterly* 44, no. 3 (September 1992).

13. New conceptualizations of the frontier must be, in Fredric Jameson's phrase, "situation-specific" where the frontier is understood as an imperial site, with political and national tracings that interpenetrate; while Jameson might quarrel with my emphasis on binarisms, the point of this work is in

his phrase to "remember a war" by extending the political and geographical meaning of the frontier to the South; see Jameson's Foreword to Roberto Fernńdez Retamar's *Caliban and Other Essays*.

Said might call frontier situations "contrapuntal," a term that suggests the composition of hybridity. Mary Louise Pratt's model of "contact zones" and Renato Rosaldo's conception of the border as a "zone" where U.S. and Mexican cultures implode into one another are important revisions that come out of a transnational idea of America. Gloria Anzaldúa's influential in *Borderlands/La Frontera: The New Mestiza* reclaims the frontier from the monolingual triumphalist narrative through a critical practice that is both dialectical and personal.

For a valuable reconsideration of Said in the Pan-American context, see Silvia Spitta's *Between Two Waters: Narratives of Transculturation in Latin America*, which discusses Said's contrapuntal metaphor in terms of Latin American anthropological theories of "transculturation."

14. See Annette Kolodny, "Letting Go Our Grand Obsessions: Notes Toward a New Literary History of the American Frontiers," *American Literature* 64, no. 1 (March 1992): 1–3. One critic who has been successful at this type of work is Eric Cheyfitz, whose *The Poetics of Imperialism* has been immensely helpful as a guide to the type of criticism that successfully "interrogates language . . . for the complex intersections of human encounters." Amy Kaplan and Donald Pense's edited volume, *The Cultures of U.S. Imperialism*, along with Cathy N. Davidson and Michael Moon's *Subjects and Citizens: Nation, Race, and Gender from* Oroonoko *to Anita Hill*, are indications that this kind of work is taking hold. Lawrence Buell has also been an important critic in the work of revising the notion of the frontier in American studies, seeking to understand Melville especially as a "post-colonial" author.

Other works that have informed my own thinking include James Axtell, *The European and the Indian: Essays in the Ethnohistory of Colonial North America*; Richard Slotkin, *Regeneration through Violence: The Mythology of the American Frontier, 1600–1860*; Robert Berkhofer, *The White Man's Indian* and *Salvation and the Savage*; Walter Prescott Webb, *The Great Frontier*; and Richard Drinnon, *Facing West: The Metaphysics of Indian-Hating and Empire-Building*. For some of the more literary explorations of the frontier tradition and its relation to imperial ideology, see Henry Nash Smith's *The Virgin Land* and Leo Marx's *The Machine in the Garden*; while still captive to some of the more insidious myths of continental emptiness and essential naturalism, both works are crucial in the revisionary work of American cultural studies.

15. See Diana Sorensen Goodrich, *Facundo and the Construction of Argentine Culture*, 6–13, for a similar view of frontier thinking but from the critical perspective of Argentinian nationalism.

16. Edwin Fussell makes this case convincingly, pre-Drinnon. The frontier, as a mode of thinking about the world's spaces, implied a "meta-physics": "Dialectic was the all-but-universal mode of reconciling opposites . . . real or imaginary dichotomies spotting the gray debris of Cartesian confusion

and Kantian clarification" (*Frontier: American Literature and the American West,* 19).

17. Perhaps because of the proliferation of revisions of the frontier as an imperial site, I am aware that it is difficult to use the word "imperialism" carefully. This is especially true for a study that derives so much of its techniques and perspectives from multiple sources – New Historicism, cultural studies, and deconstruction. I would hope that it is clear exactly where I position myself in current debates about imperialism, neocolonialism, and cultural domination. This study, in its historically attentive close readings, is about the fierce dominations that U.S. empire has visited (and continues to visit) upon the people of America – particularly Indians. To investigate the logic of American responsibility is to enable my critical reassessment of Martí's provocation. Imperialism as a moral issue, the physical agony of the historical past, is the spine of my own Melvillean "black letter text."

18. I borrow this distinction from Spivak. See her "Neocolonialism and the Secret Agent of Knowledge" (interview with Robert Young), *Oxford Literary Review* 13, nos. 1–2 (1991): 220–51.

19. Benedict Anderson writes of this process with primary emphasis on South American mestizo hegemony over indigenous people: "In this vein, more and more 'second-generation' nationalists, in the Americas and elsewhere, learned to speak 'for' dead people with whom it was impossible or undesirable to establish a linguistic connection. This reversed ventriloquism helped to open the way for a selfconscious *indigenismo,* especially in the southern Americas. At the edge: Mexicans speaking in Spanish 'for' pre-Columbian 'Indian' civiilations whose languages they do not understand" (*Imagined Communities,* 198–9).

20. The early American situation bears fruitful comparison to that of Irish nation-building. David Lloyd in his essay "Adulteration and the Nation: Monologic Nationalism and the Colonial Hybrid" discusses the implications of a "decolonizing nationalism" on genre in Irish literature. See Alfred Arteaga, ed., *An Other Tongue: Nation and Ethnicity in the Linguistic Borderlands,* 53–92.

21. This is generally true of diplomatic historians such as Graebner and Merk. But there is a countertradition that seeks to identify the roots of American empire in Jacksonian America and before. William Appleman Williams is of course one of the earliest and most comprehensive historians of this school.

22. Angela Miller, in *Empire of the Eye,* makes this point without the psychoanalytic framework I suggest: "To Anderson's crucial definition [nationalism as a 'print language'], I would add the essential role played in the American context by visual images in creating a community transcending bonds of clan, caste, or religion, and working across space and time . . . Images were thus central to the formation of American nationalism" (8).

23. I rest much of this argument on Lacan's notions of *méconnaissance* and *jouissance.* Still, it should be obvious that I am using them as suggestive descriptions of a slightly different identification process. The national

thinker is no (metaphorical) infant – he imagines himself as both new and old. Thus, he brings critical consciousness to identity formation. Still, the fundamental struggle between the coherent potential of national identity and the neocolonial, international domain of difference is helpfully described by Lacanian concepts.

Lacan offers a crisis-inflected summary of the effect of such self-alienating processes in "The Function and Field of Speech and Language in Psychoanalysis": "Does the subject not become engaged in an ever-growing dispossession of that being of his, concerning which – by dint of sincere portraits which leave its idea no less incoherent, of rectifications that do not succeed in freeing its essence, of stays and defences that do not prevent his statue from tottering, of narcissistic embraces that become like a puff of air in animating it – he ends up by recognizing that this being has never been anything more than his construct in the imaginary and that this construct disappoints all his certainties? For in this labour which he undertakes to reconstruct *for another*, he rediscovers the fundamental alienation that made him construct it *like another*, and which has always destined it to be taken from him by *another*" (*Ecrits*, 42).

24. Witness the neocolonial narratives that have sprung up in the wake of the fall of the Eastern bloc; proto-American narratives and identities – the middle class, mafia, consumption – play themselves out in the discourse of market development, merely on foreign territory.

25. Bhabha describes this psychological economy in his anatomy of stereotypes: "The fetish or stereotype gives access to an 'identity' which is predicated as much on mastery and pleasure as it is on anxiety and defence, for it is a form of multiple and contradictory belief in its recognition of difference and disavowal of it. This conflict of pleasure/unpleasure, mastery/defence, knowledge/disavowal, absence/presence, has a fundamental significance for colonial discourse. For the scene of fetishism is also the scene of the reactivation and repetition of primal fantasy – the subject's desire for a pure origin that is always threatened by its division . . ." (*The Location of Culture*, 75). See also his more general discussion of Lacan and the Imaginary in *The Location of Culture*.

26. Variations on this Lacanian approach to nationalist thinking have been posited by Bhabha (the narrated nation) and, in a strictly American context, by Lauren Berlant (the National Symbolic) in *The Anatomy of National Fantasy: Hawthorne, Utopia, and Everyday Life.*

27. For Prescott this model seems exceptionally well suited since it describes the crisis implicit in passing into the juridical implications of primitive fantasy and border-making between civilized and barbarian. For Melville, the model applies in that he is acutely aware of the recognition of difference and the aporetic qualities of the nation thus produced. Finally, for Whitman the frontier is a construct that tends to reverse its lenslike effects – identity falls within the body rather than without. Thus there is the need to both recognize the body and dematerialize it in the name of surmounting that frontier and maintaining its identifying power.

28. For an excellent overview of the status of recent historical and sociological debates about American exceptionalism, see Michael Kammen, "The Problem of American Exceptionalism: A Reconsideration," *American Quarterly* 45, no. 1 (March 1993): 1–43. It should be obvious that exceptionalism means many things to many disciplines and to different historical periods. I take it as a given that nationalist Americans think of their state and culture as excepted from the metanarratives of corruption and cruelty that accompanied other great nations. I advance an argument here about how they justify this view.

29. See Bercovitch's *American Jeremiad* and *The Rites of Assent*, for influential accounts of American exceptionalism – its amazing cultural ability to absorb and discipline challenges to the state and culture – as a function of residual Puritan ideology and cultural forms.

30. The work of Jack P. Greene has been exemplary in this regard. His insistence on viewing Atlantic colonies in a North-South framework is a model for critically understanding the dialectics and contestations of the New World and America. See also the work of Peter White, Raymond Dolle, and Norman Grabo.

31. Alfred Arteaga, in his introduction to *An Other Tongue: Nation and Ethnicity in the Linguistic Borderlands*, describes this East-West dominant narrative as a means to establish chronological precedence in the New World over and against the Spanish and mestizo, so that the Spanish West appears to come "historically after" the Anglo arrival.

Chapter 1. Commencements

1. Madison directed the United States' first declared war fought in the name of establishing the nation's fragile international power, if not its "rising glory." According to Philip Marsh's *Philip Freneau: Poet and Journalist*, 25, Madison was ill and did not actually attend the ceremony. Burr was an imperialist visionary, at one point scheming to coordinate Mexican and Cuban insurgencies to help him found republics in the West. He embodies the conflicts inherent in an Ahab-like imperial ego that takes seriously the individualism at the core of America's nationalist ethos.
   See the bibliography for publication facts for all works cited.

2. See Hans-Joachim Lang, "The Rising Glory of America and the Falling Price of Intellect: The Careers of Brackenridge and Freneau," in Winfried Herget and Karl Ortseifer, eds., *The Transit of Civilization from Europe to America: Essays in Honor of Hans Galinsky*, 131–43. Henry Nash Smith also mentions this poem as a crucial ideological vision of empire; see *The Virgin Land*, 9.

3. I regret that I repress a reading of the 1771 poem as a collaborative effort. I also neglect, though acknowledge, the performative aspect of the 1771 poem as against its reappearance in 1786 embedded within and enhanced by the post-Revolutionary milieu of print culture.

I should further note the changes relative to Freneau's status as author and politician: by 1786, Freneau has consolidated not only many of his republican tendencies, if not his identitarian quandaries, but also his authorial powers. His subscription list for the 1786 volume of poetry is impressive and spans the colonies from the Carolinas northward.

4. For an interesting assessment of hybridity see *New Formations* no. 18, (Winter 1992). The essay by Smadar Lavie informs much of my own thinking about the idea of "border hybridity" in a framework where nation and empire are inseparable and in constant flux. See Lavie, "Blow-ups in the Borderzones," 84–106. For a comprehensive collection of essays on such issues in a specifically North American context, see Frank Shuffelton, ed., *A Mixed Race: Ethnicity in Early America.*

5. I thank the Library Company of Philadelphia for their help in locating this 1772 reprint.

6. Lawrence G. Friedman, in *Inventors of the Promised Land*, discusses what he calls "the rising glory of America" poem in similar terms. He points out that the desire for international redemption is a sublimation of the hard facts of domestic cultural and political life (13–16).

7. See Marsh, *Philip Freneau*, 8–10.

8. Jacob Axelrad, *Philip Freneau, Champion of Democracy*, 34.

9. See such widely divergent chronicles (from the standpoint of reproach) as Bartolomé de Las Casas's *History of the Indies*, Garcilaso de la Vega's *Royal Commentaries of the Incas*, Felipe Guáman Poma de Ayala's *New Chronicles*, Bernal Díaz del Castillo's *True History of the Conquest of Mexico*, and even Cortés's *Letters from Mexico.*

10. As Shields puts it: "The Black Legend tells of how agents of the greatest power in the Old World, Spain, came into the New World and found a people living in paradisiacal innocence. The land that these people inhabited was a place of wonders blessed with luxuriant flora, astonishing animals, gorgeous minerals. The people apportioned the materials of this world with '*orden y concierto*' (order and harmony), governing themselves with simple justice. The Spaniards justified their dealings with the people of the New World as expanding the dominion of the Book and the Cross, their actions proved that the true god was gold and their task the enslavement of the native population to serve in the mines . . . In sum, the Black Legend tells of the conquest of innocence and simplicity by evil and hypocrisy" (*Oracles of Empire*, 177).

For a discussion of Arcadia in early modern utopian thought, see J. C. Davis, *Utopia and the Ideal Society: A Study of English Utopian Writing, 1516–1700*. Davis is particularly useful for making distinctions between the varieties of utopian thinking I engage, e.g. Arcadianism as opposed to millenarianism. Other works of interest are William Brandon, *New Worlds for Old: Reports from the New World and their Effect on the Development of Social Thought in Europe, 1500–1800*; and Frank E. Manuel, ed., *Utopias and Utopian Thought.*

11. The late eighteenth-century American standard on the subject was William

Robertson's *History of America* (1777), though other literature, such as Dryden's plays about South American Indians, had been popular earlier.

The Legend, as an important mobilizing literary genre, probably played a significant role in disseminating nationalist discourses within Protestant European countries. See Anderson, *Imagined Communities*, 40.

12. See Mary Louise Pratt, *Imperial Eyes: Travel, Writing and Transculturation.* Pratt's concept of "anti-conquest" partly describes the phenomenon I sense in Freneau: "The main protagonist of the anti-conquest is a figure I sometimes call the 'seeing-man,' a . . . label for the European male subject of European landscape discourse – he whose imperial eyes passively look out and possess" (7).

13. Savagism was theorized by Roy Harvey Pearce in *Savagism and Civilization: A Study of the Indian and the American Mind.* According to Pearce, it was an unsystematized belief comfortably held by many in the eighteenth century that said that Northern Amerindians were not native aboriginals and therefore merely an obstruction to American destiny. It also held that the Indian must be removed for the ultimate good that was civilization.

14. The American debate over monogenetic versus polygenetic racial origins persisted well into the nineteenth century, figuring strongly in slavery debates. See John Irwin's *American Hieroglyph: The Symbol of the Egyptian Hieroglyphics in the American Renaissance*, 59; see also Reginald Horsman, *Race and Manifest Destiny*, 44–52.

15. In his essay "Identity: A Latin American Philosophical Problem," *Philosophical Forum* 20, nos. 1–2 (Fall–Winter 1988–9), Leopold Zea quotes Arnold Toynbee on just this issue: " 'When we Westerners speak of "Natives," ' wrote Toynbee, 'we implicitly take the cultural color out of our perception of them. We see them as trees walking, or as wild animals infesting the country in which we happen to come across them. In fact, we see them as part of the local flora and fauna and not as men of like passions with ourselves; and seeing them thus as something supra-human, we feel entitled to treat them as though they did not possess ordinary human rights.' . . . The Indian, the native, as any native in any region of the earth beyond the centers of culture and civilization . . . is outside what is considered the only expression of humanity" (35–6).

16. See Emmerich de Vattel, *The Law of Nations or the Principles of Natural Law*, 3:38. I first came across this quotation in Wai-Chee Dimock's *Empire for Liberty*. For an excellent discussion of the legal discourses surrounding the Indian in Spanish America and in post-Revolutionary legal thought see Robert A. Williams, Jr., *The American Indian in Western Legal Thought.*

17. Quoted in Paul Carter's *Revolt Against Destiny: An Intellectual History of the United States*, 30.

18. John P. McWilliams, in *The American Epic*, makes a similar argument while discussing Joel Barlow's *The Vision of Columbus/Columbiad*: "[Barlow's] subject [the agricultural virtuousness of the Incas] . . . would be cherished by forward-thinking republicans everywhere" (58).

19. See Robert Berkhofer's discussion of the Noble Savage in *The White Man's Indian*, esp. 72–96, for an excellent and wide-ranging treatment of the broad cultural significance of the Indian in American civil ideology. See also Richard Slotkin's discussion of the relationship between myths, history, and natural law in his essay "Myth and the Production of History," in Myra Jehlen and Sacvan Bercovitch, eds., *Ideology and Classic American Literature*, 81–2.

20. The line does not appear in "RGA" 1786.

21. It is worth noting once again that the commercial aspect of the 1771 poem was played down in the 1786 version when Freneau was more radically republican.

22. See Shields's discussion of Whig poetry of commerce (*Oracles of Empire*, 16–7) and his analysis of Columbus in this tradition (32).

23. I am not convinced by the argument that Freneau excised all disparaging passages about Indians in the later version of the poem. It does not hold up to scrutiny, as the poem merely becomes more pro-agriculture and less pro-commercial, and, in a way, a more sophisticated imperial screed. (Such critics blame Brackenridge for the origin of most of the anti-Indian rhetoric; he was probably the author of most of the commercial verse.) This claim was made originally by Pearce in *Savagism and Civilization*, 182; see also Daniel Marder's introduction to *A Hugh Henry Brackenridge Reader: 1770–1815*, 25.

24. France's status as heroic supporter of the Revolution is more ambiguous when applied to the frontier in 1786.

25. This in spite of the fact that Washington and Freneau had a great deal of personal animosity toward one another. Indeed, it was Washington who famously referred to Freneau as "that rascal." An alternative reading of the passage could find Washington ironically written into British history because of his Federalism, to point up his status as an imperial dupe.

26. The *OED* cites 1841 as the earliest American usage of "native" as a synonym for "non-European." But I have seen the word used in this punning sense, in the early seventeenth-century poetry of Roger Williams, and I suspect it might be found elsewhere.

27. A comparison with Bercovitch's concept of the jeremiad is in order, where the ambiguity between history and rhetoric is "translated into promise," and this myth-making provides "self-justification" and "social cohesion." See *American Jeremiad*.

28. Russel B. Nye, in *The Cultural Life of the New Nation, 1776–1830*, points to 1765 as the important moment when British Americans began to self-consciously differentiate an American nationality within the imperial realm. It was the need for "recognition" by the British that most influenced American meditations on their identity. My point here is to bring into view the contested identities that asked for recognition as "American."

29. In the British American tradition of the Black Legend, Columbus came to be horrified by what became of his discovery in the hands of Spanish colonialists. But his historical sorrow had more to do with his personal misfortunes than anything else.

30. For instance, the term "Columbard" as a synonym for "American" became prevalent, particularly in the years after independence. The tricentennial of Columbus's voyage was observed in several cities in 1792. Columbia University took its name around the same time. Other epic treatments of the theme were attempted by Barlow and Richard Snowden, both of whom wrote *Columbiads*. Caleb Bingham authored *The Columbian Orator* (1797). *The Columbian Magazine* saw a popular and extended run from 1786 to 1792, and it was purposeful in its project of literary nationalism. Matthew Carey's *American Museum* contained a chapter entitled "Columbian Parnassiad," and Charles Brockden Brown had it in mind to write a history of Peru. Benjamin Spencer calls the popularity of the term "Columbians" a part of the "campaign for an American literature" (*The Quest for Nationality: An American Literary Campaign*, 59–60). For an excellent, more recent analysis of "Columbus" as a signifier, see William Spengemann's chapter, "Columbus: The Early American History of an English Word," in his *A New World of Words*.

Chapter 2. Diplomacy

1. For a comprehensive evaluation of the more recent work on the historicism of Jeffersonian republicanism, see *William and Mary Quarterly* 43 (January 1986), especially Lance Banning's "Jeffersonian Ideology Revisited: Liberal and Classical Ideas in the New American Republic," 3–19, and Joyce Appleby's "Republicanism in Old and New Contexts," 20–34.
   See the Bibliography for publication facts for all works cited.
2. See Abdul JanMahommed, "The Economy of Manichean Allegory: The Function of Racial Difference in Colonialist Literature," in Henry Louis Gates, Jr., ed., *"Race," Writing, and Difference*, 83.
3. There were two important versions of *The Vision of Columbus*, one completed in 1787 and the other a revised edition printed in Paris in 1793. The 1793 version contains many of the changes that would be fleshed out more radically in *The Columbiad* (1807), and for that reason I deal only with the 1787 version. See Arthur L. Ford, *Joel Barlow*, 68.
4. Once in Europe, his status as an American who had much to offer the international republican cause was quickly solidified. Barlow's sense of himself as New World prophet of republicanism is evident in a journal entry from October 3, 1788: "I presume there are not to be found five men in Europe who understand the nature of liberty and theory of government so well as they are understood by five hundred men in America. The friends of America in London and Paris are astonished at our conduct in adopting the New Constitution. They are as intemperate in their idea of liberty as we were in the year seventy-five." Americans are figured paternistically here, older and wiser than their "intemperate" European disciples. The entry's arrogance of historical wisdom, as we will see, can be read as a product of *The Vision of Columbus*, which he had just completed. Quoted in M. Ray

Adam's "Joel Barlow, Political Romanticist," *American Literature* 9 (May 1937): 117–18. This piece provides a comprehensive account of his time abroad and the variety of philosophical battles his cosmopolitan ways gave rise to.

5. See Thomas J. Schlereth's *The Cosmopolitan Ideal in Enlightenment Thought: Its Form and Function in the Ideas of Franklin, Hume, and Voltaire, 1694–1790*, which provides much of the basis for my own thought on the cosmopolitan currents of eighteenth-century intellectual and political life. Schlereth explains that the New World was seen as a product of the exploration-obsessed Renaissance, and that there was a sense of historical continuity between the New World and Europe's own imaginative awakening. This connection was crucial to the reification of the exotic; as Schlereth puts it: "The literature of discovery, exploration, and travel had enormous impact upon the European imagination and fostered this exoticism" (21).

6. In the 1780s Barlow began to embrace a new philosophy of history, espoused most notably by Condorcet and Paine. William C. Dowling's essay "Joel Barlow and *The Anarchiad*," *Early American Literature* 25 (1990): 18–33, from which this summary of "progressive linearism" has been borrowed (24), is a nuanced and carefully argued explication of the political theories that underlie Barlow's literary evolution. Dowling holds that in the latter half of the 1780s Barlow chose between two visions of history, "progressive linearism" and the cyclical theory, a more conservative view in line with the proto-Federalism exemplified by Dwight. Dwight is then the more religious millenarian while Barlow is the more secular; but Dowling complicates this breach by arguing that Barlow is hard-pressed to free himself of the language of cyclical history and classical civic humanism so that his movement toward radical republicanism is a much trickier and less dramatic fissure than has been thought. Ultimately, Dowling makes the case for the theoretical continuities that lie beneath the rhetorical surfaces of Federalism and republicanism.

Another extremely useful discussion of the role of the epic in the articulation of American history is John Griffith's "*The Columbiad* and *Greenfield Hill*: History, Poetry, and Ideology in the Late Eighteenth Century," *Early American Literature* 10 (1975–6): 235–50.

7. Quoted in Benjamin T. Spencer, *The Quest for Nationality*, 22.

8. Quoted in Ford, *Joel Barlow*, 46.

9. See Schlereth, *The Cosmopolitan Ideal*, 62–72, for an elucidation of the relationship between varieties of cosmopolitan philosophy and typically cosmopolitan brands of history.

10. John McWilliams in *The American Epic* has amply demonstrated the difficulties Barlow encountered with his struggle to redefine the epic in a new republican and American context. I am refining the terms of that struggle, taking into account the racial strains on Barlow's conception of the epic and then discussing those strains as they relate to Barlow's construction of ancient America.

11. For Barlow the only reliable source in English for New World history was

William Robertson's *History of America* (1777); he bemoans the fact that it has not been reprinted in the colonies. Much of his knowledge of pre-Columbian America was also based on the Spanish American historian Garcilaso de la Vega (*Royal Commentaries of the Incas*) and French *philosophe* Jean François Marmontel (*The Incas*). He also pays tribute to Don Alonzo de Ercilla's epic poem on pre-Columbian civilization, *Araucana*. Somewhat regretfully, Barlow believes an extensive historical introduction is needed to familiarize Americans with this neglected part of their own history. Barlow's version of events reflects – as might be expected given the biases of his sources (Robertson especially) – the standard lionization of Columbus (and to a lesser extent Isabella) at the expense of imperial Spain.

12. Leon Howard makes this point comprehensively in *The Connecticut Wits* and in the essay "The Late Eighteenth Century: An Age of Contradictions," in *Transitions in American Literary History*; in a similar vein, Gregg Camfield argues in "Joel Barlow's Dialectic of Progress," *Early American Literature* 21 (1986): 131–43, that Barlow in his prose "relished a good paradox against all the natural 'laws' of Enlightenment epistemology"(131).

13. Dwight, in an inaugural sermon delivered as president of Yale College, used the word "visionary" to disparage the fantasies of optimism that he associated with republican thinkers: "In this age of innovation, visionary philosophers have . . . discovered that men are naturally wise and good, prone to good government . . ." One can almost hear the corrosive irony and contempt in his caricature of optimistic republicanism. But Barlow, who was undergoing a conversion from Calvinist Federalism to radical republicanism in the course of the writing of *The Vision of Columbus*, would seem inclined to the visionary, if for no other reason than to petulantly experiment with the philosophy of the opposition. The word "visionary" was thus a mark of progressivism when used by Barlow, a code word for social change as a national *and* transnational ideal, in contrast to a static and reactionary nationalism denoted by the word "patriotic" adhered to so fervently by the likes of Dwight.

14. Barlow makes it clear that the poem would not be possible without the history that must be written as an accompaniment to the English language's new epic: "Doctor Robertson's history of [South America] . . . is not yet reprinted in America, and therefore cannot be supposed to be in the hands of American readers in general: and perhaps no other writer in the English language has given a sufficient account of the life of Columbus to enable them to understand many of the necessary allusions in the following Poem" (*Works*, 2: 107). This absence in the market for published historical narratives is lamentable.

15. As such, the trope can be read as the playing out of the Pocockian conflict between "value and personality on the one hand, history and society on the other, in its first and secular form" (J. G. A. Pocock, *The Machiavellian Moment*, ix). Pocock suggests that, indeed, the conflict between history and the corruptions of empire culminated in a "utopian perception of global space in America"(ix).

16. Perhaps even more importantly, we glimpse in the essay just how and why the legendary Inca acquired his own authoritative and utopian identity. In the process, we gain an object lesson in the poetics of bestowing a national identity upon a growing populace. The essay makes available that which had been known only to readers of unwieldy and often untranslated South American, Spanish colonial histories (Garcilaso de la Vega's *Royal Commentaries* in particular). Barlow, in recirculating this history, is acutely aware of the nationalizing process inherent in the marketing of popular histories.

17. The critical debate about the constitution of American national authority is interesting to note in this context. Michael Warner's argument in *The Letters of the Republic* about the centrality of the public sphere as a print phenomenon to anchor constitutional authority is now countered by Christopher Looby's more performative, voice-centered argument in *Voicing America*. Manco, as a model for revolutionary discourses of authority, seems to present problems for both sides.

18. This seems to jibe with Cathy Davidson's comment on Barlow in *Revolution and the Word*. She notes his having worked "almost as hard as Webster to promote copyright laws and to recognize art as a commodity" (34). This link with Barlow's historicism deserves more treatment than I give here, but it is worth noting as well the relationship between art as commodity and art as *martial* commodity.

19. Solon and Numa are also mentioned, but are not analyzed since Barlow believes Athens and Rome were already established societies and thus did not provide the "means nor the opportunity of shewing their talents in the business of original legislation" (*Works*, 2: 178).

20. As we will see in the next chapter, this formulation of savagist surprise will echo in much of Prescott's evaluations of the achievements of the Aztec civilization. Race and reason seem to conflict in the prospect of Indian social organization/nationalization and thereby erupt into locutions of surprise.

21. See Stephen J. Greenblatt's famous discussion of this Machiavellian interpretation of Indian otherness, "Invisible Bullets: Renaissance Authority and its Subversion," in *Shakespearean Negotiations: The Circulation of Social Energy in Renaissance England* (Berkeley: University of California Press, 1988).

22. *The Columbiad* precipitated a controversy arising from the questioning of transatlantic authenticity. In 1810, a series of letters were published between Barlow and H. Gregoire, a member of the National Institute of France and the Bishop of Blois. The letters consist of a mutually respectful critical exchange over the alleged sacrilegiousness of *The Columbiad*. Gregoire's criticism of the moral object of the poem prompts Barlow's defense, a revealing discussion of his philosophy of poetry; the defense directly addresses his proprietary view of history.

The printers of the volume begin by affirming the authority of both men, but particularly that of Barlow: "The literary fame of the writers is established in both hemispheres. *The Columbiad*, of itself, refutes the opinion of the Abbé Raynal and other European visionaries, who have maintained that our soil and climate is unpropitious to genius." In Barlow's initial presentation of a copy of the poem to the French National Institute, he is careful to profess his modesty, intending the gift only as a demonstration of the advances of American typography. In his offering though, he once again conflates the individual talent with that of the nation and casts his conflation in the language of commerce. "France can fear no rival in any thing; but in the fine arts, as in literature and science, all rivals are friends. True knowledge, whether physical or moral, will teach us more and more that the real interests of all nations are common and reciprocal."

Nonetheless, Barlow's poem occasioned great distress for Gregoire, who deemed it anti-Catholic. Interestingly, Barlow's most passionate and effective defense is his editorial view of history, his sense that he has, in fact, merely constructed his poem and its moral objects out of received historical materials: "It is not from vanity that I speak; my book is not a work of genius; the maxims in it are not my own; they are yours, they are those of good men that have gone before us both; they are drawn from the gospel, from history, from the unlettered volume of moral nature, from the experience and the inexperience of unhappy man in his various struggles after happiness; from all his errors and all his objects in the social state. My only merit lies in putting them together with fidelity. My work is only a transcript of the tablet of my mind imprest with these images as they pass before it" (*Works,* 1:545).

Barlow's most remarkable confession in this regard is that the materials of history were not properly his own. This distanced relationship to a historical domain, always subject to the transactions of the commercial mind, is the very source of his authenticity, his authority, and his innocence. Given his "latitude of reason" – which stretches the epic vision of the poet to global proportions – he has played the role of metahistorical editor where history is an objective form of national capital. With this purchase on an unprecedented range of texts, Barlow (including the Incas of "the unlettered volume of moral nature") can make unique, and finally exculpating, claims to visionary mimesis.

23. Larzer Ziff's *Writing in the New Nation* explains the emergence of this universalizing republicanism by pointing to the need for national authority recognized on a worldwide scale: "those features of American culture that seemed to indicate national inferiority to traditional cultures were actually signs of the international culture of republicanism that was to spread worldwide. What appeared, that is, to be typically American would eventually prove to be not that but typically modern" (135–6). This "international culture of republicanism" also bore a religious dimension that in Barlow's case was an important part of his training as a Calvinist Federalist at Yale. In *Visionary Republic,* Ruth Bloch has traced the development of American political universalism in the 1790s in terms of the enduring discourse of religious millennialism. She distinguishes the millennialism of the 1790s from that of the 1780s, a distinction that speaks to the force and direction of Barlow's own beliefs: "Less moderate and nationalistic than the millen-

nialism of the 1780's, the political millennialism of the following decade set its sights on the fundamental republican transformation of the entire world and projected an even more universalistic perspective on the future than the earlier revolutionary millennialism of the 1770's" (151).

24. This redemptive and providential closure is religious in nature, but it is also fundamentally historical and materialist in practice and theory. As William Dowling has shown, Barlow had by *The Vision of Columbus* developed a fairly sophisticated materialist philosophy. Barlow's republicanism had evolved a notion of history that was fully progressive, that no longer took part in the cyclical millennialism of Barlow's own Calvinist background.

25. While he was revising the poem, Barlow befriended Robert Fulton and with him undertook to sell machines for naval warfare to the U.S. government. The 1807 edition of *The Columbiad* bears this relationship out explicitly. After an engraved portrait of Barlow, based on a painting by Fulton, there is a loving dedication to Fulton that personalizes the transactional terms of literary obligation. The dedication thus differs in obvious ways from the dedication to Louis XVI in *The Vision of Columbus*:

"My Dear Friend, This poem is your property. I present it to you in manuscript, that you may bring it before the public in the manner you think proper. This letter will explain to them my motives for offering you such a testimony of my attachment; an attachment which certainly comprises all the good affections that the virtues and talents of one man can inspire in the breast of another . . .

"These are motives of affection and precaution; but I am likewise impelled by a motive of justice. My poem, having grown up under your eye, much benefited by your observations, as well as by those of my excellent wife, is to come forward, I find ornamented by your taste. You designated the subjects to be painted for engravings; and, unable to convince me that the work could merit such expensive and splendid decorations, you ordered them to be executed in my absence and at your own expense. So that the whole work, as committed to the publisher and estimated by its cost, is chiefly yours already. For my proportion has cost me nothing but that leisurely and exhilarating labor in which I always delight.

"Take it then to yourself; and let it live, as long as it is to live, a monument of our friendship: you cannot need it as a monument of your fame. Your inventions and discoveries in the useful arts, the precision and extension of your views in the physical sciences and in their application to the advancement of society and morals, will render it proper that the lines you have selected and written under my portrait would be transferred to yours. Posterity will vindicate the right and fix them in their place.

"Continue to be happy, my Fulton, as your various merit entitles you to be. Continue to enhance that merit by well directed labors for the good of mankind; and since this address will not outlast the poem to which it is prefixed, I leave you to take some other method to unite my memory more durably with your own" (Barlow, *The Columbiad*).

26. Dowling astutely perceives the authorial importance of Manco Capac to

Barlow's epic ambitions in the two poems when he writes of *The Columbiad*: "Manco Capec [*sic*], as the enlightened lawgiver of a barbarous people, prefigures the role of Barlow himself in *The Columbiad*, the difference being that Manco Capec, as the inhabitant of a darker age, had been compelled to accomplish through ideological subterfuge what is left to Barlow, as the disembodied voice of progressive history revealed as such, to declare as objective truth" (*Poetry and Ideology*, 115–6).

27. This fetish is borne out even more explicitly by his elaborate footnote to a couplet about Benjamin West in Book Eight. In that note he mentions each of the 299 finished historical paintings West had compiled and given to Barlow personally in 1802. He goes so far as to specify where each collection is housed.

Elsewhere in his footnotes to *The Columbiad* Barlow discourses on the role of the alphabet and written culture in the production of history. He refers to "three stages of improvement in the graphic art or the art of communicating our thoughts to absent persons and to posterity by visible signs" (*Works*, 2: 789). Each of these stages shares the gerund "painting": painting ideas (hieroglyphs), painting sounds (writing), and painting phrases (sentences). My point here is that, to a certain degree, painting and portraiture were important facets of his theory of representation. I would suggest further that Barlow was beginning to attempt the kind of representational evaluation, in the wake of a print culture explosion in the United States, that occupied Prescott's later struggle with New World history.

28. I thank the Library Company of Philadelphia for their help in locating this text and for granting permission to reproduce the paintings and signatures.

29. Of course, this view would be drastically revised in the stark prophecy of war and mass slaughter expressed in the later poem, "Advice to a Raven in Russia." The poem is about Napoleon, who turned the might of modern empire and colonial methods on Europe itself, to Barlow's horror. Barlow witnessed the Russian retreat firsthand on a peace mission for the U.S. government.

30. *The Pennsylvania Gazette* for January 2, 1782, carried a similar report with the same editorial attitude. I should also point out that part of the colonial refusal to endorse the South American rebellion could have been strategic, since Spain was by 1782 an ally of the colonies.

31. Interestingly, Adam Smith holds out the admittedly remote possibility that commerce may serve to restore the native's ability to assert sovereign claims. See *The Wealth of Nations*, 591.

Chapter 3. Noctography

1. For this assessment to be accurate some context is in order. Freneau's and Barlow's national imaginary was fundamentally different from Prescott's. Freneau and Barlow were Jeffersonian republicans, while Prescott was a

Federalist. For Freneau and Barlow, Spain was the national entity that lay on the other side of a western and southern border – a direct hemispheric contender; for Prescott, Spain was a failed colonial empire, sympathetic in its ineptitude, cooperative in the historical projects he undertook. The South American ideal, as an ideal of innocence destroyed, was replaced to a certain extent by a reversion to Spanish apologies and a strong desire at least to render New World history with rhetorical evenhandedness and scientific objectivity. Prescott and Irving both communicate the sense that ancient America and particularly its story of imperial conquest needed to be reclaimed from the Jeffersonian interpretive tradition and refigured given the crises of their own era.

See the Bibliography for publication facts for all works cited.

2. This may be the greatest difference between the nineteenth-century Federalist romantic and the eighteenth-century republican classicists. A new aesthetic gained force wherein history was to be a novelistic item of mass consumption. Prescott paid special attention to "bringing history to life," filling it with intriguing psychologies and astoundingly bad decisions; for the individual reader he promised an altogether entertaining and inwardly felt experience of the exotic past, Hispanic and pre-Columbian.

This sensualist school of history writing was, of course, intimately linked to martial literature (which has, interestingly, connections with Barlow's military aesthetic). Prescott speaks of Scott's appeal: "[Scott] had a natural relish for gunpowder; and his mettle roused, like that of the war-horse, at the sound of the trumpet" (*Miscellanies*, 225). The martial aspects of romantic history resonate with the reader in search of masculine traits within history. Instead of telling readers how to feel, writers like Scott and also Irving strove for intuitiveness and immediacy; Prescott calls the sensual aspect of militarism the intensest form of readerly contact with history (*Miscellanies*, 107).

William Howard Gardiner wrote to Prescott on the eve of the publication of the *Conquest of Mexico*, predicting the work's popularity in the book marketplace on the basis of its figurative quality as opposed to what Hayden White calls the "compilation of facts" associated with scientific historicism: "I have read it through – and have no hesitation in saying that it is destined to be more popular even than its predecessor – not because it is more meritorious (for what do *the people* know about that?) – but because the subject and the manner of treating it make an excellent substitute for one of Scott's best historical novels. It's as good as fiction – which ought to be highly gratifying to the compiler of facts" (213). Prescott remarks in a letter that the *Conquest of Mexico* "is as much a child's story as much as any of Monk Lewis's tales of wonder" (*Correspondence*, 147) thereby positing a middle-class reader subject to awe in much the same way that the Aztec was captive to the fantasy of the supernatural. (Needless to say, this is something of a bizarre claim considering the bloody facts of the conquest, which are not spared by Prescott.)

3. Samuel Johnson, *Lives of the English Poets*, 1: 73.

4. See George Ticknor, *Life of William Hickling Prescott*, 81–2; see also C. Harvey Gardiner, *William Hickling Prescott: A Biography*, 124–7.
 David Levin's *History as Romantic Art: Bancroft, Prescott, Motley, and Parkman* is the preeminent work on interpreting and culturally placing Prescott within the context of American romantic historiography. Much of my work here is an expansion of, and occasionally a supplement to, Levin's insights.

5. The work of Irving and Prescott – not to mention James Fenimore Cooper (one of this book's largest omissions) – represents a crucial moment in the history of American romanticism and its growth out of a transitional political culture. Exploring the relationship between Irving and Prescott and the transitional political culture in detail is not my aim here, however. My focus on Irving and Prescott at the outset of this chapter is intended to ground an investigation into the compositional poetics of Prescott's South American romance histories. Prescott, as we will see through the issue of composition, has much to teach us about the formation of nineteenth-century political and literary culture.

6. Prescott had a less admiring estimation of Irving as a scientific historian, and he maintained a kind of genteel rivalry with him (see Gardiner, *Prescott: A Biography*, 149–50). Prescott's other models were Voltaire (he admired his categorical and systematic approach), Scott ("the true romantic historian"), Gibbon (a great stylist), and perhaps most of all the Abbé de Mably (who invested his work with drama and political didacticism) (Charvat and Kraus, *Prescott: Representative Selections*, xxxviii–xxxix). The influence of Harvard hispanicist George Ticknor, later his biographer, was almost as important as Irving's. A year after Ticknor's return to Harvard from Europe, Prescott decided on a life of scholarship; in January 1826 he settled on Spanish history, for it contained "the germs of the modern system of European politics." Of Ticknor's authoritativeness in the field, "[I]t was said, not six men in Europe were capable of reviewing" (Charvat and Kraus, *Prescott: Representative Selections*, xxviii) his *The History of Spanish Literature* (1849).

7. Charvat and Kraus also describe the rivalry between Irving and Prescott. The opening of the Spanish archives in 1780 produced new literary territory to be colonized competitively. "Prescott and Irving seem to have marked out provinces for themselves almost simultaneously. A month after Prescott decided on his subject ... At Edward Everett's suggestion ... Irving began a translation of [Navarrete] which he soon turned into a supposedly original *Life and Voyages of Columbus* (1828). A year later he brought out his *Conquest of Granada*, which, Prescott said, 'superseded all further necessity for poetry, and unfortunately for me, history.' Thus Prescott found that two of the most brilliant portions of his story had been robbed of their novelty while he was making his 'tortoise-like progress.' A more serious situation was averted later when Irving, upon learning that Prescott was at work on the *Conquest of Mexico*, gave up his own plans in that field" (*Prescott: Representative Selections*, xxxiii–xxxiv).

8. See Donald A. Ringe's *The Pictorial Mode: Space & Time in the Art of Bryant,*

Irving, and Cooper. Ringe points out that Irving's obsession with and advancement of the pictorial style was part of a general literary tendency in the period. Also helpful is Wendy Steiner's *Pictures of Romance: Form against Context in Painting and Literature.* For a more art historical approach to the same topic, see Bryan J. Wolff, *Romantic Re-Vision: Culture and Consciousness in Nineteenth-Century American Painting and Literature;* Angela Miller, *Empire of the Eye;* and David C. Miller, ed., *American Iconology: New Approaches to Nineteenth-Century Art and Literature.* For a Derridean exploration of this cluster of issues, see Michael Phillipson, *Painting, Language, and Modernity.*

9. Twentieth-century readings of Prescott have tended to assert the ethnocentrism of a nationalist project in Prescott's romances while neglecting the tangle of race and writing that structured his histories. John Ernest, in an important revaluation and reinterpretation of Prescott's work, points out that two of Prescott's most eminent critics, Ringe and David Levin, have shown him to be a nationalist and ethnocentrist without ideological or textual complications. Ernest goes on to demonstrate the limits of such claims by arguing that Prescott had a sophisticated understanding of the constructed moral content of his romance. Situating Prescott's writing in the period of the U.S. war with Mexico, Ernest emphasizes the ambivalence Prescott betrayed about "the political and ethical sense of mission that this romance can inspire – indeed, that he intends it to inspire" ("Reading the Romantic Past: William H. Prescott's *History of Mexico,*" *American Literary History* 5, no. 2 [Summer 1993]: 233). Thus, Ernest would have us look for the ways Prescott constructs his romance as a "metahistorical commentary, not on the character of the conquest itself but rather on the attempt to read and interpret the text of the past" (233). My own reading here attempts to build on this valuable insight while keeping in view the racial and nationalist quandaries that result in a conflicted textual metahistory that asks its readers to be distrustful of its own inspiration. Where Ernest reads for Prescott's "dialogical relation to the past" (in the words of Dominick LaCapra), I read for the agonistic conflict and ambivalence inherent in the self-conscious mode of representing otherness. For similar readings of Prescott see Inga Clendinnen, " 'Fierce and Unnatural Cruelty': Cortés and the Conquest of Mexico," *Representations* 33 (1991): 65–100; and Daniel Cooper Alarcon, *The Aztec Palimpsest: Mexico in the Modern Imagination.*

10. Irwin's work has been crucial to explaining how the decipherment of Egyptian hieroglyphics – indeed the entire issue of decipherment – affected the hermeneutic disposition of the American Renaissance. What Irwin leaves out of his analysis regarding the American relationship to these insights are the post-colonial, imperial dimensions of decipherment and representation for the American.

11. Gardiner (*Prescott: A Biography*) points to the influence of Peter Stephen DuPonceau's "Essay on Indian Languages" and Alexander von Humboldt's *Researches concerning the Institutions of the Ancient Inhabitants of America,* while Charvat and Kraus's Introduction to *Prescott: Representative Selections* is exhaustive in locating content sources for the secondary historical reading.

12. Ernest explains that the elements of Prescott's dialogism – on the one hand a romance epic and on the other a legalistic and scientific sifting of textual evidence – resolve finally into a story about the ascendance of the historian himself, "acting on behalf of a nation struggling for self-realization" ("Reading the Romantic Past," 236).

13. By 1843, the date of publication of *The Conquest of Mexico*, the United States was fully embroiled in its own conquest of Mexico, and it would not be long before a U.S. general fully appropriated and enacted the conquest trope of Cortés and laid siege to Mexico City itself. By 1843, the United States had intervened *globally* over thirty-six times. For a comprehensive account of early American imperial involvement, see William Appleman Williams's *Empire as a Way of Life*.

14. After a delay in which he was occupied by an article on Irving's *Conquest of Granada*, Prescott began composing *Ferdinand and Isabella* in 1829. It was published in 1837. He then proceeded to write the *History of the Conquest of Mexico* (1843) and the *History of the Conquest of Peru* (1847).

15. This scheme was derived from a number of sources, among them: Greppo's *Essay on the Hieroglyphic System of M. Champollion* (1829), Champollion's *Précis du Système Hieroglyphique des Anciens Egyptiens* (1824), and Warburton's *Divine Legation* (1811).

16. Ticknor writes of the fiction of visibility associated with the noctograph: "The chief difficulty in the use of such an apparatus is obvious. The person employing it never looks upon his work; never sees one of the marks he is making. He trusts wholly to the wires for the direction of his hand. He makes his letters and words only from mechanical habit" (*Life of Prescott*, 118).

17. Irwin quotes a passage from Foucault's *The Order of Things* that resonates with this sense that the world, now geographically revealed and claimed, may be successfully "read": "the face of the world is covered with blazons, with characters, with ciphers and obscure words – with 'hieroglyphics,' as Turner called them. And the space inhabited by immediate resemblances becomes like a vast open book; it bristles with written signs; every page is seen to be filled with strange figures that intertwine and in some places repeat themselves. All that remains is to decipher them" (Foucault, *The Order of Things*, 25).

18. See Edward Said, "Nationalism, Human Rights, and Interpretation," *Raritan* 12, no. 3 (Winter 1993): 26–51. Said's discussion of a distinction made by Perry Anderson in the *London Review* between the concepts of national character and national identity is especially useful for thinking about the historical construction of national "characters."

19. See Pagden, *The Fall of Natural Man*, 27–108, on the transformation of Amerindians in South America from "nature's slaves" to "nature's children."

20. See Roy Harvey Pearce, *Savagism and Civilization: A Study of the Indian and the American Mind*.

21. For a more elaborate description of this process, see Edward W. Said, *Beginnings: Intention and Method*.

22. Here I am departing somewhat from John Irwin, who describes a double story inhering in the hieroglyph, linguistic history and the objective, human history. Irwin views the hieroglyph as a more enabling figure for American Renaissance writers. "The attempt to discover the origin of man through language inevitably leads to the hieroglyphics, to that basic form of signification in which the physical shape of the sign is taken directly from – indeed, is like the shadow of – the physical shape of the object that it stands for. For the writers of the American Renaissance, the hieroglyphics and the question of man's origin are implicit in one another . . . Furthermore, because in pictographic writing the shape of a sign is in a sense a double of the physical shape of the object it represents, like a shadow or a mirror image, the essays and stories from this period dealing with the hieroglyphics and human origins are always, in one way or another, 'double' stories" (*American Hieroglyph*, 61). I would argue that, while important to understanding Prescott, the double story is necessarily inflected by self-conscious discourses of race.

23. I want to be clear in stating that Prescott has many powerful moments of revulsion toward the Spanish conquest that betray an important moral conscience. My point in the current argument is to suggest how his narrative poetics complicates this moralism.

24. Anthony Pagden points out that the dominant mode of interpreting the Indian's Otherness was to try to remove it. That is, the tendency was to appeal to (quoting Foucault) " 'restrictive figures of similitude' " in human behavior. See *The Fall of Natural Man*, 5. It may be instructive to see Foucault's discussion of the late eighteenth-century empiricist transformation from the *taxinomia*, an order of two-dimensional knowledge based on resemblance and difference, into an order with "depth in which what matters is no longer identities, distinctive characters . . . but great hidden forces developed on the basis of their primitive and inaccessible nucleus, origin, causality, and history" (*The Order of Things*, 251). Prescott evinces aspects of both Pagden's and Foucault's analyses.

    See also Wai-Chee Dimock's *Empire for Liberty*, in which she locates in Melville's work a critique of "an economy of ascription": "We might speak of this punitive representation as broadly allegorical, for it operates through a set of signifying attributes, out of which it produces both 'persons' and 'destinies.' Indeed, if we are right to detect in *Moby-Dick* a 'hideous and intolerable allegory' . . . that allegory works, I believe, primarily as an economy of ascription, as the production of narrative through the assignment of attributes" (118).

25. This awareness of usurping the authority of the conqueror is evident in a review by W. B. Lawrence of George Folsom's translation of *The Despatches of Hernando Cortés*: "though the Spanish leader may not claim the high literary rank which the Greek and Roman generals have attained as classical historians, we are not to conclude that Cortés has any occasion, even as an author to deprecate criticism. The despatches possess the attractions of romance with the certainty of truth" (*North American Review* 59 [Oc-

tober 1843]: 461). Ultimately, it is Prescott, not Cortés, who deserves praise: "The American reader will . . . have an opportunity of perusing, from the pen of one of our accomplished countrymen . . . the fullest details of this remarkable event. To Mr. Prescott, it is understood, that all documents, as well in the mother country as in America, that tend to illustrate his subject, have been laid open, and his narrative can hardly fail to render uninteresting any discussions founded solely on sources of information generally accessible, unless, like the letters of Cortés, they emanated from those directly engaged in the mighty enterprise" (488). Accordingly, Prescott fetishizes cavalier, warrior masculinity. No doubt such a desire to represent a cavalier hero reflects a certain anxiety over a perceived weakening of unsentimental, heroic masculinity within middle-class literature. The "characters thus formed" were, in a suggestive and tangible sense, male. At the same time such feudal, hierarchical fantasies probably served as symbolic relief from the commercial turmoil of Jacksonian enterprise and Federalist corporatism. As such, his histories present a type of anti-sentimental literature in which the Spanish, and even the Aztecs and Incas, are a repository of masculinity that was being threatened in contemporary America.

26. Note the apparent conflation of Roman Catholicism with sacrifice at the end of the passage. Spaniards and pre-Columbians can and must be read through their ritualized spectacles. The word "priest" acts to conjoin the two in such a reading.

   Levin calls this scene the "epitom[e]" of "Prescott's romantic art" (*History as Romantic Art*, 185), where the types of "human destiny" are brought to their suitably spectacular end.

27. Lawrence Buell's "Transcendentalist Catalogue Rhetoric: Vision Versus Form," in Philip F. Gura and Joel Myerson, eds., *Critical Essays on American Transcendentalism*, 417–19, discusses the "principle of the microcosm" as it operates in the catalogues of Emerson and Whitman. Buell points out that the microcosmic principle was essentially a unifying logic that employed symbol and analogy to understand the diversity of natural manifestations. Moreover, this principle was "not merely a matter of principle of perception" (419). I suggest that though he did not partake of transcendentalism in any direct, easily identifiable way, Prescott operated within a transcendental intellectual milieu that affected certain aspects of his philosophy. Charvat and Kraus are helpful in explaining his relationship to Unitarianism and Federalism, both of which he had had a long though uneasy history with. As a New England, Harvard aristocrat, schooled and rooted in the fundamentals of these philosophies, Prescott may be understood discursively as a product of these movements.

28. In a review of Madame Calderón de la Barca's *Life in Mexico* (1842) that appeared in the *North American Review* (January 1843), Prescott ends with a typically romantic, orientalist compendium. It is an expansive microcosmic cataloging of the Spanish American picturesque – marvelous, excessive, voluptuous: "There is no country more difficult to discuss in all its multi-

form aspects, than Mexico ..." (147). He waxes for almost two pages on its "multiform aspects."

29. *History of the Conquest of Peru* was followed by his *History of the Reign of Philip the Second* (1855–8) and a continuation of William Robertson's *Charles V.*

30. The remainder of the preface deals with his reputation as a blind writer, which Prescott admits to being responsible for, given his plaintive conclusion to the preface of *The Conquest of Mexico.* He prefers not to be called blind, explaining his limited vision as a less severe obstacle than has been supposed. The evidence suggests, however, that his eyes were almost useless by this time.

31. Regarding the current Mexican War and the civilizations of Mexico and Peru, General William Miller, an assiduous Peruvianist and British soldier of fortune, wrote to Prescott after the publication of *The Conquest of Peru*: "The Mexicans have fallen far below what was expected of them, and their conduct during the late War has confirmed the opinion I came to long ago, namely, that they are a very inferior People to the *South* Americans. It was lucky for the Invaders that they had not Gauchos, Guasos, Llaneros, or even Lambayeguanos of Peru, to contend against. I firmly believe that a couple of bold and cool-headed *Caudillos* who knew how to do their work properly, each at the head of about 500 followers, might have sufficed to have prevented the go-a-head Volunteers, and hand-ful of Regulars, from entering the Capital of Montezuma, or if they did enter it, to prevent their escape" (*Papers of Prescott,* 259).

32. W. B. Lawrence expressed a different facet of this comparison in a discussion in the *North American Review* of the relevance of the history of the Spanish empire to a contemporary North American's view of Mexico.

"The constant succession of internal dissensions and military revolutions in those extensive regions of our continent, that formerly acknowledged allegiance to the king of Spain ... has almost extinguished the sympathetic feelings which, twenty years ago, led the people of the United States, with entire unanimity, to demand the admission of the Southern Republics of America into the great family of nations. But not to refer to occurrences in our immediate vicinity, that indicate political changes more portentous than any that have taken place since the first European colonization, we need scarcely remind our readers ... that ... other sources of interest, of a wholly different character, have recently been created in those countries, which were ... forbidden regions to all beyond the sphere of Spanish influence. Discoveries not of gold or silver mines, but of immense cities, once the habitations of man and the abodes of luxury and wealth, have been made, which have rendered the central regions of the American continent prolific for the researches of the historian and antiquary.

"At such a moment, the inquiry naturally arises, to what people are we to attribute the monuments, that still exist in Guatemala and Yucatan, and which evince so much architectural skill that they may be compared with some of the best works of Greek and Roman art; while, in their colossal character and style of execution, they compete with the gigantic produc-tions of Egypt. It is not surprising, when we consider the ignorance and abject condition of the natives at the present time, after a vassalage of three centuries, that doubts should be entertained whether their ancestors were capable of accomplishing what the ruins of Palenque and Uxmal attest . . ." ("Review of *The Depatches of Hernando Cortez*," 459–60).

33. For a good summary of Prescott's attitudes, see Charvat and Kraus, *Prescott: Representative Selections*, lxi–lxii.

34. Lois Parkinson Zamora points out, in her essay "The Usable Past: The Idea of History in Modern U.S. and Latin American Fiction," in Gustavo Pérez Firmat, ed., *Do the Americas Have a Common Literature?*, that the German historicism that strongly influenced Prescott (most likely through Everett, who was praised by Emerson as the great importer of German historical thought), with its "overarching transcendental idealism," was never accepted by Latin American historians, who preferred the "scientific modes of French positivism" (25).

35. If representation is consistently inflected by the terms of empire in Prescott, then the resulting problematic has a dual valence – one directed outward to the periphery and one directed back to the authorial metropole. In Jonathan Arac and Harriet Ritvo's introduction to *Macropolitics of Nineteenth Century Literature: Nationalism, Exoticism, Imperialism*, the authors cite Said's seemingly self-evident proposition regarding the hybrid tendencies of the orientalist: "In . . . *Culture and Imperialism*, Edward Said recalls a pregnant formula from J. A. Hobson's seminal study *Imperialism* (1902): Imperialism is the expansion of nationality. Exoticism, in turn, is the aestheticizing means by which the pain of expansion is converted to spectacle, to culture in the service of empire, even as it may also act to change the originating national culture" (3).

Such a formulation elegantly sets out the task of reading this particular micronarrative of empire: How did Prescott's fascination for South America-as-text accomplish its task of ideological legitimation and how did it fail? How did he, first, aesthetically "convert the pain of expansion" into "spectacle," and second, operate within and alter the "originating [U.S.] culture"?

I would suggest that Prescott's racial symbology can be viewed as a response to the conflicts of "expanding" American political and social reality. Lionel Gossman, in *Between History and Literature*, explains that a fundamental ambivalence, arising out of the crisis of national identity, inhered in the philosophical underpinnings of the European romantic historian. Gossman's analysis is useful as well for thinking about Prescott: "The role of history in the political programs of the first half of the nineteenth century was crucial. By discovering the hidden anonymous history of the nation beneath the outmoded histories of its rulers and its narrow ruling class, historians were expected to provide the legitimation of a new political order, a new state, and at the same time to impose the idea of this state on the consciousness of its citizens. Since history's objective was at once revolutionary (to furnish a basis for a new political order) and conservative (to found and authorize that order by revealing it to be the culmination of a continuous historical development, albeit a long-concealed, underground one), part of its aim was to achieve in itself a reconciliation of the investigative and disruptive practice of historical criticism and scholarship with the narrative art that establishes connections and asserts continuities" (153).

36. This appeared in *North American Review* 52 (January 1841): 75–103.

37. This is perhaps a response to critics of his conquest histories, who saw parallels in the contemporary situation of U.S.–Latin American relations. It could also be an artful, righteous-sounding mask for fears of proslavery hegemonists asserting too much power in the Union. He voted for Henry Clay in 1844, and derisively called the Mexican War "Mr. Polk's War" (*The Papers of Prescott*, 236).

38. A reading of this anti-imperialist dissent might proceed from the insights of Richard Poirier, who writes in *The Renewal of Literature: Emersonian Reflections* that a kind of imperial control is one of the primary features of the authorial impulse: "Having already argued that literature might be considered a form of technology disguised as an attack upon it, I am additionally saying that it is a form of cultural and imaginative imperialism . . . To create an ingenious plot, to control the action, to dispatch a character who gets too big for his role in the play or the novel, all this deserves the highest literary commendation, and while I cannot be supposed to applaud the same activities in historical life, I am suggesting that there is an intriguing if limited equivalence, and that this may be a clue to the kinds of human energy excited by the prospect in life of any efficient form or system" (165).

39. Analyzing the confrontation of ancient civilizations from within the emerging imperial nation can help explain the motivation behind the romantic historian's desire to "preserve" a historical Other in a dialectical narrative. One motivation was surely to control the atavistic subtexts of secular history. Such a role implied a poetics in which communication with the past was a way of negotiating threats to interpretive coherence. On this issue of muteness and interpretation within romantic historicism, see Lionel Gossman, *Between History and Literature:* "The role the Romantic historian attributed to himself was similar to that for the Romantic poet. If the poet, according to Baudelaire, was the interpreter of 'le langage des fleurs et des choses muettes' the historian was to recover and read the lost languages of the mute past . . . By making the past speak and restoring communication with it, it was believed, the historian could ward off the potentially destructive conflicts produced by repression and exclusion; by revealing the continuity between remotest origins and the present . . . he could ground the social and political order and demonstrate that the antagonisms and ruptures – notably the persistent social antagonisms – that seemed to threaten its legitimacy and stability were not absolute or beyond all mediation. Understandably . . . the historical imagination of the nineteenth century was drawn to what was remote, hidden, or inaccessible: to beginnings and

ends, to the archive, the tomb, the womb, the so-called mute peoples . . ."
(258–9).

40. Gossman explains the nexus between romantic history and the author responding to a variety of conflicting demands: "Hidden mediating links had to be disclosed between forces that were visibly in conflict: man and nature, man and his own nature, male and female, the West and the East, the post-revolutionary bourgeoisie and the people, the scholarly historian and common people to whom he owed his existence and whose history was in many cases the preferred object of his study. This could only be done, however, by bringing to light, naming, and acknowledging what the historical record had so often tried to suppress – the injustices of the past, the acts of violence by which the distinctions and discriminations (such as property, the family, and the state) that the historian himself accepted as the condition of civilization and progress had been established, and which had at each successive stage in human development (*Between History and Literature*, 258–9).

41. From "Representative Men," also quoted in Irwin, *American Hieroglyph*, 11.

42. See Philip F. Gura's "The Transcendentalists and Language: The Unitarian Exegetical Background," in Philip F. Gura and Joel Myerson, eds., *Critical Essays on American Transcendentalism*, 609–24, for a useful and related discussion of the theological significance of transcendentalist symbolic discourse.

43. The importance of "federalizing" – this centering and administering of philological and racial discourse in the romantic vision – should once again be understood in its relationship to the consolidation of U.S. power in the hemisphere. This is especially so when viewed comparatively with Spanish America's inability to do just that (though Sarmiento surely tried – and yet his model was North American). Benedict Anderson speaks to this in *Imagined Communities*: "the 'failure' of the Spanish-America-wide nationalism reflects both the general level of development of capitalism and technology in the late eighteenth century and the 'local' backwardness of Spanish capitalism and technology in relation to the administrative stretch of the empire" (63).

Chapter 4. Mutations

1. Conceptually, much of what follows is suggested by an etymological connection (etymology was, of course, a Melvillean obsession) between the terms "mute" and "mutation." The *OED* documents the evolution of the sense of "mutation" as an elision (thus a change and a muting) of the vowel in certain words. Melville's interest in the Galápagos is connected to Darwin's (and Lyell's) through the language of the historically linked, and therefore mutually determined, terms "muteness" and "mutation." I will argue more broadly that science and literature are anchored in Melville by the political and historical geography of his stories.

Some other studies that document the vexed and productive crossings of literature and science include: Bert Bender, *The Descent of Love: Darwin* and the Theory of Sexual Selection in American Fiction, 1871–1926; Peter Morton, *The Vital Science: Biology and the Literary Imagination, 1860–1900*; and John Christie and Sally Shuttleworth, eds., *Nature Transfigured: Science and Literature, 1700–1900*.

See the Bibliography for publication facts for all works cited.

2. Both *Benito Cereno* and "The Encantadas" have been the focus of a great amount of research as to their sources. Numerous accounts have linked "The Encantadas" to Darwin's *Voyage*; not so many have made the link to *Benito Cereno*. See Mary K. Bercaw, *Melville's Sources*, 5–6.

See also Mark Dunphy, "Melville's Turning of the Darwinian Table in 'The Encantadas,' " *Melville Society Extracts* 79 (November 1989): 14; and James Robert Corey, "Herman Melville and the Theory of Evolution," Ph.D. dissertation, Washington State University, 1968.

3. See Jay Leyda, ed., *The Melville Log*; and Charles R. Anderson, *Melville in the South Seas*.

4. See John Samson, *White Lies: Melville's Narratives of Facts*. Samson argues persuasively for a reading of Melville's fictions as occupying an ideologically more sophisticated and politically progressive space between fact and fiction. By calling into question the cultural grounds of both, he calls into question the cultural grounds of the political and racial. Samson places Columbus at the figurative head of the purported narrative of the factual that Melville is responding to: "In fact and by convention, every narrator insists that his is a true account, a narrative of *facts*. From Columbus on, the explorers confronted a world radically alien to what they and their societies had been accustomed – alien not only geographically but naturally and geographically" (4).

5. Lyell, the first volume of whose *Principles of Geology* was published in 1830, is crucial to understanding Melville's dual encounter with the new science and the old South America. Lyell emphasized geology as a historical science, concerned with the "causes of the processes underlying earth history" (*Principles of Geology*, xv), rejecting the anti-theoretical disposition of much geological thinking of the day. He proposed a steady-state theory of earthly change and diversity that stood in opposition to the notion of catastrophic change that foreclosed further evolution. Accepting a vast time scale for history, Lyell believed that: "geology must exclude speculations about the origins of the earth, and confine itself to an analysis of the subsequent changes that the earth has undergone" (xvi). Prefiguring Darwin's imperious but faulty vision, Lyell stressed our "failure to recognize the distorting effect of our viewpoint as subaerial terrestrial beings" (xviii). New strata "need to be intercalated into the succession previously known." Lyell concludes: "renovating as well as . . . destroying causes are unceasingly at work, the repair of the land being as constant as its decay" (473). He stresses in the end the limitations of the human ability to explain history definitively. For an interesting discussion of Melville's relationship to Lyell's geological theory, especially as it is articulated in *Mardi*, see Elizabeth Foster, "Melville and Geology," *American Literature* 17 (1945): 50–65.

6. The critical work on the Darwinian aspects of Melville's South American Pacific works is excellent. Mark Dunphy's "Melville's Turning of the Darwinian Table in 'The Encantadas,' " *Melville Society Extracts* 79 (November 1989): 14: "Merton M. Sealts, Jr. notes in his recent expanded edition of *Melville's Reading* that although Melville was 'no partisan of science himself, he had nevertheless read Darwin's *Journal* as early as 1847 . . . and drawn on it in Sketch Fourth of "The Encantadas" in 1854. In [the sketch] Melville parodies Darwin's pedantic, scientific method of quantitative analysis by lampooning one of his tables . . . Unlike Darwin, Melville feels that none of this reduction of the wonders of nature to pedantic quantification is "truly wonderful." ' " H. Bruce Franklin's "The Island Worlds of Darwin and Melville," *Centennial Review* 11 (1967): 353–70, brilliantly articulates the bourgeois appeal of Darwin's "island" theory as against Melville's. The devastating parody of empirical categorization carried out by Melville in his charts in "The Encantadas" is well analyzed by Franklin, and he points out where Melville contradicts Darwin on biological facts. Perhaps Franklin's most important insight from my perspective has to do with the civilizing trope inherent in Darwin's mode of reasoning. Franklin points out that Darwin "is looking through 'the scale of civilization' for a corresponding order in Nature. The huge discovery toward which he moves is that the analogies can be reversed: 'The varieties of man seem to act on each other, in the same way as different species of animals – the stronger always extirpating the weaker" (366).

Other scholars have noticed the Darwin-Melville relationship. Bert Bender in *Sea-Brothers* calls Melville's "biological observations" in "The Encantadas" a "kind of natural theology" (44). He also points out that Melville's "zoological meditations" on the tortoise are "far less 'scientific' or systematic than were his previous meditations on the whale" (43).

7. I do not want to press too hard into an anachronistic reading. Darwin's complete articulation of his theory of natural selection was, of course, *predated* by Melville's work. Rather, my focus is on the quotations from the *Voyage* that are suggestive in many ways that *imply* Darwinian thinking as well as more generic debates about history, savagism, and domination. My point is similar to Samson's: that Darwin's account of the voyages contains the seeds of a type of scientific thinking that Melville might have found suggestive and insightful, though significantly limited.

8. Eric Sundquist, " 'Benito Cereno' and New World Slavery," in Robert E. Burkholder, ed., *Critical Essays on Herman Melville's "Benito Cereno,"* 146–67.

9. The premises for Delano's intervention have been the stuff of diplomatic and military interventions since the time of the Monroe Doctrine. Ambiguity in national affairs is a token of distress: no colors are showing, the ship is sailing toward a reef, exhibiting uncertain movements; like a nation in turmoil, it is a figure of either danger or distress, perhaps both. Accordingly, in 1847, a writer in the *Democratic Review* declared: "It is an acknowledged law of nations, that when a country sinks into a state of anarchy, unable to govern itself, and dangerous to its neighbors, it becomes

the *duty* of the most powerful of those neighbors to interfere and settle its affairs.''

10. Interestingly, Darwin makes a great fuss over the women of Lima in his account of his voyage, finding them to be among the most beautiful and alluring he had ever seen. His quasi-orientalist eroticism was a somewhat standard nineteenth-century feature of representations of Peruvianness. Melville too is captive to this allure, but tellingly reinscribes it as a trope of truth's resistance to possession and penetration. See Deborah Pool, "A One-Eyed Gaze: Gender in 19th Century Illustration of Peru," *Dialectical Anthropology* 13(1988): 333–64, which traces the *saya-y-manta* (a black shawl) to Andalusia and North Africa.

11. One is tempted to say that the open margin is for subsequent U.S. annotations in the form of Melville's self-conscious colonizing literary textualization. In essence, Melville's story is a full – though certainly ironic – annotation to the appended legal documents from the Lima royal court.

12. See Sundquist, " 'Benito Cereno' and New World Slavery," 149.

13. On the question of simultaneity and temporality as it relates to the emergence of nationalist thinking, see Benedict Anderson, *Imagined Communities*, 22–7. This moment would seem a premodern reversion, and as such a moment where national identity slips away under the force of racially motivated violence.

14. H. Bruce Franklin makes this point quite definitively in "Past, Present, and Future Seemed One," in *Critical Essays on Herman Melville's "Benito Cereno,"* 230–46. Marvin Fisher, in *Going Under: Melville's Short Fiction and the American 1850s*, provides an incisive interpretation of the political implications of "Benito Cereno," given the context of Spanish history embodied in the legal documents from the viceroyal court: "With this view of Spanish history a modern reader blessed with greater sophistication in regard to verbal masks and legalistic deceit might more readily see the lengthy legal deposition as a contrived cover-up rather than a revelation. The deposition clearly expresses the values and reinforces the status quo of the Spanish colonial establishment – ignoring Spanish injustices and black aspiration, glossing over the civilized savagery of the Spanish to condemn black barbarities – and views that somewhat indiscriminate massacre of blacks and Spaniards by Delano's SWAT force . . . as a fortunate victory" (115).

15. I am aware that such statements about humanism are deeply problematic, given humanism's undeniable relationship with scientific empiricism and the discourses of imperialism. For excellent critiques of such humanism in the context of imperialism see Robert Young, *White Mythologies*, especially the chapter on Edward Said, "Disorienting Orientalism"; also important in this vein is James Clifford's critique of Said's humanism in *The Predicament of Culture.*

16. "*Auto-da-fé* " in its most literal sense refers to the ceremony whereby the Inquisition pronounced judgment on a heretic and executed the sentence.

17. See Elaine Scarry, *The Body in Pain: The Making and Unmaking of the World*, for the best account of the dynamics of torture, language, and belief.

18. Once again Marvin Fisher's placing of "Benito Cereno" in the context of the Spanish Inquisition (*Going Under*, 114–15) is worth noting. Fisher contrasts the, "American [as an] historical amnesiac untroubled by past; the Spaniard a much-troubled victim of physical and spiritual trauma" (114).

19. Franklin points out that the sketch of the hermit Oberlus, which I neglect to discuss here, is linked to a discourse of Caliban-like degradation – where the human is degraded below the level of nature. Hunilla functions as the more hopeful counterpoint to the absolute degradation of Oberlus, who is irredeemably animalized ("The Island Worlds of Darwin and Melville," 367).

20. Victor Wolfgang von Hagen, "Introduction," in *The Encantadas, or Enchanted Isles*, by Herman Melville.

21. Sealts gives a comprehensive list of Melville's sources for the story as they appear in his library and in local newspapers (*Melville's Readings*, 90).

22. Franklin points out in "The Island Worlds of Darwin and Melville" that Melville translates the Indian word "kentucky" in *The Confidence Man*: it means "the bloody ground" (357).

23. Samson puts it this way: "Melville's opposition to the dominant ideology of his culture redefines that ideology as 'white lies,' in that it is the less-than-true system of belief upon which the white civilization grounds its experiences, and in that it operates by a convenient acceptance of untruth, a sweeping under the ideological carpet of actions and ideas not logically or readily assimilable. In his narratives of facts Melville . . . pulls out the carpet from under the white culture to expose the clutter beneath its white lies" (*White Lies*, 12).

Chapter 5. Passage

1. Doris Sommer's fine essay "Supplying Demand: Walt Whitman as the Liberal Self," in *Reinventing the Americas*, 68–91, detects this problem in her discussion of Martí's politically dangerous love of Whitman. Sommer's essay as a whole speaks to many of the claims I make in this chapter and indeed casts the problematic of blank spaces in terms of Lacanian psychoanalytic understandings of national identity. Her focus, however, is primarily on the issue of self-love that seems to confuse self and Other and what the implications of this confusion might be for the construction of an "ideal American." She puts it aptly: "One way of approaching Whitman's accomplishment . . . is to focus on his construction of a utopian plenitude that ignores, and therefore has no need to oppose, political conflict and social hierarchies. In other words, rather than attempt to coordinate liberalism and democracy in his poetry . . . Whitman manages to sidestep the ideological competition by fixing the contestants in an uncannily static and perfect moment . . . Something about Whitman's poetry puts conflict under erasure, as Derrida uses that term; it does not deny the conflict, but neutralizes it on the page . . . How, then, can he have any real heirs? In fact, the fragility of his static construct

shatters as soon as time touches it" ("Supplying Demand," 73). My only quarrel with this assessment is the claim that Whitman ends in stasis, that he attempts to use the fixity of print to arrest the moment. I argue that he struggles to accomplish something more restless and less rooted *in print*; though, to be sure, ultimately print *does arrest* his exceptional dreams.

See the Bibliography for publication facts for all works cited.

2. See Michael Warner, *The Letters of the Republic*, and Mitchell Breitwieser, *Cotton Mather and Benjamin Franklin: The Price of Representative Personality*. For an exhaustive study of Whitman in the context of literary culture and publishing, see Ezra Greenspan, *Walt Whitman and the American Reader*.

3. See Benedict Anderson's discussion in *Imagined Communities* of the expansionary nature of the nationalist imaginary as it is produced by a similarly expansive print culture. For Whitman's most eloquent expression of the power of print, see *Democratic Vistas*, in *The Complete Poetry and Prose*, 974–5. For another view of Whitman's linguistic nationalism, see the *Notebooks and Unpublished Prose Manuscripts*, especially the following: "For the chief and indispensable condition of a political union such as ours and (only to be firmly knit and preserved, by a general interpenetration and community of social and personal standards, religious beliefs and literature, essentially the same,) is a copious and uniform language" (1682–3).

4. Historical geographies, essential reading in public education in the antebellum period, were similarly guilty of this elision of a South American historical domain. Emma Willard – author of the *Universal History in Perspective* (1844) and the *Ancient Geography* (1822), both immensely popular and, through their role in classrooms throughout the republic, key to forming public imaginings of the historical past – leaves out pre-Columbian history entirely. She, like Whitman, covers every continent and region but South and Central America.

5. See, for a good example of this ambivalence, Whitman's *Memoranda During the War [&] Death of Abraham Lincoln*, which documents over and over his doubts about the ability of history to do justice to lived experience, even as he attempts to materially account for past events in print.

6. Michael Moon's *Disseminating Whitman: Revision and Corporeality in Leaves of Grass* discusses this phenomenon in rich cultural and social detail.

7. See Michael Warner, "Whitman Drunk," in *Breaking Bounds: Whitman and American Cultural Studies*, 40.

8. Certainly this tension between the insistently performative Whitman and the print-bound Whitman is not to be underestimated. I emphasize the "print Whitman" for one type of entry into imperial consciousness, but it is certainly not the only access available. My argument here gains, I think, from the tension in Whitman's work between the voiced and the printed. For an alternative, performance-oriented analysis of imperial literary modes see Eric Cheyfitz, *The Poetics of Imperialism*.

9. See E. Fred Carlisle's *The Uncertain Self: Whitman's Drama of Identity*, one of the earliest attempts to understand the "problematic of identity" in Whitman's work.

10. See Carlisle, *The Uncertain Self,* 40–1.

11. Though "absorbing," with reference to the English language, is a term Whitman used after the Santa Fe letter in an 1885 article on American slang in *North American Review,* my point still obtains: the absorptive powers of the "second England" are worrisome as well as remarkable.

12. Benedict Anderson famously puts it this way: "If nation states are widely considered to be 'new' and 'historical,' the nation states to which they give political expression always loom out of an immemorial past" (*Imagined Communities,* 19).

13. In the letter, he also makes an oblique admission of the tragedy of Manifest Destiny.

14. I should note that one of Whitman's first published poems was called "The Inca's Daughter"; it appeared in the *Long Island Democrat* on May 5, 1840, and is a nice example of sentimental, Black Legend savagist writing. My sense is that this poem is a good indication of just how self-critical the Santa Fe letter must have been.

    For an excellent account of the role of the Native American as type and trope throughout Whitman's work, see Ed Folsom's *Walt Whitman's Native Representations,* especially the chapter "Whitman and American Indians."

15. Many critics, from Albert Weinberg to Betsy Erkkila to Walter Grünzweig to David Simpson, have sought an "imperial Whitman" in the annexationist length and breadth of his poetic line or in his glorification of the Mexican War – in the rage to catalog, appropriate, and annex. But I would suggest that an alternative place to locate these devices is within the contours of national identity, in his lifework's revisions and annexations – the printed culture of Whitman, self and national; this reading prioritizes his need "to fuse" across lines of identity and difference. See Weinberg's *Manifest Destiny*; Erkkila's *Whitman the Political Poet*; Grünzweig's "Noble Ethics and Loving Aggressiveness: The Imperialist Whitman," in Richard-Serge, ed., *An American Empire: Expansionist Cultures and Policies, 1881–1917*; and Simpson's "Destiny Made Manifest: The Styles of Whitman's Poetry," in Homi Bhabha, ed., *Nation and Narration.*

    More in line with the type of reading I am attempting (with a very different poem, at a very different moment, with very different political and social contexts in view) is Quentin Anderson's reading of "Crossing Brooklyn Ferry" in *The Imperial Self.* He is especially good at exposing the extent of the "complex of centrality" in Whitman's poem – how this self-as-universe seems to beget a kind of imperial metaphysics.

16. The author's edition I use here is in the Special Collections of Van Pelt Library at the University of Pennsylvania.

17. I should mention that the word "annexation" must have had a lingering political charge for Whitman; an "annexationist" was someone, like him, who favored the annexation of Texas during the Mexican War.

18. See Michael Moon's extensive discussion of solidity/fluidity in Whitman in *Disseminating Whitman,* which also associates the topos with the corporeality of the text (59–87).

19. In "Policy Made Personal," in Harold Bloom, ed., *Walt Whitman: Modern Critical Views*, Kenneth Burke writes, "what would Whitman do without the word 'pass'?" (33).
20. See Horace Traubel's transcription of Whitman's "autobiographical" marginalia and notes to "Passage to India" (*With Walt Whitman in Camden*, 399–401). In this text, Columbus seems to play this "gluing" role in the movement from individual author to global identity.
21. As David Simpson points out, it is D. H. Lawrence who demonstrates that Whitman's affection for death is in part a longing for nondifferentiation and an escape from heterogeneity ("Destiny Made Manifest," 177).
22. William Bedford Clark, "Whitman, Warren, and the Literature of Discovery," *Walt Whitman Quarterly Review* 10, no. 1 (Summer 1992): 10–15, points out the fatalist importance of Columbus to Whitman's identity: "Both poet and reader were called upon to assume an explicitly Columbian role, but I would suggest that Whitman's Browningesque 'Prayer of Columbus' (in which he spoke covertly in an 'impersonalized' but avowedly autobiographical persona) revealed the extent to which he was hoping against hope. To this ought to be added the vaporish affirmation at the conclusion of 'A Thought of Columbus,' according to Horace Traubel Whitman's final poem, written on his deathbed on the occasion of the fourth centenary of the Genoan's fateful encounter with the West Indies."
23. See, for instance, "Prayer of Columbus," which also first appeared in *Two Rivulets*; it is a thinly veiled allegorical lament that merely buttresses the grandiose autobiographical project of Whitman's own legend-making.
24. Once again I should point out that Whitman consistently figures that textual power in spoken terms. However, as I understand him in this text, the appeal is to eloquence *on behalf* of the charted, printed self.
25. The term "fuse" is conceptually crucial to my argument. To fuse is "to liquefy, melt . . . to blend intimately, amalgamate, unite into one whole" (*OED*). Fusion, dictated by the metaphor of the rivulets and the oceanic Columbian voyage, rather than incorporation by expansion, seems to be the process Whitman enacts.
26. I borrow this term from nineteenth-century cosmology and physical science because it expresses a representational paradox – the unobtrusive, universal medium. The *OED* gives one of its meanings as: "A substance of great elasticity and subtlety, believed to permeate the whole of planetary and stellar space, not only filling the interplanetary spaces, but also the interstices between particles of air and other matter on the earth; the medium through which the waves of light are propagated." Ether is thus analogous to the work of the poem and the role of history within it: it enables the movement of other substances *and* it is an objective substance in itself. Other reasons for the elaboration of this critical apparatus will become clear in what follows, i.e., the material/seemingly immaterial ether mirrors the work of print culture for Whitman. Whitman is, moreover, pointing to it without naming it.
27. I have based this quotation on Edward Grier's edition of Whitman's *Note-*

books and Unpublished Prose Manuscripts. There is disparity among various editions of the fragments and memoranda (cf. Richard M. Bucke, ed., *Notes and Fragments*, 76–7).

28. Again, a more formal expression of this view is contained in Whitman's *Memoranda During the War.*

29. See Doris Sommer's discussion of the trope of "melting" and "love" in *Democratic Vistas* in the context of the spread of American liberalism ("Supplying Demand," 76). On this general topic see also Moon, *Disseminating Whitman.*

30. M. Jimmie Killingsworth's "Tropes of Selfhood: Whitman's 'Expressive Individualism,' " in R. K. Martin, ed., *The Continuing Presence of Walt Whitman*, as with the language of so many critics of this poem, accounts for what I have identified as the etherlike quality of his poetics by resorting to words like "self-surpassing" and "erasing": "Ironically, the soul of this 'true son of God' is self-surpassing. The soul that had been the foundation for material progress has come by the poem's conclusion to be the principle by which that progress is discounted, surpassed, erased. In wiping the slate clean, the troping self risks all, even its own status as a foundation for further invention, further realization" (48). John Irwin, writing of Whitman's exceptional historicism and metaphysics, is similarly abstract: "In 'Passage to India' . . . Whitman suggests that the real discovery of America was the understanding that East and West are polar opposites joined by a circular path, that the journey's end leads back to its beginning. Yet the peculiar dilemma of the American condition is that though spatial movement on the surface of a sphere will reverse itself and return to the point of origin, temporal movement is irreversible. Even if one returns to the starting place, it is always a different, a later, time. The past cannot be repeated; the temporal point of origin is inaccessible. But for a people whose country began with the idea that there is a spatial solution to temporal (historical) problems, that moving to a new place means making a new beginning, the realization of the irreversibility of time must be rejected" (*American Hieroglyph*, 114).

31. We might also want to read this as what Michael Moon, referring to the fluid/solid binary that is at the core of Whitman's boundary-making and differentiation, calls "wash-out": "a mode of consciousness poised at the 'washed-out' boundaries of mind and body" (*Disseminating Whitman*, 59).

BIBLIOGRAPHY

Adams, M. Ray. "Joel Barlow, Political Romanticist." *American Literature* 9 (May 1937): 117–18.

Alarcon, Daniel Cooper. *The Aztec Palimpsest: Mexico in the Modern Imagination.* Tucson: University of Arizona Press, 1997.

Alstyne, Richard W. Van. *Empire and Independence: The International History of the American Revolution.* New York: Wiley, 1965.

Anzaldúa, Gloria. *Borderlands/La Frontera: The New Mestiza.* San Francisco: Spinsters/Aunt Lute, 1987.

Anderson, Benedict. *Imagined Communities: Reflections on the Origin and Spread of Nationalism.* London: Verso, 1991.

Anderson, Charles R. *Melville in the South Seas.* New York: Columbia University Press, 1939.

Anderson, Quentin. *The Imperial Self: An Essay in American Literary and Cultural History.* New York: Knopf, 1971.

Appleby, Joyce. "Republicanism in Old and New Contexts." *William and Mary Quarterly* 43 (January 1986): 20–34.

Arac, Jonathan, and Harriet Ritvo, eds. *Macropolitics of Nineteenth-Century Literature: Nationalism, Exoticism, Imperialism.* Philadelphia: University of Pennsylvania Press, 1991.

Arner, Robert. "The Connecticut Wits." In Everett Emerson, ed., *American Literature, 1764–1789: The Revolutionary Years.* Madison: University of Wisconsin, 1977.

Arteaga, Alfred, ed. *An Other Tongue: Nation and Ethnicity in the Linguistic Borderlands.* Durham: Duke University Press, 1994.

Axelrad, Jacob. *Philip Freneau, Champion of Democracy.* Austin: University of Texas Press, 1967.

Axtell, James. *The European and the Indian: Essays in the Ethnohistory of Colonial North America.* New York: Oxford University Press, 1981.

Bailyn, Bernard. *The Ideological Origins of the American Revolution.* Cambridge, Mass.: Harvard University Press, 1967.

Balibar, Etienne. "The Nation Form: History and Ideology." *Review* 8, no. 3 (Summer 1990): 329–61.

Bancroft, George. *History of the Colonization of the United States.* 2 vols. Boston: Charles C. Little and James Brown, 1841.

Banning, Lance. "Jeffersonian Ideology Revisited: Liberal and Classical Ideas in the New American Republic." *William and Mary Quarterly* 43 (January 1986): 3–19.

Barber, Benjamin R., Michael J. Gargas McGrath, eds. *The Artist and Political Vision.* New Brunswick, N.J.: Transaction Books, 1982.

Barbour, James, and Thomas Quirk, eds. *Romanticism: Critical Essays in American Literature.* New York: Garland, 1986.

Barlow, Joel. *The Columbiad.* Philadelphia: Fry and Kammerer, 1807.

The Works of Joel Barlow. 2 vols. Gainesville: Scholars' Facsimiles & Reprints, 1970.

Barnett, Louise K. *The Ignoble Savage: American Literary Racism, 1790–1890.* Westport, Conn.: Greenwood, 1975.

Barone, Charles A. *Marxist Thought on Imperialism: Survey and Critique.* Armonk, N.Y.: M.E. Sharpe, 1985.

Barrell, John. *The Birth of Pandora and the Division of Knowledge.* Philadelphia: University of Pennsylvania, 1992.

Bender, Bert. *The Descent of Love: Darwin and the Theory of Sexual Selection in American Fiction, 1871–1926.* Philadelphia: University of Pennsylvania Press, 1996.

Sea-Brothers: The Tradition of American Sea Fiction from Moby-Dick to the Present. Philadelphia: University of Pennsylvania Press, 1988.

Benjamin, Walter. *Illuminations.* Edited by Hannah Arendt, translated by Harry Zohn. New York: Schocken Books, 1968.

Bercaw, Mary K. *Melville's Sources.* Evanston, Ill.: Northwestern University Press, 1987.

Bercovitch, Sacvan. *The American Jeremiad.* Madison: University of Wisconsin Press, 1979.

The Rites of Assent: Transformations in the Symbolic Construction of America. New York: Routledge, 1993.

Berkhofer, Robert. *Salvation and the Savage: An Analysis of Protestant Missions and American Indian Response, 1787–1862.* University of Kentucky Press, 1965.

The White Man's Indian: Images of the American Indian from Columbus to the Present. New York: Knopf, 1978.

Berlant, Lauren. *The Anatomy of National Fantasy: Hawthorne, Utopia, and Everyday Life.* Chicago: University of Chicago Press, 1991.

Bhabha, Homi K. *The Location of Culture.* London: Routledge, 1994.

Bhabha, Homi K., ed. *Nation and Narration.* London: Routledge, 1990.

Bloch, Ruth H. *Visionary Republic: Millennial Themes in American Thought, 1756–1800.* New York: Cambridge University Press, 1985.

Bloom, Harold, ed. *Walt Whitman: Modern Critical Views.* Philadelphia: Chelsea House, 1985.

Brackenridge, Henry Marie. *Voyage to South America; performed by order of the American government, in the years 1817–1819, in the frigate Congress.* Baltimore: The Author, 1819.

Brandon, William. *New Worlds for Old: Reports from the New World and their Effect on the Development of Social Thought in Europe, 1500–1800.* Athens: Ohio University Press, 1986.

Breitweiser, Mitchell R. *Cotton Mather and Benjamin Franklin: The Price of Representative Personality.* Cambridge University Press, 1984.

Breuilly, John. *Nationalism and the State.* Manchester: Manchester University Press, 1982.

Bucke, Richard M., ed. *Notes and Fragments: Left by Walt Whitman.* London: A. Talbot, 1899. Folcroft Library Editions, 1972.

Buell, Lawrence. "American Literary Emergence as a Post-colonial Phenomenon." *American Literary History,* 1992: 411–13.

"Melville and the Question of American Decolonization." *American Literature* 64, no. 2 (June 1992): 215–33.

"Transcendentalist Catalogue Rhetoric: Vision Versus Form." In Philip F. Gura and Joel Myerson, eds., *Critical Essays on American Transcendentalism.* Boston: Hall, 1982.

Burke, Kenneth. "Policy Made Personal." In Harold Bloom, ed., *Walt Whitman: Modern Critical Views.* Philadelphia: Chelsea House, 1985.

Burkholder, Robert E., ed. *Critical Essays on Herman Melville's "Benito Cereno."* New York: Hall, 1992.

Camfield, Gregg. "Joel Barlow's Dialectic of Progress." *Early American Literature* 21, no. 2 (Fall 1986): 131–43.

Carlisle, E. Fred. *The Uncertain Self: Whitman's Drama of Identity.* East Lansing: Michigan State University Press, 1973.

Carr, Helen. *Inventing the American Primitive: Politics, Gender and the Representation of Native American Literary Traditions, 1789–1936.* Cork: Cork University Press, 1996.

Carter, Paul. *Revolt Against Destiny: An Intellectual History of the United States.* New York: Columbia University Press, 1989.

Charvat, William, and Michael Kraus, eds. *William Hickling Prescott: Representative Selections.* New York: American Book Company, 1943.

Chevigny, Bell Gale, and Gari Laguardia, eds. *Reinventing the Americas: Comparative Studies of Literature of the United States and Spanish America.* Cambridge University Press, 1986.

Cheyfitz, Eric. *The Poetics of Imperialism: Translation and Colonization from The Tempest to Tarzan.* New York: Oxford University Press, 1991.

Chiappelli, Fredi, ed. *First Images of America: The Impact of the New World on the Old.* Berkeley: University of California Press, 1976.

Christie, John, and Sally Shuttleworth, eds. *Nature Transfigured: Science and Literature, 1700–1900.* New York: Manchester University Press, 1989.

Clark, Harry Hayden, ed. *Transitions in American Literary History.* Durham: Octagon Books, 1954.

Clark, William Bedford. "Whitman, Warren, and the Literature of Discovery." *Walt Whitman Quarterly Review* 10, no. 1 (Summer 1992): 10–15.

Clendinnen, Inga. " 'Fierce and Unnatural Cruelty': Cortés and the Conquest of Mexico." *Representations* 33 (1991): 65–100.

Clifford, James. *The Predicament of Culture: Twentieth-Century Ethnography, Literature, and Art.* Cambridge, Mass.: Harvard University Press, 1988.

Columbus, Christopher. *The Diario of Christopher Columbus's First Voyage to America 1492–1493.* Translated by Oliver Dunn and James E. Kelly. Norman: University of Oklahoma, 1989.

Corey, James Robert. *Herman Melville and the Theory of Evolution.* Ph.D. dissertation, Washington State University, 1968.

Cortés, Hernán. *Letters from Mexico.* Translated and edited by Anthony Pagden, with an introduction by J. H. Elliott. New Haven: Yale University Press, 1986.

Darwin, Charles. *The Autobiography of Charles Darwin, 1809–1882.* Edited by Nora Barlow. New York: Norton, 1969.

The Voyage of the Beagle. Harvard Classics, volume 29. New York: P. F. Collier, 1909.

Davidson, Cathy N. *Revolution and the Word: The Rise of the Novel in America.* New York: Oxford University Press, 1986.

Davidson, Cathy N., and Michael Moon, eds. *Subjects and Citizens: Nation, Race, and Gender from Oroonoko to Anita Hill.* Durham: Duke University Press, 1995.

Davis, J. C. *Utopia and the Ideal Society: A Study of English Utopian Writing, 1516–1700.* Cambridge University Press, 1981.

Degler, Carl N. *In Search of Human Nature: The Decline and Revival of Darwinism in American Social Thought.* New York: Oxford University Press, 1991.

Derrida, Jacques. *Margins of Philosophy.* Translated by Alan Bass. Chicago: University of Chicago Press, 1982.

Diaz del Castillo, Bernal. *True History of the Conquest of Mexico.* Translated by A. P. Maudslay. Farrar, Strauss & Cudahy, 1956.

Dimock, Wai-Chee. *Empire for Liberty: Melville and the Poetics of Individualism.* Princeton: Princeton University Press, 1989.

Dowling, William C. "Joel Barlow and *The Anarchiad.*" *Early American Literature* 25 (1990): 18–33.

Poetry and Ideology in Revolutionary Connecticut. Athens: University of Georgia Press, 1990.

Drinnon, Richard. *Facing West: The Metaphysics of Indian-Hating and Empire-Building.* Minneapolis: University of Minnesota Press, 1980.

Dryden, John. *The Indian Emperour, or, the Conquest of Mexico by the Spaniards (1694 edition).* Ann Arbor, Mich.: University Microfilms, International, 1980.

The Works of John Dryden. Plays: The Wild Gallant, The Rival Ladies, The Indian Queen. 1663/4 ed. Berkeley: University of California Press, 1962.

Dunphy, Mark. "Melville's Turning of the Darwinian Table in 'The Encantadas.' " *Melville Society Extracts* 79 (November 1989):14.

Emerson, Edward Waldo, and Waldo Emerson Forbes, eds. *Journals of Ralph Waldo Emerson, with Annotations.* Cambridge, Mass.: Riverside Press, 1913.

Emerson, Everett, ed. *American Literature 1764–1789: The Revolutionary Years.* Madison: University of Wisconsin Press, 1977.

Erkkila, Betsy. "Whitman and American Empire." Unpublished article.

Whitman the Political Poet. New York: Oxford University Press, 1989.

Erkkila, Betsy, and Jay Grossman, eds. *Breaking Bounds: Whitman and American Cultural Studies.* New York: Oxford University Press, 1996.

Ernest, John. "Reading the Romantic Past: William H. Prescott's *History of the Conquest of Mexico.*" *American Literary History* 5, no. 2 (1993): 231–49.

Everett, Edward. "Review of *Essay on the Hieroglyphic.*" *North American Review* (January 18, 1831): 95–127.

Fisher, Marvin. *Going Under: Melville's Short Fiction and the American 1850s.* Baton Rouge: Louisiana State University Press, 1977.

Folsom, Ed. *Walt Whitman's Native Representations.* Cambridge University Press, 1994.

Ford, Arthur L. *Joel Barlow.* New York: Twayne, 1971.

Foster, Elizabeth. "Melville and Geology." *American Literature* 17 (1945): 50–65.

Foucault, Michel. *The Order of Things: An Archaeology of the Human Sciences.* New York: Vintage Books, 1973.

Franklin, H. Bruce. "The Island Worlds of Darwin and Melville." *Centennial Review* 11 (1967): 353–70.

"Past, Present. And Future Seemed One." In R. E. Burkholder, ed., *Critical Essays on Herman Melville's "Benito Cereno."* New York: Hall, 1992.

Freneau, Philip. *The Last Poems of Philip Freneau.* Westport, Conn.: Greenwood, 1976.

The Poems (1786) and Miscellaneous Works (1788) of Philip Freneau. Delmar, N.Y.: Scholars Facsimiles & Reprints, 1975.

"The Rising Glory of America," written with Hugh Henry Brackenridge. Philadelphia: Joseph Crukshank, 1772. Reprint, Library Company of Philadelphia.

Friedman, Lawrence G. *Inventors of the Promised Land.* New York: Knopf, 1975.

Fussell, Edwin. *Frontier: American Literature and the American West.* Princeton: Princeton University Press, 1965.

Galeano, Eduardo. *Memory of Fire.* Translated by Cedric Belfrage. New York: Pantheon Books, 1978.

Garcilaso de la Vega. *Royal Commentaries of the Incas, and General History of Peru.* Translated by Harold V. Livermore. Austin: University of Texas Press, 1987.

Gardiner, C. Harvey. *William Hickling Prescott: A Biography.* Austin: University of Texas Press, 1969.

Gates, Henry Louis, Jr., ed. *"Race," Writing, and Difference.* Chicago: University of Chicago Press, 1985.

Gibson, Charles. *Spain in America.* New American Nation Series. New York: Harper & Row, 1966.

Goodrich, Charles A. *History of the United States of America from the First Discovery to the Fourth of March, 1825.* New York: Russell Robbins, 1825.

Goodrich, Diana Sorensen. *Facundo and the Construction of Argentine Culture.* Austin: University of Texas Press, 1996.

Gossman, Lionel. *Between History and Literature.* Cambridge, Mass.: Harvard University Press, 1990.

Grabo, Norman S., Russel B. Nye, eds. *American Thought and Writing*. Boston: Houghton Mifflin, 1965.

Graebner, Norman. *Empire on the Pacific: A Study in American Continental Expansion*. 2d ed. Santa Barbara, Calif.: ABC-Clio, 1983.

Graebner, Norman, ed. *Manifest Destiny*. Indianapolis: Bobbs-Merrill, 1968.

Politics and Crisis of 1860. Urbana: University of Illinois Press, 1961.

Green, Martin. *Dreams of Adventure, Deeds of Empire*. New York: Basic Books, 1979.

Greenberg, Bruce L. *Some other World to Find: Quest and Negation in the Works of Herman Melville*. Urbana: University of Illinois Press, 1989.

Greenblatt, Stephen J. "Invisible Bullets: Renaissance Authority and Its Subversion." In *Shakespearean Negotiations: The Circulation of Social Energy in Renaissance England*. Berkeley: University of California Press, 1988.

Marvelous Possessions: The Wonder of the New World. Chicago: University of Chicago Press, 1991.

Greene, Jack P. *The Intellectual Construction of America: Exceptionalism and Identity from 1492 to 1800*. Chapel Hill: University of North Carolina Press, 1993.

Interpreting Early America: Historiographical Essays. Charlottesville: University Press of Virginia, 1996.

Greenspan, Ezra. *Walt Whitman and the American Reader*. Cambridge University Press, 1990.

Griffin, Charles C. *The United States and the Disruption of the Spanish Empire, 1810–1822; A Study of the Relations of the U.S. with Spain and with the Rebel Spanish Colonies*. New York: Columbia University Press, 1937.

Griffith, John. "The *Columbiad* and *Greenfield Hill*: History, Poetry, and Ideology in the late Eighteenth Century." *Early American Literature* 10 (1975): 235–50.

Grinde, Donald A., Jr., and Bruce E. Johansen. *Exemplar of Liberty: Native America and the Evolution of Democracy*. Los Angeles: American Indian Studies Center (UCLA), 1991.

Gross, Seymour L., ed. *A Benito Cereno Handbook*. Belmont, Calif.: Wadsworth, 1965.

Grünzweig, Walter. "Noble Ethics and Loving Aggressiveness: The Imperialist Whitman." In Ricard-Serge, ed., *An American Empire: Expansionist Cultures and Policies, 1881–1917*. Aix-en-Provence: Université de Provence, 1990.

Guamán Poma de Ayala, Felipe. *Nueva crónica y buen gobierno; selección [por] Felipe Guamán Poma de Ayala*. Versión paleográfica y prólogo de Franklin Pease G. Y. Lima: Casa de la Cultura del Perú, 1969.

Gura, Philip F., and Joel Myerson, eds. *Critical Essays on American Transcendentalism*. Boston: G. K. Hall, 1982.

Guttman, Allen. "Washington Irving and the Conservative Imagination." *American Literature* 36, no. 2 (May 1964): 165–73.

Haberly, David T. "Form and Function in the New World Legend." In Gustavo Pérez Firmat, ed., *Do the Americas Have a Common Literature?*. Durham: Duke University Press, 1990.

Habermas, Jürgen. *The Structural Transformation of the Public Sphere*. Translated by Thomas Burger. Cambridge: MIT Press, 1989.

Hagen, Victor Wolfgang von. "Introduction." In *The Encantadas, or Enchanted Isles*, by Herman Melville. Edited by Victor Wolfgang von Hagen. Burlingame, Calif.: William P. Wreden, 1940.

Hanke, Lewis. *Aristotle and the American Indians: A Study in Race Prejudice in the Modern World*. London: Hollis & Carter, 1959.

Herbert, T. Walter. *Marquesan Encounters: Melville and the Meaning of Civilization*. Cambridge, Mass.: Harvard University Press, 1980.

Herget, Winfried, and Karl Ortseifen. *The Transit of Civilization from Europe to America: Essays in Honor of Hans Galinsky*. Tübingen: Gunter Narr Verlag, 1986.

Hietala, Thomas R. *Manifest Design: Anxious Aggrandizement in Late Jacksonian America*. Ithaca, N.Y.: Cornell University Press, 1985.

Hobsbawm, Eric, and Terence Ranger, eds. *The Invention of Tradition*. Cambridge University Press, 1983.

Horsman, Reginald. *Race and Manifest Destiny: The Origins of Amerian Racial Anglo-Saxonism*. Cambridge, Mass.: Harvard University Press, 1981.

Howard, Leon. *The Connecticut Wits*. Chicago: University of Chicago Press, 1943. "The Late Eighteenth Century: An Age of Contradictions." In Harry H. Clark, ed., *Transitions in American Literary History*. Durham: Octagon Books, 1954.

Hulme, Peter. *Colonial Encounters: Europe and the Native Caribbean 1492–1797*. London: Methuen, 1986.

Hunt, Michael. *Ideology and U.S. Foreign Policy*. New Haven: Yale University Press, 1987.

Irving, Washington. *The Life and Voyages of Christopher Columbus*. 1889 ed. 3 vols. New York: AMS Press, 1973.

The Sketch-Book of Geoffrey Crayon, gent. 1890 Putnam ed. New York: AMS Press, 1973.

Irwin, John. *American Hieroglyph: The Symbol of the Egyptian Hieroglyphics in the American Renaissance*. Baltimore: Johns Hopkins University Press, 1980.

JanMohammad, Abdul. "The Economy of Manichean Allegory: The Function of Racial Difference in Colonialist Literature." In Henry Louis Gates, Jr., ed., *"Race," Writing, and Difference*. Chicago: University of Chicago Press, 1985.

Jefferson, Thomas. *Writings*. New York: Library of America, 1984.

Jehlen, Myra. *American Incarnation: The Individual, the Nation, and the Continent*. Cambridge, Mass.: Harvard University Press, 1986.

Jehlen, Myra, and Sacvan Bercovitch, eds. *Ideology and Classic American Literature*. Cambridge University Press, 1986.

Jennings, Francis. *The Invasion of America: Indians, Colonialism, and the Cant of Conquest*. New York: Norton, 1975.

Johnson, Barbara. *A World of Difference*. Baltimore: Johns Hopkins University Press, 1987.

Johnson, Samuel. *Lives of the English Poets*. 2 vols. New York: E. P. Dutton, 1925.

Jones, Dorothy V. *License for Empire: Colonialism by Treaty in Early America*. Chicago: University of Chicago Press, 1982.

Kammen, Michael. "The Problem of American Exceptionalism: A Reconsideration." *American Quarterly* 45, no. 1 (March 1993): 1–43.

Kaplan, Amy, and Donald E. Pease, eds. *The Cultures of U.S. Imperialism.* Durham: Duke University Press, 1993.

Kelley, Robert. *The Cultural Pattern in American Politics: The First Century.* New York: Knopf, 1979.

Killingsworth, M. Jimmie. "Tropes of Selfhood: Whitman's 'Expressive Individualism'." In Robert K. Martin, ed., *The Continuing Presence of Walt Whitman: The Life after the Life.* Iowa City: University of Iowa Press, 1992.

Kolodny, Annette. *The Lay of the Land: Metaphor as Experience and History in American Literature.* Chapel Hill: University of North Carolina Press, 1975.

"Letting Go Our Grand Obsessions: Notes Toward a New Literary History of the American Frontiers." *American Literature* 64, no. 1 (March 1992): 1–3.

Kupperman, Karen Ordahl. *Settling With the Indians: The Meeting of English and Indian Cultures in America 1580–1640.* Totowa, N.J.: Rowman and Littlefield, 1980.

Lacan, Jacques. *Ecrits: A Selection.* Translated by Alan Sheridan. New York: Norton, 1977.

Lang, Hans-Joachim. "The Rising Glory of America and the Falling Price of Intellect: The Careers of Brackenridge and Freneau." In Winfried Herget and Karl Ortseifen, eds., *The Transit of Civilization from Europe to America: Essays in Honor of Hans Galinsky.* Tübingen: Narr, 1986.

Las Casas, Bartolomé de. *An Account of the First Voyages and Discoveries Made by the Spaniards in America.* London: J. Darby, 1699.

History of the Indies. Translated and edited by Andrée Collard. New York: Harper & Row, 1971.

Lavie, Smadar. "Blow-ups in the Borderzones." *New Formation* 18 (Winter 1992): 84–106.

Lawrence, W. B. "Review of *The Despatches of Hernando Cortez,* translated by George Folson." *North American Review* 59 (October 1843): 459–90.

Leary, Lewis. "Philip Freneau." In Everett Emerson, ed., *Majors Writers of Early American Literature.* Madison: University of Wisconsin Press, 1972.

Levin, David. *History as Romantic Art: Bancroft, Prescott, Motley, and Parkman.* Stanford, Calif.: Stanford University Press, 1959.

Leyda, Jay, ed. *The Melville Log: A Documentary Life of Herman Melville, 1819–1891.* New York: Harcourt, Brace, 1951.

Lockhart, James, and Enrique Otte, eds. *Letters and People of the Spanish Indies.* Cambridge Latin American Studies. Cambridge University Press, 1976.

Looby, Christopher. *Voicing America: Language, Literary Form, and the Origins of the United States.* Chicago: University of Chicago Press, 1996.

Lyell, Charles. *Principles of Geology.* Chicago: University of Chicago Press, 1990.

Major, R. H., ed. *Christopher Columbus: Four Voyages to the New World; Letters and Selected Documents.* 1847 ed. Gloucester, Mass.: Corinth Books, 1978.

Manuel, Frank E., ed. *Utopias and Utopian Thought.* Boston: Houghton Mifflin, 1966.

Marder, Daniel, ed. *A Hugh Henry Brackenridge Reader: 1770–1815.* Pittsburgh: University of Pittsburgh Press, 1970.

Marmontel, J. F. *The Incas, or, The destruction of the Empire of Peru.* London: Printed for J. Nourse, et al., 1777.

Marsh, Philip M. *Philip Freneau: Poet and Journalist.* Minneapolis: Dillon Press, 1967.

The Works of Philip Freneau: A Critical Study. Metuchen, N.J.: Scarecrow Press, 1968.

Martí, José. *Inside the Monster: Writings on the United States and American Imperialism.* Edited by Philip S. Foner, translated by Elinor Randall. New York: Monthly Review Press, 1982.

On Art and Literature: Critical Writings. Edited by Philip S. Foner, translated by Elinor Randall. New York: Monthly Review Press, 1982.

Texts. Translated by Carmen González. Havana: Instituto Cubano del Libro, 1995.

Martin, Calvin, ed. *The American Indian and the Problem of History.* New York: Oxford University Press, 1987.

Martin, Robert K., ed. *The Continuing Presence of Walt Whitman: The Life after the Life.* Iowa City: University of Iowa Press, 1992.

Marx, Leo. *The Machine in the Garden: Technology and the Pastoral Ideal in America.* New York: Oxford University Press, 1977.

Matthiessen, F. O. *American Renaissance: Art and Expression in the Age of Emerson and Whitman.* New York: Oxford University Press, 1941.

May, Henry F. *The Enlightenment in America.* New York: Oxford University Press, 1976.

May, Robert E. *The Southern Dream of a Caribbean Empire, 1854–1861.* Baton Rouge: Louisiana State University Press, 1973.

McWilliams, John P. *The American Epic: Transforming a Genre, 1770–1860.* Cambridge University Press, 1989.

Meinig, D. W. *The Shaping of America: Atlantic America, 1492–1800.* New Haven: Yale University Press, 1986.

Melville, Herman. *The Confidence Man: His Masquerade.* 1949 ed. New York: Grove Press, 1955.

Great Short Works. Edited by Warner Berthoff. New York: Harper & Row, 1969.

Moby-Dick: or, The Whale. Norton Critical Edition. New York: Norton, 1967.

Piazza Tales. 1st ed. New York City: Hendricks House, 1962.

Merk, Frederick. *Mission and Manifest Destiny: A Reinterpretation.* New York: Knopf, 1963.

The Monroe Doctrine and American Expansionism, 1843–1849. New York: Knopf, 1966.

Michaels, Walter Benn, and Donald E. Pease, eds. *The American Renaissance Reconsidered.* Baltimore: Johns Hopkins University Press, 1985.

Miller, Angela. *The Empire of the Eye: Landscape Representation and American Cultural Politics, 1825–1875.* Ithaca, N.Y.: Cornell University Press, 1993.

Miller, David C., ed. *American Iconology: New Approaches to Nineteenth-Century Art and Literature.* New Haven: Yale University Press, 1993.

Mogen, David, Mark Busby, and Paul Bryant, eds. *The Frontier Experience and the American Dream: Esays on American Literature.* College Station: Texas A & M Press.

Moon, Michael. *Disseminating Whitman: Revision and Corporeality in Leaves of Grass.* Cambridge, Mass.: Harvard University Press, 1991.

Morse, Jedidiah. *The American Universal Geography.* 6th ed. Boston: I. Thomas and E.T. Andrews, 1798.

Morse, Richard M. *New World Soundings: Culture and Ideology in the Americas.* Baltimore: Johns Hopkins University Press, 1989.

Morton, Peter. *The Vital Science: Biology and the Literary Imagination, 1860–1900.* London: George Allen and Unwin, 1984.

Murrin, Michael. *The Allegorical Epic: Essays in its Rise and Decline.* Chicago: University of Chicago Press, 1980.

Myers, Andrew B., ed. *Washington Irving: A Tribute.* Tarrytown, N.Y.: Sleepy Hollow Restorations, 1972.

Nnolim, Charles E. *"Benito Cereno": A Study in Meaning of Name and Symbolism.* New York: New Voices, 1974.

Norton, Anne. *Alternative Americas : A Reading of Antebellum Political Culture.* Chicago: University of Chicago Press, 1986.

Nye, Russel B. *The Cultural Life of the New Nation: 1776–1830.* New York: Harper & Brothers, 1960.

O'Gorman, Edmundo. *The Invention of America: An Inquiry into the Historical Nature of the New World and the Meaning of Its History.* Bloomington: Indiana University Press, 1961.

O'Sullivan, John L. "Annexation." *Democratic Review* 17 (July-August 1845): 5–10.

———. "The Great Nation of Futurity." *Democratic Review* 6 (November 1839): 426–30.

Pagden, Anthony. *The Fall of Natural Man: The American Indian and the Origins of Comparative Ethnology.* Cambridge University Press, 1982.

Pagden, Anthony, ed. *Hernan Cortés: Letters From Mexico.* New Haven: Yale University Press, 1986.

Paltsits, Victor Hugo. *A Bibliography of the Separate & Collected Works of Philip Freneau, Together with an Account of His Newspapers.* New York: Dodd, Mead, 1903.

Parrington, Vernon Louis. *Main Currents in American Thought: The Colonial Mind (1620–1800).* Vol. 1. New York: Harcourt, Brace, 1927.

Pearce, Roy Harvey. *The Continuity of American Poetry.* Princeton: Princeton University Press, 1961.

———. *Savagism and Civilization: A Study of the Indian and the American Mind.* Baltimore: Johns Hopkins University Press, 1965.

Pérez Firmat, Gustavo, ed. *Do the Americas Have a Common Literature?* Durham: Duke University Press, 1990.

Phillipson, Michael. *Painting, Language, and Modernity.* London: Routledge & Kegan Paul, 1985.

Pocock, J. G. A. *The Machiavellian Moment: Florentine Political Thought and the Atlantic Republican Tradition.* Princeton: Princeton University Press, 1975.

Poirier, Richard. *The Renewal of Literature: Emersonian Reflections.* New York: Random House, 1987.

Pool, Deborah. "A One-Eyed Gaze: Gender in the 19th Century Illustration of Peru." *Dialectical Anthropology* 13, no. 4. (1988): 333–64.

Pratt, Mary Louise. *Imperial Eyes: Travel Writing and Transculturation.* New York: Routledge, 1992.

Prescott, William. *Biographical and Critical Miscellanies.* Philadelphia: J. B. Lippincott, 1895.

The Correspondence of William Hickling Prescott, 1833–1847. Transcribed and edited by Roger Wolcott. New York: Da Capo Press, 1970.

History of the Conquest of Mexico and History of the Conquest of Peru. Modern Library. New York: Random House, 1936.

The Literary Memoranda of William Hickling Prescott. Edited by C. Harvey Gardiner. Norman: University of Oklahoma Press, 1961.

The Papers of William Hickling Prescott. Edited by C. Harvey Gardiner. Urbana: University of Illinois Press, 1964.

"Review of *Life in Mexico during a Residence of Two Years in that Country,* by Madame Calderón." *North American Review* 56, no. 118 (January 1843) : 137–49.

Remini, Robert V. *Andrew Jackson and the Course of American Empire, 1767–1821.* New York: Harper and Row, 1977.

Retamar, Roberto Fernández. *Caliban and Other Essays.* Translated by Edward Baker. Minneapolis: University of Minnesota Press, 1989.

Reynolds, Charles. *Modes of Imperialism.* New York: St. Martin's Press, 1981.

Richardson, William D. *Melville's "Benito Cereno": An Interpretation with Annotated Text and Concordance.* Durham: Carolina Academic Press, 1987.

Ringe, Donald A. *The Pictorial Mode: Space and Time in the Art of Bryant, Irving, and Cooper.* Lexington: University Press of Kentucky, 1971.

Robertson, William. *History of America.* Dublin: Printed for Messrs. Whitestone [etc.], 1777.

Rogin, Michael P. *Subversive Genealogies: The Politics and Art of Herman Melville.* New York: Knopf, 1983.

Rosaldo, Renato. "Ideology, Place, and People without Culture." *Cultural Anthropology* 3, no. 1:77–87.

Rosenblum, Nancy L. *Another Liberalism: Romantics and the Reconstruction of Liberal Thought.* Cambridge, Mass.: Harvard University Press, 1987.

Runden, John P., ed. *Melville's Benito Cereno.* Boston: D.C. Heath, 1965.

Said, Edward W. *Beginnings: Intention and Method.* New York: Columbia University Press, 1976.

Culture and Imperialism. New York: Knopf, 1993.

"Nationalism, Human Rights, and Interpretation." *Raritan* 12, no. 3 (Winter 1993): 26–51.

Orientalism. New York: Pantheon Books, 1978.

Saldívar, José David. *The Dialectics of Our America.* Durham: Duke University Press, 1991.

Samson, John. *White Lies: Melville's Narratives of Facts.* Ithaca, N.Y.: Cornell Press, 1989.

Sanford, Charles L. *The Quest for Paradise: Europe and the American Moral Imagination.* Urbana: University of Illinois Press, 1961.

Sauer, Carl Ortwin. *Sixteenth Century North America: The Land and the People as Seen by the Europeans.* London: University of California Press, 1971.

Scarry, Elaine. *The Body in Pain: The Making and Unmaking of the World.* New York: Oxford University Press, 1985.

Schlereth, Thomas J. *The Cosmopolitan Ideal in Enlightenment Thought: Its Form and Function in the Ideas of Franklin, Hume, and Voltaire, 1694–1790.* Notre Dame, Ind.: Notre Dame University Press, 1977.

Sealts, Merton M., Jr. *Melville's Reading.* Columbia: University of South Carolina Press, 1988.

Shields, David S. *Oracles of Empire: Poetry, Politics, and Commerce in British America, 1690–1750.* Chicago: University of Chicago Press, 1990.

Shuffelton, Frank, ed. *A Mixed Race: Ethnicity in Early America.* New York: Oxford University Press, 1993.

Simpson, David. "Destiny Made Manifest." In Homi Bhabha, ed., *Nation and Narration.* London: Routledge, 1990.

Slotkin, Richard. *Regeneration Through Violence: The Mythology of the American Frontier, 1600–1860.* Middletown, Conn.: Wesleyan University Press, 1973.

Smith, Adam. *The Wealth of Nations.* Modern Library. New York: Random House, 1937.

Smith, Anthony D. *Theories of Nationalism.* 2d ed. New York: Holmes and Meier, 1983.

Smith, Henry Nash. *The Virgin Land: The American Land as Symbol and Myth.* Cambridge, Mass.: Harvard University Press, 1950.

Smith, Peter, ed. *Christopher Columbus: Four Voyages to the New World.* Gloucester, Mass.: Corinth Books, 1978.

Snowden, Richard. *The Columbiad: or, A Poem on the American War.* Philadelphia: Jacob Johnson, 1795.

Somkin, Fred. *Unquiet Eagle: Memory and Desire in the Idea of American Freedom, 1815–1860.* Ithaca, N.Y.: Cornell University Press, 1967.

Sommer, Doris. "Supplying Demand: Walt Whitman as the Liberal Self." In Bell G. Chevigny, ed., *Reinventing the Americas: Comparative Studies of Literature of the United States and Spanish America.* Cambridge University Press, 1986.

Spencer, Benjamin T. *The Quest for Nationality: An American Literary Campaign.* Syracuse, N.Y.: Syracuse University Press, 1957.

Spengemann, William C. *A New World of Words: Redefining Early American Literature.* New Haven: Yale University Press, 1994.

Spillers, Hortense, ed. *Comparative American Identities: Race, Sex, and Nationality in the Modern Text.* New York: Routledge, 1991.

Spitta, Sylvia. *Between Two Waters: Narratives of Transculturation in Latin America.* Houston: Rice University Press, 1995.

Spivak, Gayatri Chakravorty. *In Other Worlds: Essays in Cultural Politics.* New York: Methuen, 1987.
——. "Neocolonialism and the Secret Agent of Knowledge" (interview with Robert Young). *Oxford Literary Review* 13, nos. 1–2 (1991):220–51.
Steiner, Wendy. *Pictures of Romance: Form against Context in Painting and Literature.* Chicago: University of Chicago Press, 1988.
Stimson, Frederick S. *Origines del Hispanismo Norteamericano.* Vol. 29 of Colección Studium. Mexico City: Ediciones de Andrea, 1961.
Stuart, Reginald C. *United States Expansionism and British North America, 1775–1871.* Chapel Hill: University of North Carolina Press, 1988.
Sundquist, Eric. " 'Benito Cereno' and New World Slavery." In Robert E. Burkholder, ed., *Critical Essays on Herman Melville's "Benito Cereno."* New York: Hall, 1992.
Takaki, Ronald. *Iron Cages: Race and Culture in Nineteenth-Century America.* New York: Knopf, 1979.
Thomas, M. Wynn. *The Lunar Light of Whitman's Poetry.* Cambridge, Mass.: Harvard University Press, 1987.
Ticknor, George. *Life of William Hickling Prescott.* Boston: Ticknor and Fields, 1864.
Todorov, Tzvetan. *The Conquest of America: The Question of the Other.* Translated by Richard Howard. New York: Harper & Row, 1984.
Traubel, Horace. *With Walt Whitman in Camden.* Boston: Small, Maynard, 1906.
Turner, Frederick Jackson. *The Significance of the Frontier in American History.* New York: Ungar, 1963.
Vattel, Emmerich de. *The Law of Nations or the Principles of Natural Law* (1758). Translated by Charles G. Fenwick. Washington, D.C.: Carnegie Institution Classics of International Law, 1916.
Warner, Michael. *The Letters of the Republic: Publication and the Public Sphere in Eighteenth-Century America.* Cambridge, Mass.: Harvard University Press, 1990.
——. "Whitman Drunk." In Betsy Erkkila and Jay Grossman, eds., *Breaking Bounds: Whitman and American Cultural Studies.* New York: Oxford University Press, 1996.
Webb, Walter Prescott. *The Great Frontier.* Austin: University of Texas Press, 1964.
Weinberg, Albert K. *Manifest Destiny: A Study of Nationalist Expansionism in American History.* Baltimore: Johns Hopkins University Press, 1935.
Whitaker, Arthur P. *The United States and the Independence of Latin America, 1800–1830.* 1941.
White, Hayden. *The Content of the Form: Narrative Discourse and Historical Representation.* Baltimore: Johns Hopkins University Press, 1987.
Whitman, Walt. *The Complete Poetry and Prose.* Edited by Justin Kaplan. Library of America, 1965.
——. *The Early Poems and the Fiction.* Edited by Thomas L. Brasher. New York: New York University Press, 1963.
——. *Leaves of Grass.* Norton Critical Edition. New York: Norton, 1965.

Memoranda During the War [&] Death of Abraham Lincoln. Edited by Roy P. Basler. Bloomington: Indiana University Press, 1962.

Notebooks and Unpublished Prose Manuscripts. Vol. 5: *Notes.* Edited by Edward F. Grier. New York: New York University Press, 1984.

Two Rivulets. Author's edition (1876), in Special Collections Van Pelt Library, University of Pennsylvania, Philadelphia.

Williams, Robert A., Jr. *The American Indian in Western Legal Thought.* New York: Oxford University Press, 1990.

Williams, Stanley T. *The Spanish Background of American Literature.* Hamden, Conn.: Archon Books, 1968.

Williams, William Appleman. *Empire as a Way of Life: An Essay on the Causes and Character of America's Present Predicament Along With a Few Thoughts About an Alternative.* New York: Oxford University Press, 1980.

The Tragedy of American Diplomacy. New York: Norton, 1988.

Williams, William Appleman, ed. *From Colony to Empire: Essays in the History of American Foreign Relations.* New York: Wiley, 1972.

Wood, Gordon S. *The Creation of the American Republic, 1776–1787.* Chapel Hill: University of North Carolina Press, 1969.

Wolff, Bryan J. "How the West Was Hung, Or, When I Hear the Word 'Culture' I Take Out my Checkbook." *American Quarterly* 44, no. 3 (September 1992).

Romantic Re-Vision: Culture and Consciousness in Nineteenth-Century American Painting and Literature. Chicago: University of Chicago Press, 1982.

Young, Robert C. *Colonial Desire: Hybridity in Theory, Culture, and Race.* New York: Routledge, 1995.

White Mythologies: Writing History and the West. New York: Routledge, 1990.

Zamora, Lois Parkinson. "The Usable Past: The Idea of History in Modern U.S. and Latin American Fiction." In Gustavo Pérez Firmat, ed., *Do the Americas Have a Common Literature?* Durham: Duke University Press, 1990.

Zamora, Margarita. *Language, Authority, and Indigenous History in the Comentarios Reales de los Incas.* Cambridge University Press, 1988.

Zea, Leopold. "Identity: A Latin American Philosophical Problem." *Philosophical Forum.* 20, nos. 1–2 (Fall–Winter 1988–9): 33–43.

Ziff, Larzer. *Writing in the New Nation: Prose, Print, and Politics in the Early United States.* New Haven: Yale University Press, 1991.

INDEX

	DATE DUE		